Raza Rising

Raza Rising

Chicanos in North Texas

Richard J. Gonzales

Number 10 in the Al Filo: Mexican American Studies Series
Roberto R. Calderón, Series Editor

UNT Press

Denton, Texas

10 9 8 7 6 5 4 3 2 1

Permissions:

University of North Texas Press
1155 Union Circle #311336
Denton, TX 76203-5017

The paper used in this book meets the minimum requirements of the American National Standard for Permanence of Paper for Printed Library Materials, z39.48.1984. Binding materials have been chosen for durability.

Library of Congress Cataloging-in-Publication Data

Names: Gonzales, Richard J., 1950- author
Title: Raza rising : Chicanos in north Texas / Richard J. Gonzales.
Other titles: Al filo ; no. 10.
Description: Denton, Texas : University of North Texas Press, [2016] |
Series: Number 10 in the Al filo, Mexican American studies series |
Includes bibliographical references and index.
Identifiers: LCCN 2015048893| ISBN 9781574416329 (cloth : alk. paper) | ISBN 9781574416411 (ebook)
Subjects: LCSH: Mexican Americans--Texas--Social conditions. | Mexican Americans--Texas--Fort Worth--Social conditions.
Classification: LCC F395.M5 G67 2016 | DDC 305.868/720764--dc23
LC record available at http://lccn.loc.gov/2015048893

Raza Rising: Chicanos in North Texas is Number 10
in the Al Filo: Mexican American Studies Series

The electronic edition of this book was made possible
by the support of the Vick Family Foundation.

To Dora, La Bailadora

Table of Contents

List of Photos

List of Tables

Preface

Raza Rising is the result of years of research, interviews, observations, and just growing up Chicano. With the explosive growth in the numbers of Chicanos and other Latinos in North Texas and this country in the late twentieth and early twenty-first centuries, I find an understanding of Chicano history, culture, and aspirations imperative if we are to thrive. Stimulated by the dearth of scholarly and popular works by and about Chicanos, especially in North Texas, I decided to work this fallow field.

I extend gratitude to the *Fort Worth Star-Telegram*, their administration and editorial staff for allowing me to write as a guest columnist, 2001–2007. I appreciate their courage in opening their editorial pages to a community writer to expound often on Chicano affairs. Their editing support and advice polished my writing to a professional level. I'm especially grateful to Javier J. Aldape and Bob Davis for giving me the break to write with the pros. Paul Harral, then editorial director, provided guidance on how to write well, accurately, and convincingly. Writing for the *Star-Telegram* taught me the importance of our First Amendment rights and how newspapers help safeguard democracy.

Through the support of my wife and children who endured my rants about Chicano issues, I was able to persevere on this writing discipline.

I'm grateful to all the community residents who shared openly their opinions, feelings, histories, and observations. Their trust and confidence that I would use their information in an honorable manner humbled me.

Dr. Roberto R. Calderón, associate professor of history at the University of North Texas, provided *mucho* editing, mentoring, and emotional support in this writing quest. He's an outstanding intellectual, teacher, and promoter of Chicano writers. Karen DeVinney, Assistant Director/Managing Editor for the University of North Texas Press, provided expert, and insightful editing of this book. She taught me the difference between newspaper and book writing.

I'm indebted to my parents, siblings, and my extended Gonzales family for their emotional support. We are truly *familia.*

Finally, I wish to acknowledge all my teachers, especially Father Albert Gallegos, OSM, poet-priest, for dedicating their lives to this noble profession. They sparked a love of learning, reading, and writing in a Chicano boy's heart and head.

Raza Rising

Introduction

The Chicanoization of the United States has dawned in the twenty-first century. Climb with me to the top of *La Raza* pyramid to gaze upon the future.

Young Chicanos will swell the ranks of workers, taxpayers, and voters as the Anglo population ages, retires, and leaves financial wealth to their children. The world these privileged children will face daily is a world quite different from their elders. Surrounded by bicultural, bilingual neighbors, classmates, and coworkers, they'll commute to work, driving alongside or riding trains in a Mexican-spiced *mundo*. With windows rolled down, they'll hear Spanish-language stations playing hot salsas, reporting *noticias*, or advertising *ventas*. Their children will attend schools where teachers will encourage them to enroll their young in dual language classes. Even in private schools, Chicano, white, and black students will study and play diversity games to learn how to live not melted but blended. To bequeath not only a greenback legacy, consider leaving your young with the knowledge and skills to live in an expanding Mexican American world. You will truly give them an advantage.

Research-laden future gazers have predicted the approaching wave of Latino numbers. In the twenty-first century, Latinos are the largest ethnic minority group in the USA. As Steve Murdock, former US Census Bureau Director, has said, if you wish to see what the country will look like in the future, study Texas. Former State Senator Leticia Van de Putte has added if you wish to see what *Tejas* will look like in fifteen years, visit San

Antonio. I offer, if you wish to discern whether Chicanos assume fiscal, legal, and political power equivalent to their numbers, study North Texas.

Photo 1. 20,000 Immigration Reform Protestors

Courtesy of the Delsa P. Pérez Collection, Genealogy, History, and Archives Unit, Fort Worth Library.
The protesters were marching from Tarrant County Courthouse, along Main Street Fort Worth, Texas, April 9, 2006,

We must never forget the past civil rights struggles shouldered primarily by African Americans; however, the future of this country's first-world status will depend increasingly on the ability of Mexican Americans to ascend in greater numbers to board rooms, elected offices, and college classrooms. America's Wall Street future is inextricably tied to the fall and rise of *La Raza* in the twenty-first century.

Unless decisive social and political actions are taken to raise academic and economic levels for Chicanos, Texas and the rest of the country will face a regression to the days when most Americans didn't graduate from high school. In a world competing fiercely for technological and economic dominance, an American future hosting a large, under-educated, Mexican American populace will prove daunting in maintaining the title of the richest country in the world. When poverty sweeps in, its sister witches of crime, urban decay, and social unrest fly in close behind.

Raza Rising was written on multiple levels: as a primer for readers with a passing knowledge of Mexican Americans and as a research-based, in-depth study of current and anticipated challenges. Students, policy makers, and elected officials will benefit from factual and personal observations that reflect on economic, educational, political, and historical issues.

I use interchangeably the terms Chicanos and Mexican Americans. As a child of the 1960s, "Chicano" is more familiar and self-identifying. At times I'll use the more general term Latino to include other Hispanics such as Cubans, Central Americans, and South Americans living in this country. However, the focus of this book is on Chicanos, United States citizens and residents of Mexican heritage, and Mexicans.

To avoid the temptation of overwhelming readers with facts and numbers, I sought to humanize the Chicano/Mexican experience. Autobiographical accounts of my personal rise from the poverty of Chicago tenement homes to middle-class life in a Texas suburb are weaved into the text. I share personal observations of historical and current events to spark the readers' insights to living Chicano proud in the United States. The book will probably incite emotional responses in hopes the readers will not only understand but empathize with Mexican American ascendancy.

Raza Rising seeks to take readers deep into *Latinolandia*. They will have opportunities to examine their own attitudes and preconceived notions about *La Raza*. Open minds and hearts will assist readers to see and feel the future. By the end of the book, readers will emerge steeped in facts about Mexican Americans, knowledgeable about the realistic, Chicano America challenges, and armed with practical twenty-first century solutions.

A current dearth of published books about Mexican Americans in North Texas calls for *Raza Rising*. Notable exceptions are *Más Allá Del Río Bravo: Breve Historia Mexicana del Norte de Texas* by Manuel García y Griego and Roberto R. Calderón and *Stories From the Barrio: A History of Mexican Fort Worth* by Carlos Cuellar. As a freelance, weekly, opinion columnist for the *Fort Worth Star-Telegram,* 2001–2007, I researched Mexican American issues impacting the nation, Lone Star State and North Texas. Large city newspapers could point to their Spanish-language inserts as proof of their coverage of Latino news. However, they were addressing a predominantly immigrant population and not the majority of Mexican American citizens who preferred English. Some Tarrant County Chicanos called me *la voz de los Chicanos*—the Chicano Voice. I was never presumptuous to assume the sobriquet, but realized the writing gig was a precious opportunity to chronicle the Chicano life and strife for all readers.

The column raised some Anglos' ire and many Mexican Americans' pride. I was vilified in letters to the editor, threatened in personal emails, ostracized in my day job, and loved by many in the Chicano community. The balancing act tilted to my favor. Some pieces were translated into Spanish and published in *Diario La Estrella*, the *Fort Worth Star-Telegram's* Spanish language insert. Several papers throughout the country reprinted my articles, including the *Houston Chronicle* and *Detroit Free Press.*

Combining reportage and personal experiences, this book is divided around four themes: Education—School Blues, History—Chicano Roots, Politics—Raza Rising, and Culture—*La Gente.* Each themed section divides into chapters providing focused, analytical discussion. For example, the Education section starts with my recounting of my academic experience in Chicago followed by a closer look at Reading, Policy, Innovators, Foreign Language Skills challenges and solutions. Each section concludes with a summary. This method balances memoir and analysis, emotion and logic, personal and group experiences. I intend to humanize Chicano life supported by research and scholarly discussion to create an enlightening read.

The themes can stand alone as a focus of study. However, the book as a whole provides a comprehensive review of the challenges that Chicanos and non-Chicanos must overcome to achieve full ascendancy.

Endnotes and bibliography reflect the available data from the first seven years of the millennium, although they include some entries after 2010 to bring the data up to date. Issues written about then are as relevant today. We have the benefit of hindsight to observe how sadly little has changed and how much work remains.

Raza Rising offers a high ground personal and factual look at Mexican Americans in the hope we will develop a deeper understanding and ardor for their emergence in the United States.

Adelante to *Raza Rising.*

SECTION 1

SCHOOL BLUES

As I boy, I learned about the shame that my father Joseph Gonzales had for not completing his high school education when I heard him lie in conversations with others that he had graduated from Lampasas High School in Texas. My father's educational fate was little different from that of other Mexican American youth growing up in Texas during the early twentieth century. A son of migrant workers, he followed the migrant trail throughout south and west Texas, picking cotton, vegetables, and fruit. His father Bernabé Gonzales was born in México and emigrated as a boy to Texas. Illiterate and unskilled, my grandfather worked in manual labor jobs throughout his life moving his family wherever he found work.

My mother Delfina Reyes, on the other hand, was born in Waukegan, Illinois, and graduated from Harrison High School in Chicago, Illinois. Her parents, born in México, followed the well-worn immigrant trail but went farther north, working in the Midwest's factories and foundries.

Photo 2. Joseph Gonzales with author on left and brother Rubén Gonzales on right, 1953

Author's personal collection.

Photo 3. Delfina Gonzales with author on left and brother Rubén Gonzales on right

Author's personal collection
Photo was taken in front of Metropolitan Cathedral of the Assumption of the Most Blessed Virgin Mary into Heaven in México City, 1955.

Both my parents had the foresight to understand that in this country a strong work ethos was not enough to excel. A post-high school education was vital to join the middle class ranks and to purchase all the luxuries that come with that status.

My mother and father saved and sent most of their children to Chicago Catholic parochial schools. Dressed in a white shirt, blue tie, and dark slacks, I attended classes taught by nuns and priests schooled in spirituality, discipline, and high expectations. We were taught that God expected us to excel, titling our school papers JMJ for Jesus, Mary, and Joseph. Anything short of our best work was disrespectful to the Holy Family. To reinforce this lesson, the teeth-gritted nuns and priests applied whacks and smacks to the behinds and hands of those who failed to heed. I often saw the nuns' rosary beads girded around their waists sway as their arms played back and forth with each swing. They were determined to impress upon us that the consequence of lazy learning was physical pain. I don't think they realized how prophetic their lessons were in light of the gang violence, poor physical and mental health, and incarceration many Mexican American dropouts suffered.

In a sense, my parents' educational destinies were a tale of two cities: one small, rural, and southern, the other large, urban, and northern. Chicago was an immigrant city, accustomed to new waves of ethnics struggling to live the American Dream. Although racism pervaded the city, the Catholic schools strived to teach all children, regardless of race and class. In the cold winters of the blustering north, we colored children learned to listen well if we were to survive the racist climes. I admired the white students and their ease with language, numbers, and self-confidence. But in time, I learned my brain worked as well as theirs and in some cases better. I welcomed the academic competition and except for adolescent angst forgot all semblance of shame and skin consciousness. I chose Latin over Spanish, took Advanced Placement in college English and joined readers' theater dramatizing the great works. I even flirted with the idea of entering an acting career.

Photo 4. St. Charles Borromeo Elementary School 5th Grade Classroom

Courtesy of Archdiocese of Chicago's Joseph Cardinal Bernardin Archives and Records Center.
Photo was taken in 1960, for the St. Charles Borromeo Diamond Jubilee Pamphlet, 1885–1960.

Powerful socioeconomic currents that swept my dad away from the classroom and into the labor force much too young sealed my father's fate. With no Chicano academic role models, born into a family that didn't read or write, he learned that hard, physical labor was the only way to earn a living without a degree or trade. After he dropped out, he sought a way to improve his lot by attending barber school in San Antonio and for several years operated his own shop. I, of course, received free burr haircuts for a regretfully long time while my male classmates were allowed to duckbill their hair until the nuns demanded more appropriate hair length like "four-eyes Gonzales."

In the early twenty-first century, many Mexican American students were overwhelmingly urban with moms and dads working long hours in low-paying jobs. The Texas rural, bucolic setting may have changed but the academic achievement was dismally the same.

Educational shame swept the Chicano community with Mexican American boys and girls dropping out in droves while their white classmates moved on. State and national standard testing scores and Advanced Placement class enrollment exposed a wide achievement gap between Chicanos and Whites. The nuns and priests dedicated to raising the lower-class students to middle-class educational standards were fewer and harder to find. With Texas ranked nationally as thirty-eighth in per-pupil school funding, according to US Census Public Finances Report of 2009, the school bell was tolling a sorrowful knell.[1]

The following chapters address educational issues that offer Chicanos challenges to close the achievement gap and to excel in academia. These include Reading, Policy, Foreign Language Skills, and Education Innovators.

These lessons will add to your understanding of the academic Río Grande that Mexican Americans must vault if this country will stay competitive with the rest of the world. Together, we can revive César Chávez's *Si Se Puede*/Yes We Can spirit to instill the *ganas*/desire in students, teachers, parents, policy makers, and residents to graduate millions of Mexican American scholars by 2030.

Chapter 1

Reading

My affinity for books started in my early schooling in Chicago. I helped the nuns of St. Charles Borromeo Elementary School to unbox new shipments of library books, catalog, and shelve them. The smooth feel and fresh smell of new books in hand was enjoyable. I suspected that it pleased the nuns as well, because they spoke to me about how important it was to take care of books and, more importantly, to read them.

Elementary school was challenging; my nun teachers and librarians must have known that for boys and girls from the Chicago inner-city, where many lived in tenement homes and both parents earned just enough to put food on their table most days of the week, an education was our freedom pass from poverty.

Pursed-lipped sisters were tough in order to harden us for the rigors of overcoming language barriers and violence (street gangs were rampant). They instilled a hardy faith in books. Bless these demanding nuns who worked with thousands of inner-city children, preaching and teaching this message of freedom and faith. They were educational missionaries working to give children a belief in their skills to search and learn.

Photo 5. St. Charles Borromeo Teachers in Front of School Entrance

Archdiocese of Chicago's Joseph Cardinal Bernardin Archives and Records Center.
The photo was taken in 1960, for the St. Charles Borromeo Diamond Jubilee Pamphlet, 1885–1960.

As a teen, I escaped from inner-city libraries to the grandest library of the prairie city: the Chicago Public Library at Washington Street and Michigan Avenue. Built in 1897 in a classical-revival style exterior with a classical Greek and Italian Renaissance interior of mosaics, marbles, bronze, and two stained-glass domes, that library was a place where I could pretend to be a Chicago book prince in a palace overlooking majestic Lake Michigan.

On hot, sultry, or snow-covered days, I rode the subway from the west side, passing rows of tenement buildings and Greek, Italian, Black, Chinese, and Mexican American neighborhoods. I rode past cathedrals, taverns, and smokestacks into the magical land by the lake where architects like Frank Lloyd Wright, Louis Sullivan, William Holabird, and Mike Roche built buildings that blended art, function, and nature.

The subway was my freedom train from the wilds to a station stop of culture and beauty.

I would sit in the grand reading room, sunlight pouring in at an angle from wide, ceiling-high windows onto the roomful of readers. I took my place in the brotherhood of books seeking information, wisdom, and respite from the roiling hustle-bustle of the City of the Big Shoulders.

We were Americans living the American Dream that permitted us to read uncensored books, to decide on what was propaganda and truth, to discern the difference between good and bad ideas, to read the controversial and orthodox.

One of my favorite haunts was a large chamber called Preston Bradley Hall, where a 38-foot Tiffany dome—said to be the world's largest—shimmered the room with filtered, blue-tinted light. Tiffany lamps were suspended from the ceiling like golden earrings on a beautiful woman. Mosaic medallions, scrolls, rosettes, and zodiacs adorned the walls and arches that led from one room to another.

Inlaid across the edge of the ceiling were the names of great writers and philosophers of the world. Amid the names were inscriptions in ten languages professing the wisdom of the ages. Profound words swelled a barrio kid's thoughts.

I walked outside of the library and a few, long blocks along Michigan Avenue to the statue of Union General John Logan, mounted on his horse and holding high a captured enemy flag. It struck me as ironic that we had played at the feet of this Civil War hero, but my family and millions of other Northern minorities were still enslaved in ignorance.

In the land of Lincoln, we had lost our freedom of expression because we didn't know how to write or read well in Spanish or English. We hadn't learned to master our books. We must act like eagles teaching their young to fly from the nest—the book pages are their wings to keep them from falling. They just need to learn to flap them often to reach dizzying heights.

I struggled to illustrate for a fourteen-year-old son the glories of libraries. Perhaps he needed a subway tour of Chicago, a visit to the palace of the common man and woman, a walk to Grant Park.

He said, "Libraries are for nerds."

I told him, "I'm the prince of nerds," and continued reading.

Photo 6. Dolores Huerta Elementary School students celebrating the arrival of Dolores Huerta, Fort Worth, May 2014

Courtesy of Emerico Pérez, Emerico Photography.

Like any skill, the earlier you start encouraging reading, the more likely the child will develop a reading habit and overcome any book lover stigma. For children from un-literate families, reading was a foreign activity that many youth never adopted as a self-initiated fun adventure equal to sports and TV. The odds were stacked against literacy for low-income minorities; if we were to convert Chicano children to book-carrying pleasure and serious readers, parental involvement was vital. Father and mother encouragement and mentoring propelled the child to take up the book. I found the Early Childhood Matters Program in Fort Worth, Texas, an excellent reading program to teach parents and children how to read and grow together.

Timing was important in instilling a desire to read and learn. The earlier that the Chicano child acquired the habit of picking up a book, looking at and turning the pages, pronouncing words and making sense of what is read, the quicker they're prepared for school and the world.

The solution to school dropouts, juvenile delinquency, welfare, and prison might be as simple as reading to an infant.

How so? Prison administrators looked at third-graders' reading levels to project the number of prison beds that they would need, said Roza Abbasi, a librarian who worked with parents in an Early Childhood Matters (ECM) class at the North Tri-Ethnic Community Center in Fort Worth.

She offered parents and children, including infants, library cards as their get-out-of-jail card. When a parent read to a child, it freed that young, developing brain to absorb words, concepts, and images needed to prepare for school. The human brain was the only organ that hasn't fully developed at birth, said Sandra Lamm, an early childhood coordinator. In fact, she said in an interview with the author, "85 percent of the brain's architecture is formed before children enter school."

Words, ideas, and colors must fill the brain's cells as its synapses begin to fire, form and connect. Timing is vital. More than anyone else, the parents or primary caregiver must nourish the child's brain daily. They can begin by reading to the child in the womb and continuing through childhood.

Some enlightened parents might assume that this was common knowledge. So why the need for programs such as ECM, which Fort Worth sponsors? Lamm cited research in an interview with the author to reveal that many parents lacked basic knowledge on how to prepare their children for school: More than 40 percent of children in low-income Fort Worth neighborhoods weren't able to pass a simple readiness screening when they entered kindergarten—a test that included knowledge such as reading progresses from left to right.

The Fort Worth school district spent more than $5 million each year to re-educate children who were held back in kindergarten or the first or second grades. Children who were behind when they entered school stayed behind and many dropped out.

Two mothers who attend ECM classes described how they used words to nourish their children's minds. Rosa Medina boasted how she had learned to become a better mother in the year she had been enrolled. Before, she would tell her children not to bother her or would sleep in the mornings. Now, aware of the importance of talking with her children, she devoted all of her attention to them when they asked her to read or talk.

Reyna Cabera said that she read to her sixteen-month-old grandson, whom she cared for while her daughter worked. In a corner where the books were kept, she found her grandson asleep with a book draped over his head. Although two of her children graduated from college, she realized she could have offered them so much more attention if she had read to them.

Lamm said that as the mothers came to classes over time, they began to dress better, speak up, and carry themselves with more confidence. Once they developed better parenting and teaching skills and realized the influence they had over their children's futures, their self-esteem rose.

Lamm's goal through the ECM program was to build a "scaffold of support around the child." The scaffolding began with parents but required the support of city-sponsored programs that taught motivated parents how to raise healthy, smart, and socially adept kids.

In 2004, Fort Worth had the foresight to seek federal and local funding, such as a $687,000 grant from the US Department of Health and Human Services, to allow experts like Lamm to reach out to parents. The city was paying staff salaries, which allowed the ECM program to continue after that grant ended in 2006. Call it a return on investment that paid off in smart kids for a smart city.

Enlightened, motivated teachers in our inner-city schools open the world of reading to Chicano students. I accepted an invitation from North Side High School Spanish teacher Juliet Wells in Fort Worth to speak to several of her Spanish language classes. A school comprised of mostly Chicano students, North Side High was an old school with a rich, Western tradition, taking the steer as their school mascot. Unbeknownst to the teacher, I had taught English and History classes years ago at North Side High as my first job out of college. Drafted away by the Army, I taught only one year but as I walked down the school hall I recalled the challenges teachers faced at a low-income, minority-dominated school.

In the first class, I felt excited to stand before the class of adolescent Mexican American students. By the end of the third class, my words sputtered, thoughts wandered, legs ached and enthusiasm waned. Teaching high school students was hard work, requiring mental, physical, and creative prowess. I learned that teaching was not for the faint-hearted or dull-witted. Teaching required nimbleness of feet, mind, and speech, a fondness for children and thick skin. Possessing the encyclopedic knowledge of Carl Sagan and wry wit of Woody Allen would make the job easier.

It also helped if the students took notes, listened, completed their homework, read, spoke up, and possessed a passion to learn.

How do we make the “have-not” students of North Side High School equal in academic excellence to the "have" students of Highland Park High School, a prestigious, mostly Anglo school in Highland Park, Texas?

The answer: good teachers motivating eager students open to learning. And we must believe that economically disadvantaged students possess the brainpower to learn well.

Marva Collins of Chicago believed it so. She had taught in the City of Big Shoulders' schools for 14 years before leaving to create the Daniel Hale Williams Westside Preparatory School.

Collins had been frustrated by the public schools' attitude toward inner-city children. Her school took a handful of them, many who had been considered impossible to educate, and gave them wings.

Collins wrote slogans daily on the blackboard: "Character is what you know you are and not what others think you are." "He who eats my bread does my will." "Speak the speech trippingly on the tongue."

Jaime Escalante of Los Angeles challenged his students at Garfield High School to find the *ganas*, or desire, to master calculus and pass an Advanced Placement exam in the subject. He had them stand as he quizzed them on their understanding of the formulas. Escalante led his students to the proof that they were smart.

Collins and Escalante knew that the magic lay in the nurturing of a passion for learning and respect for children's ability to learn. We can build palatial schools with shimmering labs in the bowels of the barrio, but if teachers fail to inspire learning, we've built castles of false hope. We've deceived the community and robbed the poor.

At career day at North Side High, soldiers in fatigues, architects, code enforcers, day care owners, writers, and other professionals stormed the classes. Ms. Wells introduced me as someone who "*lucha con sus palabras*," or fights with his words.

The students didn't appear impressed. But I was, as I observed the large cards of conjugated regular and irregular verbs along the tops of the walls, Spanish-language newspapers, a map of the world with Spanish-speaking countries highlighted, illustrations of historical events in Mexican American culture, photographs of Mexican American heroes. A walk into the classroom was a trip to Latinolandia where the Spanish-language virus was contagious.

More importantly, Wells moved gracefully among the students, encouraging them to ask questions, to volunteer to read aloud, and to stay alert.

She was a Fort Worth native who had attended the University of Texas at Austin and worked as a journalist for several years before changing careers. She seemed to possess the characteristics of a good teacher; she was enthusiastic, challenging, prepared, encouraging, accepting of cultural diversity, smart, and fluent in Spanish.

I picked the closest student to stand and read aloud one of my columns. My upbringing in a family of big mouths made it difficult to accept the silence of Chicano lambs. As he read haltingly in heavily accented Spanish, I thought that I had made a mistake and embarrassed the student. But he plugged away, stumbling, grappling with words until he got them trippingly out.

I asked for volunteers after that.

Wells thanked me for my presentation and was especially pleased that I had chosen the first student. "He never reads," she said.

"Oh," I said, glad that I hadn't apologized.

Perhaps I've unleashed a literary lion. Perchance, I inspired.

Chicanos can look for inspiration in their quest to improve their child's reading and academic skills from early Mexican history. Learning for Mexicans is in the blood.

In the days of the Aztecs, it was expected that all children would go to school. Jacques Soustelle wrote in *The Daily Life of the Aztecs* that fathers and mothers educated their sons and daughters and later enrolled them in either the *calmecac* for priesthood or high office of the state or the *telpochcalli,* the school for ordinary citizens.[2]

In the *calmecac*, students learned about architecture, the writing of glyphs, mathematics, the charting of the stars, the ways of the warrior and others. Some would study theology to prepare for the strenuous, self-sacrificing life as a priest who honored many gods.

Historians proposed theories about the dominance of the Aztecs over the other Indians in central México. Some cited their formidable armies; others said their political alliances and riches gave them control. I proposed that their stress on education and service to their people won them superiority.

As we observe Hispanic Heritage Month in September and October with parades, dancing, banquets, and speeches, let's reflect on one truth: Education is the primary quality that will help Chicanos thrive in the capitalist, global economy of the twenty-first century.

Although Chicanos were the fastest-growing minority group in the United States, they continued to lag woefully in the classroom. What a disgrace to hear of Mexican American youth gunning down a group of students at Sunset High School in Dallas on August 20, 1996, the second day of the school year, as reported by Jason Sickles and Alexi Barrionuevo in the *Dallas Morning News.* Did Mexican American teens devalue schools to where they became just another drive-by killing ground?

School administrators and teachers received criticism for perceived failures to meet the needs of the Mexican American student. Although some complaints were valid, there continued to be a shameful absence of Chicano parents in the academic lives of their children. Chicano parents should know their child's subjects and teachers more than how to dance the *macarena.*

Photo 7. Dolores Huerta Elementary students of Fort Worth, Texas

Courtesy of Emerico Pérez, Emerico Photography.
The students are celebrating the arrival of Dolores Huerta to their tenth anniversary celebration of the school's opening, May 2014.

Instead of Mexican American parents watching the Dallas Cowboys on Sundays with the gang, they should read with their children about how the vaquero Tejanos introduced ranching and cattle raising to Texas or how the buckskin-wearing Anglo settlers quickly adopted the chaparrals, lassos, rodeos, mustangs, and vocabulary of the Tejanos. Instead of praising the athletic prowess of Oscar De La Hoya, Juan González, or Iván Rodríguez, Mexican American parents could point out the educational and political achievements of Lorenzo De Zavala, José Ángel Gutiérrez, and Dolores Huerta. The Chicano child may learn about these role models from their teachers, but when they hear it from their parents, it takes on an emotional resonance that few teachers can match.

One easy but powerful parental activity that will have lifelong impact is reading with or to a Mexican American child. Encouraging reading as a habit early in life is a gift that the Chicano child desperately needs. If parents don't like to read, they should fake it for their children's sake. If Chicano fathers and mothers don't know how to read, they should take night classes and learn. Above all, the child should see the parent in the act of reading. The reading symbiosis between Mexican American parent and child can be one of the most intimate and joyful experiences in the short time they have with one another. It's an example that will stay with the child for life.

Too often in trips to the local library, I've not seen Chicano fathers but have seen a few Chicano mothers with their children. I propose that a powerful demonstration of Mexican American male acceptance of familial responsibility would be a million-man march to the library.

Padres should take their children by the hand and journey through the portals of this literary wonderland. If the parent is embarrassed by his unfamiliarity with the library, he should go alone at first and learn its layout and offerings. I have found librarians eager to help anyone with the desire to read and learn.

For the truly adventurous Chicano parent, I recommend the fine art of writing. Too few Mexican Americans write novels, short stories, plays, biographies, or opinion pieces. However, few other activities can organize one's thoughts or express the range of emotions and beauty that this life offers.

Mexican American parents can help their children to become proficient in writing by encouraging them to write letters to relatives, friends or even letters to the editor of local newspapers. A fun writing activity for the aspiring scribe is to write a journal or diary of one's observations, feelings, or thoughts. However, time must be made for writing—which may mean limiting television viewing. Again, if the Chicano parent practices writing, the child will do so as well.

Aztecs considered a person educated when they possessed a good heart and a wise face.[3] The educated Aztec had the wisdom to contribute their skills for the glory of the empire, tempered with the desire to serve with compassion.

Let's strive to make our Mexican American heritage flourish beyond Hispanic Heritage Month and into the multicultural, technologically complex world all year long. Our Chicano heritage flowers by the parent taking the Chicano child by the hand and marching bravely off to school.

Chapter 2

Policy

In an effort to hold schools accountable for the students' learning, states across the country implemented high-stakes testing. Some parents and legislatures questioned the validity of the tests and claim that the tests hampered teaching and student learning.

Please answer the following multiple-choice statement: Forty thousand seniors failed the Texas Assessment of Knowledge and Skills (TAKS) and did not graduate in 2007 because:

a.) School administrators and teachers failed to teach to all socioeconomic levels.

b.) Legislators delayed too long in implementing equitable school finance reform.

c.) Distracted or uneducated parents failed to stress the importance of education.

d.) Unmotivated students spent too little time reading and studying.

e.) All the above.

If you selected "e," you chose correctly. If you answered incorrectly, volunteer at a local school for a day.

Reporter Katherine Cromer Brock, *Fort Worth Star-Telegram,* wrote on May 12, 2007, that the Texas Education Agency documented 13 percent of seniors didn't pass TAKS in 2006; in 2007, that increased to 16 percent. Although the students might have passed all their course work, the law required that they pass the TAKS to receive a high school diploma. They either passed the tests in the summer or joined the ranks of those who wander around, looking for work that doesn't require a diploma. The non-degreed will find a harsh world, competing with the undocumented for low-skilled jobs.

The US Labor Department data reflected that median weekly income in 2014 for US households without a diploma was $488 with a high school degree, $668, and with a bachelor's degree, $1,193. The lesson learned: If you like money, get as many degrees as possible.[4]

Those who've passed the high-school equivalency test could consider joining the military, choosing between shovel or rifle, brooms or bullets. Recruiters were eager to sign on young men and women for then-President Bush's surge in Iraq and later, Obama's war in Afghanistan. If they took the patriotic route, most eventually returned to a civilian life that demanded degrees to compete successfully in a knowledge-based economy. War had a way of motivating young men and women to think seriously about their studies.

Data was not released as to the ethnicity of the 40,000 students failing TAKS. But based on historically high dropout rates among Chicanos and blacks and low SAT scores displayed in the *Fort Worth Star-Telegram's* "Measuring Up" Web site on May 13, 2007, it was likely that the non-graduates were mostly ethnic minorities.

Schools and teachers were easy scapegoats for the failure of these students. Educational professionals trained and committed to careers teaching and helping students overcome academic hurdles. School districts spent millions on computers, books, and consultants to help all students pass TAKS tests. Critics complained that high-stakes tests force teachers to teach to the test—after all, their careers hung in the balance. Four little letters stifled creativity and joy of teaching and learning: T-A-K-S.

State Senator Florence Shapiro, R-Plano and State Representative Rob Eissler, R-The Woodlands, filed bills during the eightieth legislative session to phase out TAKS and replace it with end-of-course exams. They affirmed the need for schools' accountability but prefer tests as one marker of several that measure the students' academic performance.[5]

"The TAKS test has outlived its welcome," said Shapiro. She preferred timely tests that measured students' in-depth understanding of the course.[6]

"It is important to give students multiple pathways to graduation," said Eissler.[7]

Whether at the end of course or year, students still were expected to master the material. And to understand well, Mexican American students had to catch up to Anglo students in literacy.

In 2004, the National Center for Education Statistics presented long-term trends in reading gaps between Mexican American and Anglo students, measuring the reading capabilities of students on a scale of zero to five hundred.[8]

From 1975 to 2004, the reading score gap for seventeen-year-old Mexican Americans narrowed from a forty-one-point difference lower than Anglos to twenty-nine points. It took twenty-nine years for the gap to narrow by twelve points.[9]

Must we wait another twenty-nine years for the reading gap to disappear? Can we afford to wait that long, given the demographic shift to a minority-majority state? Urgent educational reforms that crossed the learning divide for the majority of Texas students were imperative if we were to thrive as a smart state.

Please choose the correct response to the following statement. The solution to graduating all high school students is:

a.) Challenge and engage all students in the learning process.

b.) Reach out to a diverse community for support and resources.

c.) Fund all Texas schools equitably.

d.) Hire more minority teachers to act as positive role models for students.

e.) All of the above.

If you chose "e," give yourself a star as an education advocate and thank a teacher. If you answered incorrectly, re-read this section.

In 2012, TAKS was replaced by the end-of-year State of Texas Assessments of Academic Readiness or STAAR. Originally, students were required to pass STAAR to graduate. However, after considerable pressure, the Texas Legislature in 2015 decided to allow students who couldn't pass one or two of the five STAAR tests but passed their course work an alternative path to graduation. Through a determination by an individual graduation committee (IGC), students could be found eligible to receive a high school degree. In November, 2015, Bill Hammond, CEO of the Texas Association of Business, said his association's survey of the one hundred largest Texas school districts found that 86.4 percent of the students asking for IGC reviews were granted approval to receive a high school diploma. He said, "It is unconscionable to allow our students to leave our public schools unprepared, yet that is what we are doing."[10]

In addition to holding our schools accountable, we should examine the de facto re-segregation that swept our schools. What chances of educational success do minority children have if they attend schools that were predominantly minority? As American society becomes increasingly diverse, our children will face the challenge of living and working in a world of many colors and cultures. This country's major metropolitan centers teemed with immigrants, diverse languages, and customs.

Private schools may prepare affluent Anglo students to go into elite universities, but eventually these students will enter a society startlingly different from their alma maters. Whether they're physicians, entrepreneurs, architects, or writers, Anglos will work alongside or provide service to non-Anglos.

How do we prepare Anglo children to interact with other children if the majority of their classmates are Anglo? How do we foster competition among minority children in an economy driven by knowledge if the majority of their classmates drop or flunk out?

Some complain that America's minorities don't come out of their ethnic enclaves or forsake their Spanish or Ebonics for Standard English. It's difficult to communicate in the school of Babel. But there is a common language that can be learned only in schools that foster interracial mixing and high minority achievement: the language of respect and competition learned through daily interaction with people of another race or culture. There is no guarantee that the races will interact in integrated schools, but the opportunity is certainly greater if they are sitting in the same classroom.

Despite the *Brown vs. Board of Education* ruling of 1954 and subsequent federal enforcement, a major American school problem is regressing to apartheid school systems. Fort Worth and Arlington, Texas, school districts are minority-majority, with minority student populations of 86 percent and 74 percent respectively for the 2010–2011 school year. Educational research consistently shows that black and Mexican American students in predominantly minority schools don't receive competitive, quality education. These schools tend to have high concentrations of poverty, social and health problems, and limited resources. Minority students in predominantly minority schools tend to score lower on standardized tests and have a more difficult time getting into college than Anglo students.[11]

As documented in a report by Erica Frankenberg of Harvard University, "A Multiracial Society with Segregated Schools: Are We Losing the Dream?" separate schools were still unequal. The report cited a Texas study tracking millions of students over time in which researchers found that black children, particularly high-achieving blacks, attending schools with large percentage of blacks were learning in an environment that didn't encourage academic achievement.[12]

According to findings by researcher Gary Orfield in his study "Resegregation in American Schools," Mexican American student segregation has increased over the years to where Hispanics were more segregated than blacks. Like African Americans, Chicanos in segregated schools tended to experience more poverty, high dropout rates, low average levels of competition, and low levels of college admission.[13]

Thus, it was surprising to read comments by Mansfield, Texas, school officials reported by Eva-Marie Ayala, March 27, 2005, in the *Fort Worth Star-Telegram* by then Timberview High School Principal Alfred Ray, that the school's racial makeup—67 percent minority—didn't hurt the students. The newspaper reported that the student enrollment exceeded the projected minority count of 50 percent in its first year. With the increasing demographic changes in Mansfield, minority enrollment will only increase. In this article, Mansfield School Board President Joy Keller was quoted from an e-mail that Timberview's racial makeup will not affect its quality: "I expect Timberview to continue to grow into a cohesive, exciting place of learning with a quality education being provided to all students."

It truly would excite many if half of the black and Mexican American students transferred to Mansfield High School, a majority Anglo school, and half of that school's Anglo students transferred to Timberview.

Timberview student body Co-President Eric McGinnis talked about "the school's diversity does nothing but help the students" in this same *Fort Worth Star-Telegram* article.

He was right about diversity helping students, but unfortunately, the Harvard studies show that the current minority-majority enrollment at this high school will academically and socially harm the students. At the time that school administrators considered attendance zones for Timberview and Mansfield, the district's superintendent and board fumbled an opportunity to turn the resegregation tide around.

Faced with a Department of Education investigation, they will need to justify school attendance zones that clearly shielded Mansfield High School's Anglo students from black and Chicano students. Such a school policy as determined by the Supreme Court on May 17, 1954, had the implication that minorities were inferior. After sixty years of *Brown*, surely we've learned that school apartheid was not only un-American but that it failed us all.

This failure to provide superb education to all students has dire results for this country as it competes to keep its technological edge. These economic times call for far-sighted planning that develops Chicano brain power.

The economic need for more Chicano scientists was made clear at a conference focusing on the demand for a strong United States technological workforce of the future. James D. Spaniolo, former president of the University of Texas at Arlington, likened the current United States technological workforce crisis to the space race of the 1950s and 1960s. The US was caught flat-footed when Soviet scientists launched Sputnik, the first satellite to orbit the Earth. In the brain race, America rallied its schools and students to pursue math and science studies. The crowning victory over the Soviets, celebrated across the world on television, came when Neil Armstrong set foot on the moon and planted the US flag there in July 1969. More than forty years later, new challengers to US technological dominance have arisen across the world. In the near future, Chinese or Indian astronauts may plant their flags alongside the Stars and Stripes. At the Regional Workforce Development Summit at UTA in June 2005, business, civic, science, and education leaders discussed the current US technological crisis. Tegwin Pulley, Texas Instruments' vice president for workforce development, diversity, and work-life strategies, said that the United States produces 60,000 electrical engineers a year. China graduates three times and Europe and India twice that many annually.

The number of computer science students has dropped by 60 percent in the early twenty-first century across the United States. Pulley said that the country has half the number of engineers it had in the 1980s. She warned that as a result, America will not have the technology workforce required to keep pace with technological growth and foreign competitors.

"We're missing the economic boat of the future," she said. "This is a threat to the economic health of the US."

Steve Palko, retired president and co-founder of XTO Energy Corporation, cited a study that predicted that the United States would become a nation of brokers. Instead of producing the technology needed by foreign countries, America would subcontract to India and China for the hard- and software components. Soon these countries will realize that they don't need US middlemen. This country, says Palko, will become a nation celebrated for its wonderful movies and entertainment.

He advised that the United States needed a change in value systems. Too many youths and families viewed education as an entitlement; instead, they should cherish it as a glorious opportunity provided by this nation to achieve their dreams.

Look at "the single most important economic development issue, and that is: How do you get people to complete post-secondary education and dramatically increase minority participants? What is the wisdom of reducing the funding at the university and college level? What's the wisdom of reducing the percentage of dollars for the K-12 institutions?" Palko asked. He bemoaned the failure of Texas legislators to pass a school finance reform bill and chastised special interests with selfish motives.

Spaniolo envisioned a way for progress. "Education is the biggest lifter in income and personal satisfaction," said the UT-Arlington president. "We can't make progress until we change political reality. We need to change the belief that equates increased taxes with poison. We need to be willing as citizens to make this commitment to pay the price to invest in our future."

In the fifty years since the Cold War, a diversity war of sorts arose across the land.

Steve Murdock, former Texas state demographer, described the changing face of the state and country at the conference. His colored maps, pie graphs, bar charts, and population projection statistics painted a picture of a Texas and a United States that illustrates the widespread proliferation of Mexican Americans. In contrast to an aging and shrinking Anglo population, the Mexican American population was younger and growing. Murdock suggested that to see what the country will look like in the future, look around Texas.

To maintain a technological edge and economic dominance over the world, US citizens must stop denying their country's demographic diversity. To compete successfully in a global market, US teachers, politicians, business leaders, media figures, and scientists must accept Mexican Americans and other minorities as their intellectual and social equals and invest the necessary techno-bucks.

Two-tier educational systems — private schools with rich, vibrant curriculums for the affluent and poorly funded public schools overly tested and regimented for the rest — presented an opportunity to the Chinese, Indians, and other smart foreign competitors. Hard-nosed realists must face the fact that the brain trust of tomorrow must increasingly come from Mexican American youths.

The formula was simple: Chicanos plus technological education equals national prosperity.

Steven Murdock's keen analysis of this country's and state's demographic future warranted closer examination. His research sounded the alarm that Chicano growth offered challenges and opportunities that policy makers must face. Ignoring population facts was a fool's errand.

Like a prophet, Steve Murdock traveled the state preaching to audiences about demographic trends. He said, "demography is a divine call. We know it is because there is a Book of Numbers in the Bible and it's all about census."

He admitted that, as Texas state demographer, he became preachy about our need to face our quickly changing racial and ethnic population. We ignored such trends at our social and economic peril. Texas' substantial population growth called for planning. According to US Census estimates, Texas grew by 2 million people, or 9.6 percent, in 2000-2005. This was second only to California's 2.2 million (6.7 percent) for the same period.[14]

After reviewing the 2010 US Census for Texas, Murdock said, "It's basically over for Anglos," according to Gary Scharrer as posted on Chron.com, February 24, 2011. Murdock, director of the Hobby Center for the Study of Texas at Rice University, said that the Texas population was divided between the old and aging Anglo and the young minority. He said that most of the population growth was natural with 22 percent of the growth from out-of-state migration. To compute natural population growth, subtract the total number of deaths from the total number of births in a region, state or country. This natural population calculation doesn't include people who immigrate into or emigrate from the country.

What's most telling was the change in non-white student population. He predicted that by 2040, 20 percent of the state's public school enrollment will be Anglo. With Mexican American educational achievement lagging behind Anglos, the demographic shift will have dire consequences on the Texas economy.

A review of the three largest school districts in Tarrant and Dallas counties, Tables 1–3, proves Murdock's point. In all three districts, Latinos are the majority or plurality.[15]

Table 1. Dallas ISD by Race/Ethnicity

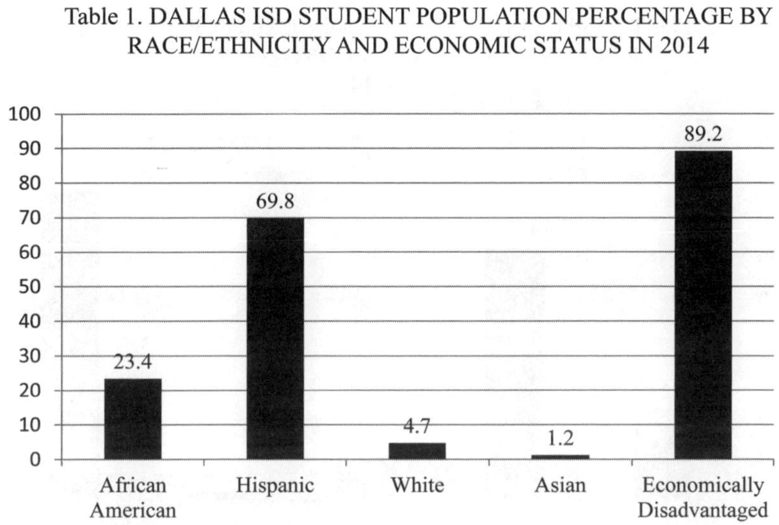

Source: Texas Education Agency

Table 2. Fort Worth ISD by Race/Ethnicity

Table 2. FORT WORTH ISD STUDENT POPULATION PERCENTAGE BY RACE/ETHNICITY AND ECONOMIC STATUS IN 2014

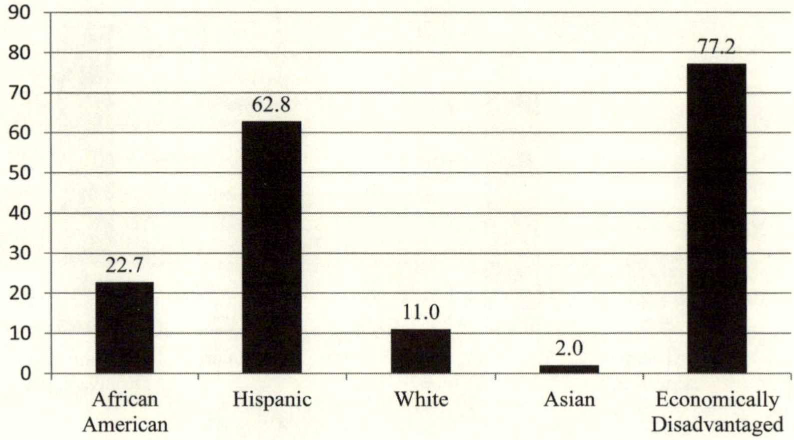

Source: Texas Education Agency

Table 3. Arlington ISD by Race/Ethnicity

Table 3. ARLINGTON ISD STUDENT POPULATION PERCENTAGE BY RACE/ETHNICITY AND ECONOMIC STATUS IN 2014

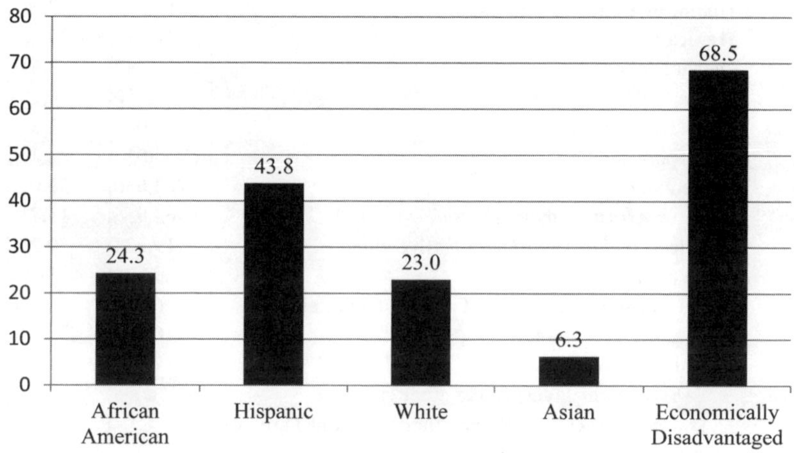

Source: Texas Education Agency

Murdock preached that the growth of the non-Anglo population was the most important factor affecting the future of Texas and the country. He projected that by 2040, Mexican Americans will become the majority in Texas. The following US Census data, Tables 4–9, show the 2013 population distribution for the Dallas-Fort Worth metropolitan areas as well as Dallas and Tarrant counties and the cities of Fort Worth, Dallas, and Arlington.[16]

Table 4. Dallas-Fort Worth-Arlington Metroplex, 2013

Table 4. DALLAS-FORT WORTH-ARLINGTON METROPLEX 2013

Total population	6,575,833	6,575,833
Hispanic or Latino (of any race)	1,813,509	27.6%
Mexican	1,544,933	23.5%
Puerto Rican	37,147	0.6%
Cuban	11,350	0.2%
Other Hispanic or Latino	220,079	3.3%
Not Hispanic or Latino	4,762,324	72.4%
White alone	3,284,636	50.0%
Black or African American alone	963,956	14.7%
American Indian and Alaska Native alone	19,621	0.3%
Asian alone	360,009	5.5%
Native Hawaiian and Other Pacific Islander alone	6,173	0.1%
Some other race alone	10,789	0.2%
Two or more races	117,140	1.8%
Two Races including Some other race	6,099	0.1%
Two races excluding Some other race, and Three or more races	111,041	1.7%

Source: US Census Bureau, 2009-2013 5-Year American Community Survey

Table 5. Tarrant County Population 2013

Table 5. TARRANT COUNTY POPULATION 2013

Total population	1,848,423	1,848,423
Hispanic or Latino (of any race)	499,033	27.0%
Mexican	432,500	23.4%
Puerto Rican	15,111	0.8%
Cuban	3,139	0.2%
Other Hispanic or Latino	48,283	2.6%
Not Hispanic or Latino	1,349,390	73.0%
White alone	945,390	51.1%
Black or African American alone	272,225	14.7%
American Indian and Alaska Native alone	5,860	0.3%
Asian alone	86,566	4.7%
Native Hawaiian and Other Pacific Islander alone	2,926	0.2%
Some other race alone	3,161	0.2%
Two or more races	33,262	1.8%
Two races including Some other race	1,673	0.1%
Two races excluding Some other race, and Three or more races	31,589	1.7%

Source: US Census Bureau, 2009-2013 5-Year American Community Survey

Table 6. Fort Worth Population 2013

Table 6. FORT WORTH, TEXAS POPULATION 2013

Total population	761,092	761,092
Hispanic or Latino (of any race)	260,349	34.20%
Mexican	232,479	30.50%
Puerto Rican	5,458	0.70%
Cuban	1,104	0.10%
Other Hispanic or Latino	21,308	2.80%
Not Hispanic or Latino	500,743	65.80%
White alone	314,642	41.30%
Black or African American alone	142,467	18.70%
American Indian and Alaska Native alone	2,426	0.30%
Asian alone	26,261	3.50%
Native Hawaiian and Other Pacific Islander alone	710	0.10%
Some other race alone	1,369	0.20%
Two or more races	12,868	1.70%
Two races including Some other race	565	0.10%
Two races excluding Some other race, and Three or more races	12,303	1.60%

Source: US Census Bureau, 2009-2013 5-Year American Community Survey

Table 7. Arlington Population 2013

Table 7. ARLINGTON, TEXAS POPULATION 2013

Total population	371,267	371,267
Hispanic or Latino (of any race)	104,724	28.2%
Mexican	89,181	24.0%
Puerto Rican	3,066	0.8%
Cuban	787	0.2%
Other Hispanic or Latino	11,690	3.1%
Not Hispanic or Latino	266,543	71.8%
White alone	161,422	43.5%
Black or African American alone	70,321	18.9%
American Indian and Alaska Native alone	1,222	0.3%
Asian alone	26,652	7.2%
Native Hawaiian and Other Pacific Islander alone	147	0.0%
Some other race alone	677	0.2%
Two or more races	6,102	1.6%
Two races including Some other race	189	0.1%
Two races excluding Some other race, and Three or more races	5,913	1.6%

Source: US Census Bureau, 2009-2013 5-Year American Community Survey

Table 8. Dallas County Population 2013

Table 8. DALLAS COUNTY POPULATION 2013

Total population	2,412,481	2,412,481
Hispanic or Latino (of any race)	928,418	38.5%
Mexican	795,712	33.0%
Puerto Rican	10,670	0.4%
Cuban	4,257	0.2%
Other Hispanic or Latino	117,779	4.9%
Not Hispanic or Latino	1,484,063	61.5%
White alone	785,993	32.6%
Black or African American alone	524,707	21.7%
American Indian and Alaska Native alone	4,543	0.2%
Asian alone	125,880	5.2%
Native Hawaiian and Other Pacific Islander alone	1,010	0.0%
Some other race alone	4,135	0.2%
Two or more races	37,795	1.6%
Two races including Some other race	2,071	0.1%
Two races excluding Some other race, and Three or more races	35,724	1.5%

Source: US Census Bureau, 2009-2013 5-Year American Community Survey

Table 9. Dallas Population 2013

Table 9. DALLAS, TEXAS POPULATION 2013

Total population	1,222,167	1,222,167
Hispanic or Latino (of any race)	512,077	41.9%
Mexican	452,557	37.0%
Puerto Rican	4,060	0.3%
Cuban	2,044	0.2%
Other Hispanic or Latino	53,416	4.4%
Not Hispanic or Latino	710,090	58.1%
White alone	357,744	29.3%
Black or African American alone	296,480	24.3%
American Indian and Alaska Native alone	1,781	0.1%
Asian alone	36,048	2.9%
Native Hawaiian and Other Pacific Islander alone	270	0.0%
Some other race alone	1,398	0.1%
Two or more races	16,369	1.3%
Two races including Some other race	614	0.1%
Two races excluding Some other race, and Three or more races	15,755	1.3%

Source: US Census Bureau, 2009-2013 5-Year American Community Survey

The future of Texas is strongly linked to how Chicanos fare. If we can raise Mexican Americans' level of performance in Texas, we can lift it in the rest of the country. Murdock said that outside the state, people called him the diversity demographer. He then pointed out the rapidly growing Mexican American presence in those "hotbed" Hispanic states of Utah, Idaho, and Iowa. The demographic alarms went off when Murdock discussed income and educational level comparisons. He said that the 1999 median income for Anglos was $47,162; for blacks, it was $29,305; for Mexican Americans, $29,873. Studies revealed a positive correlation between educational level and income: The more education, the more bucks.

In 2000, Texas was 45th among states whose residents age 25 or older had at least a high school diploma. In 2004 and 2009, the state was 50th.[17] In 2000, only 10 percent of Mexican Americans had completed college, compared to 32 percent of Anglos and 16 percent of blacks. In 2009, the data showed that 10.9 percent of Mexican Americans, 33.9 Anglos and 18.1 percent blacks completed college. Although there was a slight increase in Mexican American college graduates, a Texas Mexican American majority that was younger, less educated, and earning fewer dollars than other populations did not bode well for the state.[18]

Murdock recalled a group chuckling during one of his presentations about Texas' educational ranking. When he asked them about their joyous mood, they told him that they were from Mississippi and were grateful for Texas. But education was not a laughing matter when you consider the need for a learned population to stay competitive.

The swelling numbers and geographic spread of Mexicans and Mexican Americans stirred strong anti-immigration actions costing cities millions of dollars in legal fees. Anti-immigrant ordinances in Farmers Branch and threats by Arlington, Texas, resident Dave McElwee to press for similar laws in Tarrant County showed a gut-level reaction to immigrants' growing presence. They strove to legislate undocumented immigrants out of existence with José Crow laws.

Time and resources were better spent increasing the educational levels of all children in Texas, providing their families with access to affordable healthcare and passing federal laws that legalize their status. Murdock said that there was a demographic window of opportunity, with our current baby boomers' wealth and knowledge, to surpass Mississippi and all the other states in educational levels and median household incomes. He predicted that over time, the demographic makeup of Texas and the United States will become as diverse as the rest of the world. We need to ensure that our children can compete handsomely with them as well.

Bill Gates, founder of Microsoft Corporation, knew first-hand the importance of educating our future workforce to compete in the global market. He told the governors at the National Education Summit on February 2005 in Washington that "America's high schools are obsolete."[19]

He criticized high schools for their failure to prepare the majority of students for post-secondary education. The vitality of America's economic competitiveness with the rest of the industrialized world depended on getting bright kids into—and graduated from—college.

He zeroed in on the worst-kept secret in America's educational institutions: Although Anglo kids graduate prepared for college, work, and citizenship, "the other two-thirds, most of them low-income and minority students, are tracked into courses that won't ever get them ready for college or prepare them for a family-wage job – no matter how well the students learn or the teachers teach."[20]

From the mouth of the prototypical American capitalist, who knew a thing or two about parlaying intellectual capital into profit, came the bad news that high schools were shunting minority kids away from rigorous courses. They do so, Gates said, because they thought minority kids couldn't learn or weren't worth teaching.[21] This was a harsh indictment. But how else can we explain the high minority dropout rates or their dismal academic performance?

According to Achieve Incorporated, the organization that sponsored the summit, only 68 of 100 freshmen graduated from high school in four years. The Texas Education Agency calculated the Texas public school dropout rates for the class of 2010 as 11.8 percent African American, 9.6 percent Mexican American and 3.5 percent White. The Intercultural Development Research Association, an independent education research organization, calculated that the dropout rates for this class were 33 percent African American, 39 percent Mexican American and 15 percent White.[22] Despite the statistical differences, the dropout rates were alarming for Texas public schools.

Gates said that we should be ashamed of the American public school system. From the days of the little red schoolhouse to those of shiny, mall-like modern campuses, the doors of US public schools were seen as the portals to equity. Regardless of race, income, or parental educational level, children eager to learn could work their way out of poverty and into the highest levels of American society.

Some defenders of the public school system pointed to Attorney General Alberto Gonzales, son of migrant workers, and other successful minorities from humble backgrounds as proof that America's public schools worked quite well.

And they did—for a few. For most minorities, the high school experience lacked the challenge they deserved. We shamefully allowed them to live up to the caricature of the dumb Mexican fit only to work with his hands. We were good for taking orders but not for giving them.

Millions of kids like Gonzales in America's schools needed to be taught what Gates called the "new three R's":

•Rigor — All students needed to be given a challenging curriculum that prepares them for college or work. As he pointed out, it was outrageous that Anglo kids get Algebra II while minority kids learn to balance their checkbooks.

•Relevance — Ensured that courses related to students' lives and goals. Professions needed to be introduced on the elementary school level to all children.

•Relationships — Kids needed to see and know that adults care for them. They require that tough-love push on the hard subjects.

Gates said the challenge to America was to redesign our high schools to prepare all kids for college — not just the anointed Anglo few. Drawing on his worldwide travels, he bemoaned that American kids were falling behind the Chinese, Japanese, Indian, and South Korean youth. America's future depended on our schools' producing many smart Anglo, black, and Mexican American kids to keep our technological and economic advantage and to avoid the fourth R: Rage.

News media reports of violence in our communities reflected the anger that simmered in our neighborhoods. The lack of education and poverty bred a sense of hopelessness, futility, and loss that enslaved Chicanos to dead end jobs and low pay.

It will take a community effort to catch Mexican American youths before they fall too far from schools' graces. Boys and girls of all races but mostly African-American and Mexican American children in Texas soon transmuted into shadow students. They trailed behind their white peers on all standardized test scores; they comprised the negative tail of the bell curve; they were poor in money and literacy and, soon, spirit; they were sentenced to an outsider's existence, wondering and worrying about a better life.

Chronically short of cash and chances, they were condemned to the un-world: uneducated, underclass, unable, unfit, undeserving. They brood with dim awareness throughout their lives that somehow they were cheated but don't know how or by whom. But we who were educated know why so many poor whites and minorities were locked in a limbo of unskilled labor jobs. We allowed them to drop out of school and committed them and their children to a harsh life: no classroom, hence no class.

After struggling for eight primary years, thousands called it quits — the highest percentage in ninth grade. Then-Fort Worth Superintendent Thomas Tocco said at a Stay-In- School summit speech on October 15, 2002, in Fort Worth, Texas, 921 students, grades seven through twelve, dropped out in the 1999-2000 school year; another 976 dropped out for the same grades in the 2000-2001 school year. Texas Education Agency figures revealed that more than 40 percent of dropouts were Mexican Americans and more than 30 percent were African-Americans. Males drop out more often than females. Education researchers argued that this was an undercount — that the figures did'nt square with contrasts of ninth- and twelfth-grade enrollments.

There was little consolation in proving that the problem was much worse than reported. However, to marshal the necessary resources, the best count possible was needed.

In a country steeped in Horatio Alger stories of rugged individualism coupled with a tendency by some institutions to hide failures and problems, it was refreshing to hear the superintendent admit that the district probably never could beat the dropout problem alone. The social, economic, cultural, and academic hurdles were too high.

For the sake of the children, Tocco didn't attempt to save face but rather accepted the offers of help from the diverse chambers of commerce and community service agencies. Tocco should be commended for allowing the public to tour campuses during his tenure as superintendent, to study the causes, to partner with him in search of ways out of the dropout maze.

The schools are the public's business – not just from the traditional taxpayers' right-to-know-how-their-money-is-spent view but also in the American belief that a learned citizenry fosters democracy, innovation, prosperity, and tolerance. Diversity-rich America—a country of a highly educated white population holding most of the key financial, civic, and spiritual decision-making positions, while an undereducated minority population scrambles for lower-management and menial work – risks ethnic and class strife. With such an educational, financial, and political power disparity, how different is America from pre-Nelson Mandela South Africa?

Felipe Alanis, commissioner of the Texas Education Agency at the time, spoke to about 700 participants of the Stay-in-School Summit in Fort Worth on October 15, 2002. He said that half of the million children in Texas live below the poverty line. He asked the audience to imagine a balance-beam future. Missteps and a fall lead to "a large, alienated, hostile, underemployed population—was that the Texas future? Or will it be one that is bright, creative, forceful, energized and continues to keep us on the competitive edge?"

To dance on the education beam of light was the preference. This future is possible if more of us allow public education to enter our chambers of concern. The Stay-in-School Summit was a community rally by Fort Worth's chambers of commerce, Texas Christian University Chancellor

Michael Ferrari, and the Fort Worth school district to involve more of the public in the year-old Stay-in-School Initiative.

One of the plans of action was to match more mentors with potential dropout students. By developing a caring bond with students lacking in successful role models, the mentor spooned attention on children starved of personal, positive adult talk. It was also an opportunity for white mentors to develop close cross-cultural relationships that they otherwise might not experience.

Children of all colors, classes, and cultures deserved to know that they were valuable. Caring adults must guide them out from dropout shadows to learn and live in graceful school light.

At the same time, the business community must come to grips with the reality of financing quality education for all Texas students. As Texas demographics change, there are more Mexican American students entering schools who require more educational support if we are to close the Anglo-Mexican American educational gap.

IBM and the Fort Worth Independent School District (FWISD) partnered to pull heads out of the sand when dealing with public school finance. Big Blue and FWISD knew that to ensure a competitive edge and robust economy, a steady pool of talented, educated workers needed to graduate from Texas schools. The business of education required stable and reliable financing to pay for the rising costs of educating all of Texas' children.

At a morning breakfast forum in Fort Worth, Texas, on November 2004, local business, civic, and education leaders listened to sobering lessons from several school finance experts. F. Scott McCown, executive director of the Center for Public Policy Priorities (CPPP), asked for a show of hands of those not living or working in the school district where they grew up.

After most hands went up, he said it proved his point that ignorance doesn't stay put. The solution to this contagion of ignorance, he offered, was to inoculate the Texas public school system with heavy doses of a serum tax plan. McCown said that a state income tax was the best solution.[23]

A graph produced by CPPP showed that local ad valorem taxes have exceeded state spending for public schools since 1986. Property-rich school districts were better able to fund their children's education, but most Texas school districts could not—and therefore recaptured money from the richer districts through the Robin Hood plan.

Wayne Pierce, executive director of the Equity Center, said at the breakfast meeting that the Texas Legislature followed minimum dictates of the state constitution in providing funding for public school education. He said that "it's the worst that the state allows to teach your children. ... If you had a fancy car, you would never take it to a mechanic — regardless how good the mechanic—if all he had to work with were a crescent wrench. If we wouldn't do that with a car, why in the heck would we do that with our children?"[24]

John David Thompson III, an attorney with Brackwell & Patterson, posed a question to the audience raised by Steve H. Murdock, the former state demographer: Is demography destiny?

"Is the composition of our population determinate of our future? And Murdock's answer is: maybe. If we do nothing, our demographic shift will determine what our state looks like 10 years, 20 years, 40 years from now. . . . We will have a state that is less educated, less productive, more needy, more dependent on public services, more likely to be incarcerated, less desirable place to live."[25]

In a 2002 study by Murdock and his associates, "The Texas Challenge in the Twenty-First Century: Implications of Population Change for the Future of Texas," Murdock projected a Mexican American population growth of 175 percent between 2000 and 2040.

The Anglo population was expected to increase by 2.8 percent and the black population by 35.6 percent during the same period.[26]

In 1999, the median household income of Anglos exceeded that of Mexican Americans by $17,289. Murdock projected an increased lowering of household incomes. He also projected a fast-growing non-Anglo labor force that was less educated, less skilled, earning less, and in greater need of training than the Anglo population.[27] US Census data revealed that in 2013, the median difference was virtually the same at $17,307.[28]

The study estimated an additional 3.8 million students in public schools by 2040, with the majority of the enrollment increase attributable to Mexican Americans. This increase will call for more specialized programs such as bilingual and English-as-a-second-language classes. There will be increased pressure to provide financial aid to college students as Mexican American enrollment increases and household income decreases. Murdock said, "Education change will represent a significant challenge for the State of Texas."[29]

He concluded his study with alternative futures depending on how the state addressed the socioeconomic status of Mexican Americans. Given that the future of Texas will depend on how the non-Anglo population fares, it makes sense that improving the socioeconomic status of Mexican Americans and blacks will improve the chances that Texas will prosper. One key ingredient for Mexican American success was improving their educational status by having a reliable, steady source of education funding. Given the urgency of improving the education revenue stream, it was disappointing to hear the panelists admit that they didn't think any real change would take place in the next legislative session.

POLITIFACT, a fact-checking project of the *Tampa Bay Times*, examined Texas education funding for 2002–2012. They were particularly interested in a statement that then Governor Perry made on January 9, 2013. "We've had public education funding growing at three times the public education enrollment. So you've had a 70 percent increase of funding from 2002 to 2012. You've had a 23 percent increase in enrollment... I think under any scenario over the last decade, the funding that we have seen in the state of Texas for public education has been pretty phenomenal."[30]

After researching the budget numbers, taking into account inflation and a cut in local property tax rates mandated by the Texas Legislature in 2006, POLITIFACT researchers found that the actual difference between 2002 and 2012 in state education funding was 25 percent less in 2012.[31] In 2015, the Texas Supreme Court deliberated on a lawsuit filed by 600 Texas school districts against the state over state education funding. The 2015 lawsuit was the seventh filed by Texas school districts to reach the high court over school financing since the mid-1980s. A ruling was not expected until 2016.

Some thought, for political reasons, the state Legislature would await the Texas Supreme Court decision on school finance reform. And so we tarried while Texas turned browner, bigger, poorer, and dumber.

While the legislatures waited, Texas schools changed before their eyes.

At the start of the 2000 school year, Arlington, Texas, school bells signaled a remarkable change in the classroom. For the first time in the school district's existence, the predominantly Anglo faculty, administration, and trustees educated a minority-majority student body. Like the rest of the country, the Arlington school district awakened to the reality that the once invisible, marginalized Americans have transmuted into glaring visibility. What was once thought confined to the larger school districts, like Fort Worth and Dallas, suburban schools faced: the reality that ethnic minorities were moving in steady numbers to the idyllic land of once homogeneous bedroom communities.

Like California, Arizona, New Mexico, Illinois, and Florida, Texas witnessed a burgeoning Mexican American population that will force us to soon switch the minority numerical yoke onto Anglo shoulders. According to the 2010 US Census Bureau, Tarrant County had the highest percentage increase, 69.3 percent, of Mexican American population among the top six most Mexican American-populated Texas counties between 2000-2010.[32]

If it seemed that there were more Mexican Americans in neighborhoods, it was because there were and more are on the way. Census Bureau data forecast that California and Texas, the two most populous states in the union, will become minority-majority by 2025. New Mexico and Hawaii are already minority-majority. In 2005, Mexican Americans surpassed African-Americans as the second-largest ethnic group, behind only non-Hispanic whites. According to Jeffrey Passel and D'Vera Cohn of the Pew Hispanic Center, Mexican Americans will comprise 25 percent of the nation's population in 2050.[33] The growth of the ethnic minorities forced most of the presidential candidates even back in 2000 to shirk the white-bread, Norman Rockwellian persona and to strike ethnic poses. George W. Bush and Al Gore dropped Spanish words from their lips like candy dates, while Pat Buchanan and Ralph Nader partnered with ethnic, female running mates. Cameras swung and swayed at the Democratic and Republican conventions, portraying more minorities on TV than will ever be seen in an entire year of major network broadcasting.

However, in the race for the presidential candidacy for 2016, one Republican candidate seized on the growing American xenophobia to garner public support. In September 2015, Republican presidential candidate Donald Trump scolded fellow Republican candidate Jeb Bush for speaking Spanish at campaign events and told him to stop. He said, "I like Jeb. He's a nice man. But he should really set the example by speaking English while in the United States."[34] Bush responded with his statement: "We should celebrate that diversity and embrace a set of shared values, and Mr. Trump doesn't believe in those shared values. He wants to tear us apart. He doesn't believe in tolerance. He doesn't believe in the things that have created the greatness of this country."[35]

The techno-American future is ethnic — Mexican American, African-American, Asian — and will become more so each Microsoft year. The Texas Higher Education Coordinating Board (THECB) recognized the existing education gap and the need to implement innovative programs to enroll and graduate more Texans.

The *2015 Texas Public Higher Education Almanac, A Profile of State and Institutional Performance Characteristics* offered an excellent comparison review of how Texas higher public educational institutions fared in enrolling and graduating students. Sponsored by the THECB in an effort to achieve specific numerical goals to close the education gap, the report provided a transparent look at how Texas stacked up with the rest of the country and between four-year state universities and two-year colleges. With plentiful graphs and tables, the board gave a transparent accounting of their higher education efforts.

Dr. Raymund A. Paredes, Commissioner of Higher Education, stated their goals were "(1) to increase participation in Texas higher education and (2) to significantly increase the number of credentials awarded. More specifically, the participation goal was to increase college enrollment by 630,000. . . Our completion goal was to reach 210,000 undergraduate credentials awarded in 2015."[36] By 2014, their data showed that 589,741 students enrolled, 40,259 short of the goal. However, there remains an additional enrollment cycle. The credentials data reveal in 2014, 251,247 students graduated or received post-secondary certification, already meeting their 2015 goal.

A closer look of the enrollment data showed that Blacks exceeded their 2015 goal in 2014 by 55,945 students, but Latinos missed their 2014 target goal by 97,170. An additional 137,884 Latino students will need to enroll by fall 2015 for the project to reach its 2015 goal of 439,000 Latino student enrollments.[37]

The annual report also presented data by race and ethnicity on the enrollment and graduation rates for the state's public universities and community colleges. Readers can focus their study on an area of the state or specific universities and colleges. Given the urgency to meet established Latino enrollment and graduation goals as identified by the state, it served us well to examine these rates for the four North

Texas public universities. This important data gave us an opportunity to compare enrollment and graduation rates of Latino students at the University of Texas at Arlington, Texas Woman's University, University of Texas at Dallas, and University of North Texas. Table 10 shows that the University of Texas at Arlington enrolled and graduated a greater percentage of Latinos of their total student enrollments and graduations in 2014 compared to the other three area universities.[38]

Table 10. Percentage Latinos at Four-Year Universities

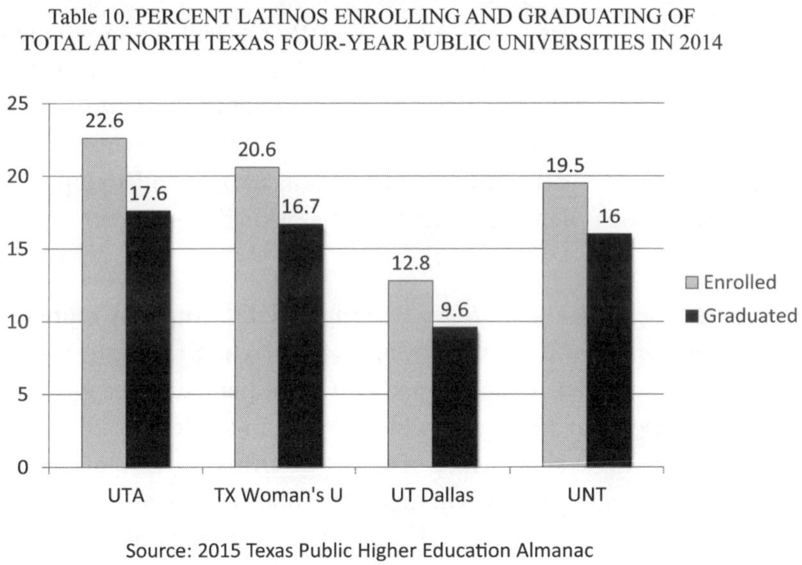

As referenced earlier, demographic projections reflected an exponential Mexican American population growth. To maintain and propel a North Texas economic boost, a comparable Chicano brain boost was required. I recommend area universities pool their resources and talents to focus their recruitment, retention, and graduation of Mexican American students in higher education. For many economically disadvantaged Chicanos, financial aid packages are required to pay their tuition, fees, room, and board. Community organizations must partner with universities to examine the obstacles to enrolling and graduating Chicanos. Financial support of Mexican American youth will close the college gap and yield an immeasurable return of investment to North Texas.

Some may never accept the reality that ethnics are their equals; however, it is the young that must be taught that their sociopolitical future is programmed to ethnicity.com. The virus of bigotry, if allowed to spread among the youth, will cause us to resemble Bosnia, Israel, or Northern Ireland—but on a much larger scale.

The challenge before us is simple: We either accept the browning of America or resist. For those who resist, daily life will become a maelstrom of frustrations as the xenophobes go to work alongside coworkers for whom they hold fear and contempt. Spanish will flow so profusely that the bigot may consider white flight to Canada, only to be stopped at the border by a French-speaking Mountie asking for *le* green card, *si vous plais.*

Another scenario, one more frightening and unfortunately more real, was that ethnic minorities will continue to fail in school and settle for low-paying, dead-end jobs. Despite their growth in numbers, proportionate numbers of Mexican Americans did not excel in academics. According to the 2012 Statistical Abstract of the US Census Bureau, about 20.8 percent of Mexican Americans in the United States dropped out of school compared to 9.1 percent of Anglos and 11.6 percent of blacks.[39] With the highest dropout rates in the country, Mexican Americans struggle to compete in a market driven by the complexity of logarithms and genome science. In a real world, faced with growing, international competition, our economic and democratic future rests on our ability to nurture the minds and esteem of all children. Arlington teachers, like their Fort Worth and Dallas counterparts, must accept the ethnic challenges before them and know that Dick, Jane, and Spot don't necessarily relate well to Yolanda, Rubén, and Jorge. We must, however, avoid the ethnocentric trap in thinking that ethnic professionals can only reach ethnic children.

Some performances by ethnic professionals, the likes of former Dallas Superintendent Yvonne González, left many ethnics with feelings of disgust and disappointment.

Instead, these brave, new ethnic times provide us with the opportunity to truly test the grand American tradition of accepting immigrants and teaching them a love for this country and the rewards that it offers to those with the skills and drive to compete well in the capitalist market. The paradox to accept is that children reciting the Pledge of Allegiance in Spanish will make America strong.

To paraphrase John Donne, the school bell tolls for us all.

Chapter 3

Foreign Language Skills

Aside from immigration, few issues raise the ire of the non-Spanish speaking population of the United States more than the freedom to speak Spanish in public. Movements to enact English as the official language of the country have periodically swept the country only to face defeat. In the meantime, some politicians point to bilingual classes and Spanish translations of government documents as divisive and unnecessary expenses. As the Mexican American population grows, the use of Spanish will increase and elicit raucous debate.

One important way to stimulate bilingualism is to encourage increased proficiency in foreign languages among all children. However, there are still some outdated attitudes that prevail.

Stories abound in the Chicano community of how Anglo and Mexican American teachers meted out physical punishment to Spanish-speaking, Mexican American students. Such a backward attitude to foreign languages not only physically and emotionally hurt Mexican American students but it arrested an understanding and acceptance of the social and economic values of a polyglot citizenry. No bilingual education or

Spanish immersion classes allowed in the land of King English! Children of the Lone Star had to learn to speak American.

The early twentieth century was a time of American isolation and arrogance. Xenoglossophobia – fear of foreign languages – ran rampant. Unfortunately, this politically charged, elitist English-language attitude lingers.

A common joke in the linguistic world: What do you call a person who speaks three languages? Trilingual. What do you call a person who speaks two languages? Bilingual. What do you call a person who speaks one language? American. Carrie Harrington, program director for foreign languages for the Fort Worth school district, said children can't afford to stay monolingual in a polyglot world.

"When you see an American child come to your class and leave your class at the end of the year more sensitive to the way other people view the world, that's a great gift," she says. "That's one of the most important things that foreign languages do. They open the world and give the kids a broader perspective other than a Fort Worth, Texas, way of viewing the world," she said in an interview with the author.

Fort Worth schools offered sign language, French, German, Italian, Japanese, Latin, and Spanish – gateways to seeing the planet's diversity and beauty. Harrington hoped to also offer Chinese and Arabic.

Along with broader vistas, foreign language study enhances understanding of English, improves listening, nurtures creativity, and slows mental losses that can occur with aging. Foreign language skills give a competitive edge in the world market. A farsighted nation recognizes that the global economy requires a sophisticated people with an ability to speak directly to the international customer. India quickly capitalized on its English speakers to lure American bucks, and as a result it has wrested call center contracts from US companies.

What a tour de force if ambitious Americans learned Hindi, Japanese, and Chinese and employed their language skills to beat foreign competitors at their own game. America's friends and foes know enough about our military might. It's time for more US presidents and diplomats to impress other countries with an ability to speak directly to them in their own tongue, showing that we're equal partners in the struggle for economic justice, democracy, and world peace. Credibility is often lost in the translation.

Despite government posturing on enforcing stricter immigration laws and cracking down on businesses that hire undocumented immigrants, bilingual workers have an edge with companies looking for Spanish-speaking sales people, customer service representatives, and social service workers. With an estimated 11 million undocumented immigrants in this country who buy cars, clothes, houses, and food, apply for loans and seek education, health care, and legal assistance, Spanish-speaking skills push a job applicant to the front of the line.

For all these reasons, the American Council on the Teaching of Foreign Languages declared 2005 the Year of Languages. Working from a 2001 European Union celebration of the Year of Languages, the ACTFL, through local events, sought to increase awareness of the richness of foreign languages and to encourage Americans to surmount language barriers and become true global citizens.[40]

America must emerge from the dark ages of English-language superiority to the enlightenment of foreign language mastery. We must learn to respect the languages of our foreign friends and foes — the former to strengthen ties, the latter to outwit them. For our own good, we must speak to the world with linguistic virtuosity.

A proven method of learning English for Spanish-speaking students is bilingual education. In conversations with two individuals encountered at a League of United Latin American Citizens' national convention in Dallas, I gained personal insight on the bilingual education issue.

The late Carlos F. Truan, state senator from Corpus Christi, recalled the physical disciplining he took in the 1940s for speaking Spanish in school.

"I and a lot of other children started in grade zero," said Texas' "Father of Bilingual Education." Motivated by his experiences of discrimination and humiliation, Truan entered politics and wrote several bills permitting Texas children to be taught in their primary language. Carmen Galindo, twenty-year bilingual teacher, said through tears that she couldn't forget the threats of punishment she received from nuns when she spoke Spanish in her South Texas Catholic school.

"For many years I thought I was dumb," she said. "My self-esteem was beaten down. Finally in the seventh and eighth grades, I learned enough English where I felt as smart as the Anglo students," she told the interviewer. Many of her friends came to her during that time, asking for help with their schoolwork, she said. Shamed from beatings in school, they told her, "If they could tell us in Spanish..." Filled with anger at watching many of her friends drop out, go to jail, and never reach their potential, Galindo earned a master's degree in education with bilingual education concentration.

The needs that Truan and Galindo expressed lie at the heart of bilingual education.

In response to critics of bilingual education, Stephen Krashen, professor of education at the University of Southern California, wrote the ironically titled book *Under Attack: The Case Against Bilingual Education.* Backed by scholarly research, Krashen found that a successful bilingual program must possess three components:

•Comprehensible input in English.

•Subject matter teaching done in the child's first language, without translation.

•Literacy development in the first language, which transfers to the second language.

Krashen explained that the knowledge gained through the first language helped the children understand the English they heard and read.[41] Wayne

Thomas and Virginia Collier of George Mason University, who found that it took non-English-speaking students who were taught exclusively in English seven to ten years to reach the age and grade-level norms of their English-speaking peers, backed his research. However, students taught bilingually reached and surpassed native English-speakers' performance across all subject areas after four to seven years when tested in English.[42]

Gilda Evans, former director of bilingual education in the Arlington, Texas, school district, said to the author in an interview that the bilingual education controversy is an "issue of access in learning."

"If you were to hand me an article in Turkish," she said, "I would thank you for the information, but I would have to tell you I don't understand." Evans said that bilingual education aims to teach the "limited English proficient" (LEP) student a public language. Evans agreed that some bilingual programs might need fixing. However, "if you discover a chemistry class that needs improvement, you don't dismantle the entire chemistry program to correct the problem."

Aware of the geopolitical position of Texas, Spanish-speaking, former president George W. Bush said at the national League of United Latin American Citizens convention in Dallas that he supported "English-plus" education, teaching in both languages. This prominent literacy advocate knew too well that a bilingual populace makes good business sense when one of the country's largest trading partners is parleying in *Español.*

Also, Bush probably was aware of the horrendous Mexican American dropout statistics. The Texas Education Agency reported that 35,813 Mexican Americans dropped out during the 1995-96 school year, accounting for 51.9 percent of all dropouts.[43] The Intercultural Development Research Association of San Antonio, an independent research agency, disclosed in their 2011 attrition report that Mexican Americans had an overall 37 percent high school attrition rate.[44]

Despite the support of scholarly research, politicians, part-time preachers, talk-show hosts, and the uninformed have blamed bilingual programs for what is wrong with Mexican American education. English-only advocates celebrated their initiative's recent successful campaign to gut bilingual education in California and believed that they were on the merry road to a monolingual millennium.

Thomas Kuhn wrote in *The Structure of Scientific Revolution* that throughout history, science has progressed by way of paradigm shifts. For example, scientists once were ridiculed for teaching the radical notion that the Earth was part of a heliocentric planetary system. It was a new scientific paradigm—a way of thinking—that had not yet been accepted.[45] Bilingual advocates, too, have advanced a new paradigm, supported by social science studies, that bilingual education is the surest and quickest route to achieve English proficiency for limited English proficient children. Science notwithstanding, bilingualism transmuted from an educational issue to a political red herring. The old paradigm of the melting pot was crumbling before the challenge of a new icon: the salad bowl. A cultural paradigm shift was sweeping the country — from *e pluribus unum* (from many, one) to *pluribus et unum* (many and one). *Ave* multicultural millennium.

The Catholic Church supported multiculturalism. In 2015, at a Saturday vigil Mass at St. Joseph Catholic Church in Arlington, Texas, the pastor explained to the mostly English-speaking congregation that Thursday evening Mass would now be held in Spanish. They could learn *Español* to participate more fully at this Mass. Like many priests, the pastor learned Spanish to reach souls and invited English speakers to stretch their linguistic skills and minds. The divinity speaks and listens in all languages.

There are some who are linguistic bigamists and even polygamists. I admit that I'm one. You see, I'm married to two languages, Spanish and English, in love with them both, till death do us part. Like many Chicanos, I was betrothed from birth to Spanish and English — I knew my linguistic brides from an early age. I courted them both, encouraged by my parents to master English and cherish Spanish. Raised partly in a Spanish-speaking world, I've developed such an attachment to the language of Gabriel García Márquez and Carlos Fuentes that on some nights I still dream in a rollicking Spanish as I did in my youth. The lyrics of Mexican melodies like *Las Mañanitas* or love songs by Trio Los Panchos stir emotional tremors along my heart's fault lines.

Likewise, I've developed a love of English that is equally deep and intense. Schooled in the tongue of William Shakespeare, I wonder what person can remain unmoved when reading stories of Ernest Hemingway or John Steinbeck. The rhymes of Langston Hughes and the lyricism of Toni Morrison sweep up from the pages into my senses like opium, hooking me into a mainlining literary junkie. Now I've got a book monkey on my back.

When the social occasion calls for it, I slip into Spanish to ease the dominant Spanish speaker, acknowledging that he or she is important and deserving of the right to be understood and speak without the embarrassment of stammer. Or when the monolingual English-speaker feels slighted or threatened by the sounds of foreign words, I will cross over to English, feeling slightly guilty of my linguistic superiority. English may be the lingua franca of the commercial world, but Spanish is the lingua amorosa of the Latin soul.

For many of us raised in the traditions of quinceañeras, padrinos, madrinas, Pedro Infante, Cantinflas, Tito Puente, Santana, Zapata, Little Joe and the Cisco Kid, speaking Spanish has rooted itself so deeply in our identity that suppression is impossible. I understand but don't accept laws to enact English as the official language of states, or rules at jobs and schools that forbid the use of Spanish by employees or students. My mother has told me of the scolding she received from nuns when they discovered on the first day of school that the little English I knew came from a regular diet of Howdy Doody.

Fellow bilinguals recall memories of slaps, paddles, and palm whacks for speaking the mother tongue in the English schools. We received the lessons early: Spanish bad, English better. Mexicans dumb, Anglos smarter. Fear of foreigners and a misguided belief that too many languages will create chaos and disloyalty and a return to some modern re-creation of the Tower of Babel fan the scare.

The xenophobes forget that in the New Testament, the Holy Spirit anointed the disciples with tongues of fire so that they could spread the word of God in many of the world's languages. I don't think the Ten Commandments were originally written in English. But monolinguals persist. They declare that bilingual education is a handicap to learning English. Total immersion in the River English will cleanse us of the taint of accent and *Español.* Although some do learn in this sink-or-swim approach, too many flounder and eventually drop out.

Administrators ignore studies that continually prove that bilingual education is the best method of keeping a child on grade level and making the crossover to English as effective as possible. No better diplomatic example of the advantages of language proficiency exists than in the charismatic Vicente Fox, former president of México. When he slips over the border, he meets and greets *Norteamericanos* in an English that shows his respect for us. I wish US presidents could get past the taco and *cerveza* level and address the Mexican Congress in Spanish on what we must do together to curb the narcotic traffic and the flow of undocumented workers. We may need to wait for the election of a Mexican American US president with a tongue of fire.

The plan by Democratic Party gubernatorial contenders Dan Morales and Tony Sánchez in 2002 to debate in Spanish raised the ire of the local English-only crowd. This linguistic skirmish awakened us to America's historical struggle with tolerance for a polyglot society.

Opponents to the use of any non-English language in government argue that English is the common language that unites us as a people. Any pandering to non-English-speakers is purely ethnic politics that discourages immigrants, especially Chicanos, from joining mainstream America and fosters separatism. They argue that like European immigrants, Mexican American immigrants should forsake their native tongue and learn English in order to partake of our land's opportunities. If history had conspired with simplistic notions, English would have been uncommonly common. Instead, the past shows that restrictive linguistic attitudes weren't part of the original American experience.

At the founding of this country, English was spoken alongside French, German, Welsh, Dutch, and hundreds of Native American tongues. The Articles of Confederation were published in German and English, while other government documents were translated into French so that many Americans and Canadians could understand the revolutionary significance of the birth of a diverse nation.[46]

When John Adams attempted to persuade the Continental Congress in 1780 to create a language academy to purify English, his plan was rejected as undemocratic and a threat to individual liberty. For the Founding Fathers who fought a bloody revolution against the tyrannical English, freedom of speech and assembly were so deeply cherished that they codified it as the First Amendment to the Constitution. They wisely held that the love of liberty, democracy, justice, and tolerance were values that united the American people more than a common language.

The age of multilingual tolerance continued through most of the nineteenth century, with bilingual education taught in French, Spanish, German, Norwegian, Italian, Polish, Czech, and Cherokee across the country. According to the National Association of Bilingual Education, at the start of the twentieth century, 600,000 American children were receiving part or all of their education in German. Proportionally, more children then were enrolled in bilingual education than is the case today.[47] The immigration of Eastern and Southern Europeans and Asians and the start of World War I saw nativism and xenophobia rise in an ugly-American splendor. Laws were enacted requiring English proficiency for public employment, naturalization, immigration and, suffrage.

Anti-German feelings fueled laws prohibiting folks to speak Deutsch in public and schools. Ironically, Northern and Western European immigrants were considered superior to Eastern and Southern European immigrants in their ability to embrace the "American Way."

The early English-only movement was stimulated more by racist, political, anti-immigrant sentiments fearful of the swelling population of new arrivals than by any patriotic zeal to welcome them into mainstream America. These attitudes persist today but are now aimed at the fastest-growing immigrant population: Mexican Americans. In the 1980s, the English-only activists roiled the public with their push to legislate English as the nation's official language. They've succeeded in shepherding English-only laws in 26 states, excluding Texas. The Arizona Supreme Court overturned in 1998 the state's official English amendment to that state's constitution.

In 1981, Sen. S.I. Hayakawa made history by introducing the first English Language Amendment to the Constitution. The California lawmaker, since deceased, also voiced agreement with the internment of Japanese-Americans during World War II. In response, an English-plus network, consisting of civil rights and educational organizations, asserted that immigrants bring with them valuable knowledge of languages and cultures that strengthen America. They heartened immigrants to keep their first languages and learn English, our customs and laws.

According to approved Resolution 15 of the 2000 LULAC National Convention, "the ability to speak languages in addition to English is a tremendous resource to our county and in today's global economy, multilingual abilities enhance the skills of our workers, making the US more competitive."[48] Like bilingual ballots and gubernatorial candidate George W. Bush campaigning in *Español*, the Morales-Sánchez Spanish debates exhibit a refreshing respect for America's rich linguistic and cultural diversity that sprouted from the time that Native Americans placed seeds in the Pilgrims' palms. Having seen the face and felt the grip of the tyrant, our Founding Fathers heard *Viva la libertad*, *Vive la liberté*, *Die Freiheit leben*, and Long live liberty as equally sweet cries in their freedom-loving ears.

That history lesson translates well in any language.

Chapter 4

Education Innovators

I learned about Chemistry Professor Ricardo Rodríguez and his work with Mexican American youth when writing about the recipients of the Hispanic Heritage Awards. Professor Rodríguez ensured that his Chemistry Summer Camp kids learn Isaac Newton's Three Laws of Motion, the four forces of flight, and how to make ice cream and slime. He also expects them to improve their English.

Since 1991, Rodríguez has concocted in his Texas Wesleyan University laboratory a three-week science camp to sharpen the analytical and language skills of inner city , fourth-, fifth-, and sixth-graders. He normally averaged eighty-five to ninety-five students per summer session. In the summer of 2013, he signed up ninety-nine students. He closed registration when he received 110 applicants because the laboratories could not accommodate any additional students. Several inner-city Fort Worth middle schools were allowed fifteen slots each to recommend students for the summer session.

He was convinced that the science lab is the gateway to better English skills and a rewarding life. In Rodríguez's labs, culture and chemistry produce a solution of success for kids and community. The professor mentioned that he often taught Spanish-dominant students in their native language to ensure that his students understood the science.

"Science is our future," Rodríguez said. "As our oil becomes depleted, who are the scientists and engineers who will build the new cars that don't run on oil?"

At the same time, he observed that the Mexican American population has exploded throughout North Texas and the country. "Who will be the physicians and nurses to communicate with the population who are English-limited?" he said. He hoped that his fledging scientists will — through his summer camp — get the thrust they need to soar into medical, nursing and engineering schools. His innovative work yielded some positive results.

Rodríguez hired handpicked, science-oriented middle and high school and college students to act as student mentors. The middle school students must have completed his summer camp before they mentored and all teachers must be bilingual. He expected the younger student mentors to learn from their older peers. He normally recruited about twenty-one students to assist him with the teaching.

As an extra benefit, the mentors met with a TWU admissions counselor to learn about college enrollment procedures and costs. Some mentors had enrolled at Brown and Dartmouth. A student teacher who started mentoring in the tenth grade graduated in 2006 from the University of Texas at Austin with a master's in biochemistry.

Rodríguez assigned a teacher to three or four students, ensuring that all students received as much individual attention as possible. An equal number of girls and boys participated in the program and the professor divided them into separate lab groups to prevent the boys from bullying the girls.

From 8:30 a.m. until 2:00 p.m., the chemistry camp students went through a daily routine of hands-on laboratory experiments, classroom lecture, and writing of observations and findings. Aware that laboratory work was their favorite activity and documentation their least, Rodríguez didn't allow them to go on to the next experiment until they finished their writing. He said about 20 percent of the students report their findings in Spanish.

The program was divided into three parts: chemistry, physics, and aerodynamics. In chemistry, they learned chemical reactions, analytical balances, chemical mixing, and how to observe chemical changes as in ice cream production.

In physics, they used yo-yos to understand the concept of pendulum movements, motions, and Newton's laws. Rodríguez was surprised to learn that many students had never made paper airplanes. He showed them how simple modifications to the planes determine whether they fly straight, in a spin pattern, sideways, up, or down. He taught them about the forces of lift, drag, thrust, and gravity that affect paper planes and jets alike. The highlight of the program was construction of water rockets that shoot three stories high.

Rodríguez bemoaned the state of science education in Texas. He noted that state standardized science scores show that Texas kids aren't receiving a good science foundation. He said that elementary school teachers aren't receiving enough science training to instill in their students a deeper understanding of science. When you add that school science classes are often too large for one or two teachers, Texas students will fall behind in the science race.

The Chemistry Summer Camp was free to the students; but wasn't a free program. Rodríguez said that the summer session program costs were $20,000 per summer. He managed to raise most of the money through donations from the Gil and Dody Weaver Foundation and Meador Chrysler, Jeep, Dodge—Fort Worth. Rodriguez donated personally $3,000 per year. The Fort Worth Independent School District contributed bus transportation and meals. Texas Wesleyan University donated the lab space and equipment throughout the existence of the summer programs.

Professor Rodríguez formulated in his lab that when you mix dedicated students with small class size, add in knowledgeable science teachers with dollops of money, you'll produce great Lone Star scientists and a vibrant state economy.

During the years that Danna Díaz was the Fort Worth Schools dropout czar, she worked relentlessly to make the educational pie bigger for all students. She strove diligently to bring the community together to keep and bring back children to school. But she couldn't do it alone.

Danna Díaz's education—formal and informal—prepared her for one of the toughest jobs in the Fort Worth school district. As the Director of Student Engagement and School Completion,, Díaz spearheaded an ambitious community effort to keep students in school. With the help of several social service agencies, volunteers, and school staff, she organized the first "iDream ... iLearn ... iWin Family Summit" on May 5, 2007, at Tarrant County College South Campus. About 200 parents and students listened as Fort Worth school district and Tarrant County College speakers encouraged them to dream big and work hard to reach their goals.

When friends asked Díaz how she was progressing, she responded, "*Estoy luchando*" — I'm fighting.

"Life is hard," Díaz said. "If we teach young people how to overcome barriers, then the world is in the palm of their hands."

She knew the dropout challenge well. In addition to her doctorate in education administration from the University of Texas at Austin, she earned a doctorate in survival in the streets and projects of New York City's Harlem. As a former gang member, pregnant teen, high school dropout, and single parent, she learned that poverty, a drug-addicted father and negative peer pressure would lead youths astray. "I know how it is to be underserved and know how it is to be a person of color ... I think that's what gives me the edge," she said.

At age seven, she aspired to become a teacher but had no idea how she would achieve the goal. As a child, she learned that Columbia University was just down the street from her neighborhood when a professor was killed in front of her elementary school. In organizing the summit, she thought that schools of higher learning should open their doors to students and parents who live nearby so that they can demystify the academic world. Students need to walk the campus, see the classrooms, and envision strolling across the stage and receiving their degrees. She helped them learn how to convert dreams to reality.

Díaz planned a second summit at the TCC Northwest Campus in the fall of 2007 and a third at Texas Christian University in the spring of 2008. Juan García, vice president for student development services at TCC South Campus, said the college was partnering with schools to help parents and students prepare for higher education. "It's important to educate the Mexican American community," García said. "We are the largest minority in the nation, but we're not represented in those numbers in the colleges and universities."

Díaz said that students drop out for several reasons. If a student falls behind academically and is retained in class, the chances of dropping out increase 50 percent. In the "High School Redesign" breakout session, a Fort Worth school district instructor said that studies have shown that a student failing the state's fifth-grade standardized test in reading will have a 90 percent chance of not graduating.

Teen pregnancy and taking a job to help the family finances increase dropout risks, Díaz said. Another factor is that modern students, steeped in technology, are more easily bored with traditional lecture teaching formats. In the "High School Redesign" session, the instructor talked about re-educating teachers on how to engage these students more effectively.

At twenty-one, Díaz earned her high school degree and pursued her dream to become a teacher. She recalled that a teacher supervisor told her that she could never be a good teacher until she mastered English. In two years after graduating from college with a bilingual education degree, she earned the Bilingual Teacher of the Year award in a Houston inner-city school.

After thirty years in Texas, she grasped the Southwest Mexican American culture well and called herself a naturalized Chicana. Her desire to serve fueled her passion. "I have to keep on moving," Díaz said. "Because if I don't do it — who will?"

The community should respond to that challenge with: "We will!"

Another educator who responded with a *Sí Se Puede*/Yes We Can attitude was Bill Betzen. After twenty-eight years working as a Child Protective Services social worker and an adoption and financial aid counselor, he knew how poverty, lack of goals, and poor education could send children into a tailspin. He had also worked several years in desolate Mexican villages where it was common for children to go only as far as the sixth grade. As adults, these uneducated villagers would emigrate from Mexico to this country without many educational experiences to share with their children born in the United States. What you don't know, you can't teach.

Behind a plastic-glass door, a school vault filled with 500 letters holds the hopes, fears, and goals of eighth-graders at Raúl Quintanilla Middle School in Dallas' Oak Cliff neighborhood. The school was named after a Mexican immigrant who came to the United States at thirteen speaking no English. Through hard work and smarts, he rose to the presidency of NationsBank in Dallas and chairman of the Dallas Hispanic Chamber of Commerce. After his death at age forty-seven, the school district honored his exemplary life and community involvement by naming the middle school for Quintanilla. At the end of the school year, their teachers gave the eighth-graders their final class assignment: continue their education, do good work, and come back in a decade with wisdom. When they return, they'll open the sealed envelopes and tell that year's eighth-graders what they've done with their lives, and how close to their goals they've come. If they do so, they'll get an A-plus in mentoring.

Inner-city children wish to know how older kids got through the trials of teenage angst, family strife, gangs, drugs, sex, gangly bodies, language and cultural differences. How do you live proud when you're poor? How do you get over the embarrassment of translating for Spanish-speaking parents when talking with doctors, teachers, and police? How do you set goals when kids are dropping out all around you?

The Achievement & Goals Archive project sprang from the frustration that computer application teacher Bill Betzen experienced watching middle school kids waste their precious time. Proud of the fact that the Dallas school district provided state-of-the-art computers and software to students, he found it painful to see unmotivated students fail to take advantage of the rich resources. If there were any program that kids would enjoy, it should be computers, he thought. "Seventh- and eighth-graders don't think ahead. I wanted them to think about the future," Betzen said.

Some of his students struggled with learning English or suffered from a poor elementary school education. He estimated that Spanish was the home language for 60 percent of his students. "They need personal attention that isn't funded by the school system," he said.

Their academic frustration and failure compounded during these crucial early years. "The Hispanic dropout rate in Dallas is 61 percent," he said, despite the district's published 1.4 percent rate for the 2003-2004 school year.

These experiences and his love of history gave him the idea that encouraging inner-city children to write their personal history and goals might give them a fighting chance to achieve. He sold the idea of a time capsule to the principal and other faculty. He convinced the local manager of the Lowe's Home Improvement Warehouse to donate the vault, plastic glass, and building material.

Quintanilla's language arts teachers had their students practice writing their letters. This writing process forced them to see beyond today, to dream about a better life.

Betzen added that no child was forced to write a letter for the vault. In the first year of the project, a pregnant student found the experience too threatening and couldn't write. Every school day, several times a day, the students pass the clearly visible vault close to the main entrance. They write letters as boys and girls to read as men and women. They learned they must seize the day.

A common goal for educational innovators is to raise Chicano youths' expectations beyond their barrio bounds. As the Mexican American population rises, new leadership must emerge from the young to lead and enrich their community. When I've spoken to Mexican American youth, I've sought to inspire them to courageous feats. However, their dearth of knowledge about Mexican American historical and ethnic identity issues surprised me. If they are to lead, further questions are raised.

Are you the ones we've waited for?

I hunger for Mexican American leaders to spring into the bullring of life and show us that courageous walk in the sand, dressed in a suit of lights before the horns of poverty, racism, and ignorance.

Are you the ones we've waited for? Do you have pride?

At this moment, I crave for the next Emiliano Zapata to state, "Better to die standing than to live on your knees," or another César Chávez to exhort, "yes, we can," or a José Ángel Gutiérrez to implore us, "vote for La Raza Unida Party."

How long will you tolerate the high dropout rates (39 percent in Texas for the class of 2010, according to the Intercultural Development Research Association),[49] the lack of Mexican American elected officials, your impoverished spirits, your jail-bird parents, brother, sisters, sons, and daughters, your depiction in the media as murderers, gang bangers, *narcotraficantes* and mambo kings and queens?

You can dance to the beat of *La Vida Loca* all night and make salsa babies but you can't make the *dinero* to raise that child in *una vida buena*. You can hit the baseball but you can't own a baseball team. You can box, run, kick, and stink but you can't speak, write, vote, or think. Better that you wash those dishes, dig those ditches, clean those restrooms, make those beds at the Holiday Inn. “Hey, *señorita*, clean my room good and I'll leave you a nice tip?” Life is simpler that way.

You say, "Hey, brown neck, that's not for me. I'm going to college; I'm going to be a lawyer, an engineer, a computer technician. I'll be the first in my family to walk across the stage in a baccalaureate cape and wield a degree sharper than any matador's sword. My cap, tassel, and gown are my suit of lights. Peddle your rant somewhere else. I'm a woman or man with a plan."

If that's your ambition and you have the fire and talent, I applaud you. We certainly need you to enter the professional schools and make your family and community proud. College is tough and takes equal parts guts and brains to make it through.

But for those who persevere and graduate, work with the Boeings, Verizons, and Motorolas of corporate America, ready to make the good money and live the life that millions in the world envy, will you become another Armani suit among an office building of Armanis?

Will you become the company man or woman spouting that what's good for General Electric is good for America? Will you move as far away as possible from us, possibly to quaint Vermont, to melt in like all good ice cream citizens into the banana split of American culture?

For didn't your teachers instruct that the American contract stated in bold print that if you study, work hard, and cause no trouble, then you will be rewarded with an El Dorado to drive around town? You signed the American deal with your sweat, toil,and time. Pay back has come. Show me the *dinero, por favor.*

If so, don't look away if you see me at the side of the road holding a sign that reads, "Will work for food."

Are you the ones, we've waited for? Are you smart enough?

I suffer from a peculiar twenty-first century ailment brought on possibly by a confluence of ozone depletion, ultraviolet rays immersion, and vapor droppings from *El Niño, La Niña, La Pinta and Santa Maria. Curanderos* (faith healers) call it *el susto* (fear). But I wish to give it a more scientific diagnosis. I call it Anorexia Latina. The symptoms are a wasting away of entire Mexican American communities because of Mexican American professionals who lack the heart to think and act as if they care for anyone other than themselves. Anorexia Latina is on a pandemic scale and will affect us at a time that America is pregnant and about to give birth to millions of beautiful Mexican American babies. (The 2010 census counted 50.5 million Latinos, the fastest growing ethnic group in the United States.)[50]

Mexican Americans are on the march and the browning of America has started. Your children will chase or be chased by bears along the Appalachian trails, hunt raccoons in Kentucky's blue hills, drive dog sleds along Alaska's glaciers, and gaze upon the craggy Stone Mountain images of Confederate heroes in Georgia.

Are you the ones we've waited for? Have you the nerve?

This middle-aged Mexican American's hair is turning gray but his crimson blood still runs hot from an insatiable craving for our people. Now with all this talk about blood and hunger, you might think that I might be some Mexican Nosferatu — the living dead. In a way, I am a vampire. I seek your young blood to satisfy this hunger for leaders. One bite from me and you'll never find rest until the social demons that infest our people are exorcised.

Who among you will have the guts to step forward to articulate the vision and represent our interests and as a consequence America's interests? You see it's not enough to score high in STARR, SAT, and GRE to earn your BA, MA, and Ph.D. You need to seed L-O-V-E. Just remember to supersize it.

My brave hearts, as leaders, much will be asked of you. Fortify yourself with knowing that your sacrifices will please God, friends, and family and your name will be on our lips after you're gone.

Are you the ones we've waited for?

SUMMARY

The School Blues section detailed the academic challenges confronting Chicano youth. Faced with a nagging educational achievement gap in comparison to Anglo students, Chicano students, parents, and the community must mobilize to stress reading at an early age, develop writing skills, and master science and math courses. At the same time, state and local policy makers must recognize the demographic realities of the changing population mix. Steve Murdock and the US Census Bureau have demonstrated the exponential growth of the Latino population. If this country and state wish to retain their economic and social first-world status, then they must fund schools and implement policies that provide Chicanos access to first-rate schools, teachers, and higher education.

Our future calls for the emergence of Chicano scientists to keep our economic ship afloat. Innovators have shown us how to reach and motivate students and parents to academic excellence. Courageous Chicano leaders must step forward to lead their community and country into a twenty-first century world of technology, diversity, and prosperity.

SECTION 2

LA GENTE

My wife scoffs at my tale that Spanish was my first language. Born in Monterrey, México, and emigrating to the United States when she was five, she speaks Spanish as a first generation American better than I, a third-generation American. I tell her that my grandmother, born in México City, cared for my siblings, cousins, and me while our parents worked in Chicago factories. She spoke only Spanish to us and in barely understandable English to others.

I explained to my wife, that my mother said that on my first day at Catholic school, the nuns scolded her for not teaching us better English. There was no bilingual education in the Chicago parochial schools in the 1950s. My brothers, sisters, and cousins received the traditional language/cultural immersion that so many modern-day English-only advocates clamor for. Sink or swim in the English language pool builds American patriotic fervor, they exhort.

We learned quickly and started the language and cultural drift toward the dominant Midwest, English-speaking world. Surrounded by English-only television, movies, radios, ads, religious doctrine, Anglo nuns and priests, classmates and music, books, lessons, and discipline, we learned quickly American ways and spoke less Spanish. We returned every day from school to our grandmother, ate her freshly baked tortillas and spoke to her in Spanish about our school day. I felt at home after a day of English consonants, lessons, religion, and discipline to the familiar Spanish sounds, love, and warmth. We learned to adapt to the two cultures and languages without much fuss or strain.

I identified family, home, and safety with my Mexican heritage and work, achievement, sin, Jesus, and heaven with the American Anglo culture. I never abandoned, felt ashamed, or regretted my Mexican heritage. This was partly due to the diverse European and African cultures pervasive in Chicago. In my youth, it was common to hear Italian, Polish, Greek, Puerto Rican Spanish dialect and African American urban English spoken often. In the 1960s, urban blacks took up the Black is Beautiful theme, revelling in their natural beauty, growing their Afro hair, raising fists and espousing African heritage as the source of all civilizations. My Mexican heritage was one among many competing for our day in the sun on the Chicago concrete prairie.

I found my bilingual, bicultural world easy and natural to travel through. I never felt any sense of inferiority or shame because of skin color or heritage as long as I lived in Chicago. In the summers, my father, a native Texan, would take us on vacation to Lampasas, Texas, in the Hill Country, to visit our Texas kin. We enjoyed the country life, the wide-open land, horses, lakes, watermelon, foot-long hot dogs, drive-in movies, Piggly-Wiggly, and Mott's department stores. Our Texas cousins seemed quieter and more reserved than their loud, rambunctious, northern relatives. I noticed there wasn't much mixing with Anglos and saw signs in stores that said they reserved the right not to serve customers. But we were always served, allowed to swim in the public pools, attended the movies and drive-ins, and ate at restaurants. I now recall that there were blacks in Lampasas but I never talked to any of them or saw them much in public. The most famous Lampasas black in the 1960s was Johnny "Lam" Jones, the outstanding high school running back. My cousin David Gonzales and Johnny became close friends and he traveled with Jones when he went to play for the New York Jets.

When my father decided that he had enough of the Chicago winters and pined for the hot Texas summers, he took a job transfer to Garland, Texas. We left Chicago and took another cultural plunge but this time into southern culture.

We found no nuns or priests to ease the transition. My siblings and I were older and found the cultural change more difficult. I quickly noticed the pervasive humility among Mexican Americans and their lack of English fluency. In college at the University of Texas at Arlington, I founded in 1970 the Association of Mexican American Students (AMAS) to instill pride among Chicano students in our culture and heritage and to encourage them to persevere in their studies. I even wrote a newsletter called *El Alacrán*, the *Scorpion*, about AMAS events, student issues and *chismes* or gossip.

Some Chicano students watched us warily from a distance, unsure about our motives and fearful about what their Anglo friends and professors would say if they knew about their association with those radical Chicanos. Today, one of the watchful claims he co-founded AMAS clandestinely but had to keep his cover lest he soil his "good Mexican" status. I perplexed two sisters whose father had the same name of Richard Gonzales and struggled reconciling the name with a student activist organization. Unfortunately, I wasn't about to change my name to ease their Oedipal distress. Rumors flew that the university administration had asked the FBI to infiltrate our group. We felt important and thought the FBI and administration paranoid.

La Raza Unida Party, led by José Ángel Gutiérrez, the United Farm Workers Movement, headed by César Chávez, and the Crusade for Justice, championed by Corky Gonzales inspired some Chicano students to raise their fists. We studied our Mesoamerican roots and took pride in learning about the Mayans and Aztecs and grew angry about the Spanish oppression of the Mexicans. We tried to improve our Spanish and searched for books by and about Chicanos and Mexicans. I set up a Mexican American heritage display in the university's main library and wrote a bibliography of the library's holdings of books relating to Mexican American culture. I was a Chicano when it wasn't cool to be Chicano.

I was attracted to the Mexicaness of my Spanish-fluent-wife-to-be whom I met in college. I wanted to connect not only amorously but also with her authentic Latina ways. She had suitors more attractive and more suave than I; however, I had the literary and intellectual edge that eclipsed the competition.

Despite the Spaniard/Mexican roots of Texas, I found the Chicano culture sidelined to a curiosity explored by academics and entrepreneurs wishing to tap Chicano dollars. Over the years since my move to Texas, the demographics have taken a dramatic shift to the Mexican currents of the Río Grande. Is demography our destiny? Perhaps. I wish the reader to step stone across the river with a deeper understanding of Chicano culture from my perspective. I wish the reader to learn Chicano beauty and rhythm and learn why many of us can't forsake our heritage for the promise of mainstream gentility. I've improved my Spanish and English; I'm a bilingual, bicultural man, a trait that many should develop if we are to live prosperously with one another in Chicanolandia.

This Culture section seeks to explicate the meaning of Chicano culture and how it impacts ethnic identity, family roles, literature, and the larger American cultures. I explain the reality of white privilege, providing testimony by white writers who are well aware of the benefits they enjoy by their favored status. The importance of cultural competency to communicate and develop relationships with Mexican Americans is developed. By the end of this chapter, the reader will understand the finesse and stress in traveling between cultural worlds.

Chapter 5

La Familia

The blue-eyed Latina yearned to find the Mexican heritage that her parents had hidden from her. She told me after a speech to her professional library association that her parents decided that a total dip in the melting pot was the American baptism needed for success in this country.

They didn't want any of that second-class, hyphenated American status— they sought the full loaf of white-bread respectability, not half. Yessirree, they wanted her to become a Yankee Doodle Dandy, too, but their wishes didn't stick. Now, as an adult with children, she longed to form soft vowels and roll r's.

She had a wistful desire to walk in the forbidden Latin Quarter; she wanted to live the Mexican American life and savor its history and culture. She sought to reattach the hyphen and cross over as an Americana to become a *Mexicana.* She wanted to mambo to the cultural rhythms that were denied her but that she felt intuitively. With the growing Chicano presence in the country and state, she'll find plenty of opportunity to fulfill this cultural attraction.

In a study released January 28, 2003, by Dallas International, a nonprofit coalition of ethnic communities and organizations, it was estimated that

35 percent of the Metroplex's population is made up of immigrants and their children.[1] The study also showed that 55 percent of the Mexican immigrants in North Texas are undocumented.

As the US Census Bureau announces the historic emergence of Latinos as the largest minority group in America, more blue- and brown-eyed Chicanos and Chicanas and non-Chicano neighbors are feeling the momentous challenge that comes with this population swell. Some middle-class Mexican American parents are faced with basic ethnic questions: Shall my children learn Spanish? Shall we live in a Chicano neighborhood? Shall I teach them the history of their ancestors? Is it possible to live in two cultures, or must I forsake the Chicano one for success?

For the Mexican immigrant, the questions are different:

Will my children forget their Spanish? Will my children lose their moral values in this permissive society? Will my family stay close-knit in a country that stresses individualism? Why do US Chicano citizens discriminate against Mexican immigrants?

The answers partly depend on the value that people place on their heritage and partly on their courage to express it in a sometimes-hostile community that feels threatened by diversity.

With 50.5 million Latinos in the USA according to the 2010 US Census, a rising socio-psychological expectation grows that Chicanos' political, social, and cultural agenda finally will draw attention. As the primo minority, Mexican Americans need not speak in hushed Spanish voices any longer when talking about Chicano issues around non-Spanish-speakers. The time has come for Chicanos to raise their voices in Spanish and English as loud as the others for all to hear.

Photo 8. Wedding Photo

Courtesy of the Delsa P. Pérez Collection, Genealogy, History, and Archives Unit, Fort Worth Library.

Ms. Maria P. Selan and Mr. Margarito R. Padilla, Black/White Wedding Outside of San José Catholic Church, Fort Worth, Texas 1926

"The Mexicans are coming! The Mexicans are coming!" – the warning once sounded by the Alamo scouts as they spied Santa Anna's army now rings in suburban schools, civic centers, churches, and the workplace. To the chagrin of Anglo, black, and Mexican American conservatives, Chicanos who should squeal with joy to assimilate or melt down have not genuflected at the melting pot.

Imagine the nerve of these immigrants who continue to speak Spanish or some other foreign tongue. They celebrate holidays that have nothing to do with American history. They cross the border undocumentedly and expect equitable treatment. Some Americans think that their version of the American Dream is the only one permitted. Ethnic amnesia prevents them from recounting their European ancestors' experiences after clearing Ellis Island.

The Irish, Germans, and Italians didn't immediately throw off the old country's ways for the new land. They lived then, and to some extent still live today, in white ethnic communities in which the sons and daughters of Ireland, Germany, and Italy paraded and feted memories of their homelands in the bosom of American cities. They were no less American for carrying the flags of their former countries.

Better to awaken to the reality of America's years of *de colores* (of colors) as 10 percent of the Mexican population lives in the United States today, according to Dallas International.[2] The days of exclusive black and white America dialogues about equality and equity are over. Set a few more chairs at the table for Asian and Chicano competitors for the American pie.

Along with accepting our country's cultural diversity, we must help Latinas caught in the twilight zone of traditional Mexican culture and the more liberal American ways. Many Latinas, especially teens, find living in a cultural competing world too bewildering and turn their confusion and resentment inward.

The Ugly Betty Latina TV character may not have been pretty or skinny by US or Mexican fashion standards, but she had qualities that may save the lives of many young Latinas: She liked herself plain, plump, and smart.

Psychological studies have consistently shown that adolescent Latinas in the United States, especially those born here, have the highest rate of suicidal thoughts and attempts of any other ethnic group. "The traditional gender-role socialization of women in Hispanic countries, the stresses associated with acculturation by the Hispanic adolescent to American society, and the intergenerational conflict that often ensues through acculturation and the shaping of a cultural identity are viewed by the present author as interacting contributants to suicide attempts among Hispanic adolescent females," wrote Luis Zayas.[3]

The National Council of La Raza (NCLR) co-sponsored a study in 2005 on six major mental health issues affecting Mexican Americans—depression, immigration and acculturation, chemical use and dependency, domestic violence, suicide, and depression and co-morbidity—and discovered what many in the barrio already knew.[4] For many Mexican Americans, the American Dream has turned into the American Nightmare.

The study wasn't an attempt to denigrate mainstream US culture. Instead, the research highlighted the effects of acculturation on Chicano families. The study cited the 2003 Youth Risk Behavior Survey that found that 35.4 percent of Latino youth and 28.6 percent of all respondents reported feeling sad or hopeless every day for two weeks or more during the preceding year.[5]

Reasons for mental illness have complex biological and environmental origins. However, the studies cited by the NCLR research indicated that the loss of traditional cultural values and beliefs was associated with increased levels of mental illness among Mexican Americans. The studies found that despite the physical, cultural, economic, and linguistic hardships that immigrants face in coming to the US, newly arrived immigrants tend to have better mental health than Chicanos born here.[6]

In 2005 National Public Radio reported on a study by Robert Crosnoe of the University of Texas at Austin that compared the ability of kindergartners from various ethnic groups to self-regulate behavior in class. Among Latino, Asian, black, and Anglo children, the newly arrived Latino children displayed the best ability to attend to teacher instruction and get along with other children.[7]

Newly arrived Mexican immigrant families still view suicide as taboo, cherish family unity over individualism, pray to the Virgin and other saints, and accept a more traditional body image. They're rich in the belief that dark skin color, Indian features, and the Spanish language are beautiful and normal. They accept that hard toil is their lot but believe that the future holds hope for their family in a country hungry for their labor.

Over the years, acculturation unravels the serape cultural blanket as children learn English and US customs quicker than their parents. Children learn that good Americans speak English without an accent, live in big homes, and drive fancy cars. (A Spanish-speaking parent recently told me that her child was punished for speaking Spanish in school.) Beauty as seen on Mexican and US television stations has a lighter hue.

Immigrant youth and their native-born Chicano peers soon learn who in our society are the real bosses. Not many look like them. The strident, anti-immigrant hostility that many children hear and see may meet the perverse patriotic needs of others, but it only adds to children's misguided belief that undocumented means that all Mexican Americans are worthless.

As our Chicano youth population increases, we must better address the mental health needs of the children of Sánchez. A concerted, widespread effort is required to accent the value of Chicano culture, starting with infants. Chicano adolescents, like all adolescents, must come to terms with their identity. The Chicano youth has the added task of integrating Chicano heritage from a belief that he or she is a product of a rich, strong culture. In a multicultural world, the child who is able to move freely between worlds is the healthiest and most beautiful youth of all.

To assist in raising healthy Chicanos, an examination of the father's role is vital for a fuller understanding of how Mexican American children thrive or suffer in *La Familia.*

The stereotypical Mexican male is a womanizing macho who likes to drink, fight, shout orders, and neglect his children. Although this image may apply to many men regardless of ethnicity, the Chicano male finds himself fending off claims of emotional abandonment and selfishness. But machismo may have lost its true meaning in the English translation.

Aztec wise men instructed children in Náhuatl to: "revere and greet your elders. Console the poor and the afflicted with good works and words. Do not mock the old, the sick, the maimed or who has sinned. Do not set a bad example, or speak indiscreetly or interrupt the speech of another. "[8] And then disrespectful, bearded men wearing metal helmets and riding horses arrived.

Since the nineteenth century, Mexican *padres* have often recited to their children some pithy advice from President Benito Juárez: "*El respeto al derecho ajeno es la paz*"' — respect for the rights of others is peace. Wars were fought into the twentieth century to extend these elusive rights and peace to Mexicans.

César Chávez, father of seven children, advised them and his followers: "I am convinced that the truest act of courage, the strongest act of manliness, is to sacrifice for others in a totally nonviolent struggle for justice."[9] His United Farm Workers union members still toil in the fields for their rights.

Today, millions of young Mexican men leave behind their wives and children in isolated towns, jump the border, live in crowded conditions, and work in the dirtiest and riskiest of American jobs for money to send to their families. They take abuse stoically because they value their responsibility as fathers and husbands more than their pride.

On pay phones, these long-distant dads explain to their children that they won't see them soon. Perhaps next year, when more terrorists are caught, the war in Afghanistan is over, and the moon is dark and river low. They know too well that sometimes wives won't wait and children grow estranged from them.

All are Mexican men speaking the common tongue of respect, duty, and courage to their wives, sons, and daughters. Caught in a world of violence, nationalism, and selfishness, struggling to raise families by word and deed, they are real men. They are machos in the ancient sense of *hombres nobles* – noble men – who will labor throughout their lives to give their children food, clothing, shelter, education, and love.

Many more Chicano fathers are needed to take on the macho roles inherited from the Mexican natives of the volcano basin. They need to don their machismo capes if they are to lead their families away from the lures of drugs, gangs, sex, and dropping out of school. Too many Chicanos have forgotten their history and lost their macho identity. They're intimidated by accusations of boorish male behavior or are ashamed of their culture. Extolling this cultural value of machismo flies in the face of modern American feminist ideals. In a country steeped in egalitarian values, America looks askance at Mexican notions of male dominance.

Women have struggled too hard and too long to allow a Ricky Ricardo to push them around or dictate their social or economic status. Talented Chicanas, excelling in school and careers, resent playing dizzy Lucy for slower-witted Chicanos. Stereotypes of the Mexican macho – a man who's physically abusive, a heavy drinker, a womanizer, arrogant – abound. Among Chicanas, such men are often referred to as *machistas.*

Javier Nájera, an Arlington businessman raised in El Paso, complained that "Little Mexican boys are taught two things for sure: how to fight and how to work. Nothing else much matters. Oh yeah, and regarding work, it better involve heavy, physical labor outside so that you can sweat and bleed."[10] Writing, reading, and the arts were supposedly for sissies. Nájera struggled mightily to overcome the narrowly scripted role.

If Chicano families are to nurture healthy, high-achieving children, then fathers must take on the role of the *hombre noble*, or the macho redux. The National Compadres Network has drawn from cultural and historical traditions of responsibility for families' wellness to devise guiding principles:[11]

•Is a man of your word

•Has a sense of responsibility for his own wellbeing and that of others in his circle

•Rejects any form of abuse: physical, emotional, mental or spiritual . . . to himself or others

•Takes time to reflect, pray, and include ceremony in his life

•Is sensitive and understanding

•Is like a mirror, reflecting support and clarity to one another

•Lives these values honestly, and with love

From the halls of Montezuma to the shores of the Trinity, fathers must talk with their children about school, drugs and sex, read books to them, attend PTA meetings, hug them, and teach them their history, culture, and languages. Machos, go home and play games with your children.

Machos must also learn to discipline their children at a time they are easily drawn into the underbelly of urban life. Like the three wise men who brought precious gifts to the Christ child, Chicano dads must bear special presents to their children. The gifts that Chicano youths require to avoid dropping out of school, teen pregnancy, gang violence, drug use, and cultural confusion are their dads' time, respect, and guidance.

As the fourth wise man, a Chicano dad must offer actions and words that are like bowls of chile peppers to his children. Chile brings tears to the eyes and enflames the taste buds. But the red and green peppers add spice that makes life more enjoyable.

Chicano dads must bite the chile pepper to offer words and actions that are hard to utter and enforce. Parents do not enjoy arguing with their children and naturally wish to avoid confrontation, tantrums, and rage. The times call for swallowing the heat and telling our children that we love them so much that we can't allow them to miss school, join a gang, or drink.

Providing food, housing, and clothes partially meets dads' responsibility. But the young require more than *huevos rancheros* to fill their bellies — they need an arm on the shoulder and a listening ear to nourish their hearts. They yearn to feel the ardor of Dad's love.

Chicano fathers must peel away the layers of demand on their time that turn them away from their children's problems. The boss, long hours, physical labor, and a strong work ethic may tempt Chicano dads to let the years and children slip by quietly. Bite the chile and make time for personal chats.

One effective way is to read together. Pick up a daily Spanish- or English-language newspaper and discuss international, national, and local news. For immigrant dads, the immigration reform bills or the DREAM Act debated in Congress are excellent conversation topics. As undocumented or legal immigrants or the descendants of such, dads can share with their children the reasons for leaving home, the trek to this country, the hardships endured, the language struggle, and the reasons for staying.

With the anti-immigration mania sweeping the country, immigrant children need to hear that they are as valued and important as any child, legal or undocumented, in this country.

Chicano dads should ask their children what the legislators and presidential candidates think about immigrants based on the news reports. They probably will say that some members of Congress and White House hopefuls hate and fear immigrants, while others prize them for their cheap labor.

The chile pepper dads should say that if they are deported, they would write and phone as often as possible until they see one another in their own million-step march. Borders, deserts, fences, "Minutemen," coyotes, and members of Congress cannot deport love from immigrant children.

With the younger ones, Chicano dads should read age-appropriate, bilingual stories to show their children the glory of speaking two languages. Accents are cool and reflect the spice in the American cultural brew. While in the United States, Chicano dads should consider expanding their idea of a father from the traditional Mexican macho lifestyle to the involved *padre*.

Brent Taylor, in his study of fathers in México and the United States, found that Mexican dads north of the border were more likely to have egalitarian views of male and female roles. They expected both sons and daughters to excel in school and attain their personal goals. They treated their wives as equal partners in their relationship and in child rearing.[12]

To truly round out their children's education, Chicano dads should show their children how to speak out courageously against social wrongs. A common complaint among the French youth of North African and sub-Saharan heritage who rioted for several nights in October and November 2007 was their alienation from mainstream French society and their own families. African parents complained that they couldn't control their children. The French youth were angry at their people's oppression in one of the world's most enlightened countries.

Algerian dads had lost control of their French children when their youth realized their dads' low social status and political puniness. They had won the Battle of Algiers but lost the fight for their children's respect. Wise Chicano fathers, take heed. Win the battle for your children's education and respect through family involvement and political change. Bites of chile-pepper love will bring tears and families together.

For a personal example of the overbearing Mexican father, I offer the story of my grandmother's decision to leave México and to journey to the

United States. In his attempt to control, my great-grandfather liberated her desire for freedom.

Sabino Puertos lacked the parental skill to nurture well my grandmother, Carmen Puertos Reyes. She represented for me all that is wonderful in México: A rebellious girl, she could not live in the traditional Mexican female docile role that her father insisted that she play. She yearned for the freedom to live her life fully without the constricting rules created by domineering men. She taught me to live courageously and without regrets.

Carmen Puertos drank, smoked, and laughed for most of her ninety-two years. When she chuckled, her open mouth revealed few remaining teeth; she never bothered with dentures. Her earlier photos show a pretty woman with thick brown hair. Time painted it gray and caused her legs to hurt when she walked. But it never took her pride, spunk, or freedom.

She cared for her grandchildren—including me—while her children worked in Chicago factories. She taught her family, in Spanish, not to be cowed by the big, blustering American city. After all, she was a *chilanga* — a native of México City who had lived in the capital during the days of dictator Porfirio Díaz and revolutionaries Emiliano Zapata and Pancho Villa. Perhaps the rebellious airs in the days of the *Adelitas* and *soldaderas*, or female warriors of the revolution, filled her with an independent spirit.

One night when she was fourteen, she stayed out late to attend a neighborhood fiesta. Fearing the wrath of her father, she ran away to a convent where her older sister was studying to become a nun.

Her father forced her to return to his comfortable, maid-tended house, where she could have lived out her years. But México was a macho country with macho men. (Her father was thirty when he married his fourteen-year-old wife, Pilar García with whom he would have nine children.) She wanted to live in the world beyond Don Puertos's reach. So she ran away again at nineteen with the help of an older brother and fled to Nuevo Laredo, Tamulipas, on the Texas-México border with a female friend to care for her aunt. She crossed the border daily and worked as a laundress at the Hamilton Hotel in Laredo. When she heard that a family was going to Waukegan, Illinois, to open a restaurant, she went along. She proudly told her children that she was never undocumented — "*No era mojada.*" She walked across the bridge spanning the Río Grande with papers for which she paid eight dollars.

A nicer story would say that life in the United States was pleasant and bountiful for her. In truth, life during the Great Depression was hard for her and millions of others scrambling for food and work. She married another Mexican immigrant, Juan Reyes, bore him four children and followed the jobs to Chicago, Lyons, Kansas, and back to Chicago.

In Kansas, she joined other Mexican women to form a mutual aid society that raised money through *jamaicas* or fairs, for the election of Mexican President Lázaro Cárdenas.

During Mexican Independence Day celebrations, she sewed Mexican dresses for her daughters and herself, splashing red, white, and green in their skirts, blouses, and hair. She played old Mexican songs and taught them to dance traditional steps that she recalled from fiestas.

When Kansas commemorated the 400th anniversary of Francisco Vásquez de Coronado's exploration for gold, Carmen Reyes and other Mexican women pooled their money to bring Mexican matadors and bulls to demonstrate the *corrida*. (The bullfighters would go through the sweeps and turns in their suit of light and crimson capes without the fatal sword plunge.)

The Kansas townsfolk easily accepted the Mexican garb, dances, customs, and Spanish. Perhaps the small number of Mexican immigrants, their hard work and neighborliness calmed any fears that they might have harbored for the children of Coronado. There was no bitter history of the Alamo and the Mexican War in Kansas; instead, they shared a memory of a conquistador traveling with his soldiers and priests in search of wealth and souls.

Life in Chicago brought disappointment and heartache for Carmen as a daughter followed in her footsteps and ran away. Despite their advanced age, Carmen and Juan Reyes adopted the runaway daughter's five children. In later years, Carmen and Juan wanted to live closer to family and she died on August 6, 1996, in Garland, Texas, close to her younger daughter, Delfina. When I asked my grandmother why she had come to the United States, she answered, "*Por la libertad* – for the freedom." She wanted the freedom to smoke, drink, marry the man she loved, and live in a country where a runaway girl could find a home. Carmen Puertos de Reyes taught her children to cherish their golden freedom in a land where conquistadores once roamed.

Photo 9. Wedding Photo of Juan and Carmen Reyes

Waukegan, Illinois, November 7, 1927. Author's personal collection.

Chapter 6

Mexican Culture

One way of warming up to the cultural shifts in this country is to take a trip to México. This will open the cultural senses to the joys of living the Mexican life. Despite the true horrors of the drug cartel wars, visitors to this beautiful country can revel in *México lindo* life if they would just suspend their native culture for a short while and embrace Mexican joy.

At center stage in a small amphitheater stood a painted white-faced clown reciting jokes and poetry to hundreds of young Mexicans, who laughed and cheered at his lyrical words. With the sounds of Pacific waves crashing on the shores of Puerto Vallarta as a backdrop, the big-footed, baggy-pants *payaso* told his audience his carefully crafted words were meant especially for this crowd tonight and no others. The audience clapped and in appreciation placed *dinero* in a hat on the stage. The clown sifted through the money, held up a coin and asked if the person who had donated the twenty-*centavos* piece wished some change.

As Americans consider vacation plans, earthly paradises can be found south of the border where Mexicans work hard to pamper tourists and to convince them that México is still a friendly, exotic land of charm and wit. Despite news coverage of corrupt Mexican government officials, the vice grip of the *narcotraficantes*, and wretched poverty, México is still a land of natural beauty, charm, grace, and warm people.

On a sunset cruise on the *Princesa Vallarta*, from one side of Banderas Bay to the seaport where *Night of the Iguana* was filmed, a band played Mexican ballads that stirred our Mexican shipmates to shout *gritos*, sing, and clap. The Americans on board appeared to enjoy the revelry but were inhibited and shy before the boisterous Mexicans. The language barrier may have kept them quietly interested and in awe of the Mexican exuberance.

A flock of white-breasted sea gulls with black wings twice as long as their bodies raced alongside the *Princesa*. Ready passengers, young and old, threw bits of their tacos and chips to the avian escorts. The gulls dived and rose in a show of agility and strength to eat on the fly, skimming ocean waves.

Through the flutter of wings, palm tree-lined shores exposed mansions of the rich. The *Princesa's* tour guide pointed to a white, palatial, towered home and claimed it was his. From the boat, we could see a woman on the veranda of his dream home, dressed in white, veils and train, beginning her married life at sunset by the bay. Her new husband stood at the doorway admiring her beauty against the rays of the sinking sun.

At the site where the guide told us that the movie was made, I could almost see Richard and Liz arm-in-arm while Ava flirted with local Mexican men.

The grace of Puerto Vallarta can best be viewed in panoramic glory from the sky, suspended in a parachute tethered by rope to a speeding motorboat. Gliding through the blue hundreds of feet above the Pacific Ocean coastline, a sky rider can watch gray-black water churn into white waves as it crashes on the brown beach. Houses with red-tiled roofs perch on the side of the Sierra Madre Mountains that sweep to the coast. For literally hundreds of suspended moments, an American tourist can wish away deadlines, bosses, sins, and failures for the joy of flying noiselessly into the face of earthly beauty.

We can almost understand the Spaniards' attraction to see such natural beauty of the New World and lust to possess it. Indeed, its richness and lushness seduced them to mate with the women and to live out their remaining days in a land named after a native people, the *Mexicas.* The Spaniards' sin was their inability to shake dusty colonial thinking of the Old World, to take off their conquistador helmet and sword, to be reborn with their mestizo children in the wild, pristine Americas.

On a Sunday evening on the *Malecón*, the main boardwalk of Puerto Vallarta, vibrant, handsome Mexicans stroll, chat, and flirt while the sounds of Cuban *meringue* singers and mariachi serenaders flow from the bars and restaurants across the street. A pickup full of youths, faces painted in green, white, and red, drives by. They shout their hopes for México's soccer team to win the World Cup.

Unlike the resort hotel staff, these Mexicans ignore tourists but allow them to join their stroll in search of laughter and companions. The clown trick to finding Mexican joy is to shortchange our foreignness and to become a Mexican for a little while.

One aspect of American life not often portrayed in the media is the Mexican immigrant life. With the millions that have crossed over *sin papeles* and the millions more who are here legally, the material for cinema adventure teems. Demographic changes in the US are partly influenced by this steady immigration. Despite political posturing about sealing the border, the business community—except for presidential hopeful Donald Trump—welcomes Latino immigrants to keep their enterprises profitable. Likewise, Mexican entrepreneurs, legal or not, wish to pursue the pot at the end of the American rainbow.

My father-in-law, Salvador Moreno, was a shining example of a Mexican hustling to turn his skills to a profitable business. Born in Monterrey, México, he immigrated to the United States and after a few years brought his family, including my wife Dora, to Fort Worth, Texas. He soon set up a tailoring business in downtown Arlington, Texas, called "Moreno's Cabellero Shop." When I moved to Arlington, Texas, in 1969 to attend college, this was the first evidence of the existence of Chicano culture in this town. My father-in-law believed in the American Dream like so many immigrants from around the world.

Francisco Álvarez, state president of the Federation of Zacatecano Clubs of Texas, called himself a Zacatejano. He was a man who loved México and the United States equally.For some who lived all their lives in one country, it may seem hard to understand how a person could cherish two flags. As he explained, it was a matter of learning and living in two cultures, two languages, two histories, two futures.

As a college student in México, he majored in linguistics and particularly enjoyed learning English. "I read Shakespeare and Stephen King," he said. He admitted that he'll never lose his Spanish accent but enjoyed the challenge of improving his English.

Once a salesman for a US company in Monterrey, México, he relished receiving his salary in dollars. He admired the efficiency and honesty of US-managed businesses — qualities he thought were lacking in a Mexican business climate that still ran on the *mordida* (the bite or bribe) and cronyism.

After the US business closed, he saw he had no future in México. Like millions of his countrymen, he came to the United States, looking for work and the good life. As a bilingual teacher in the Dallas public schools, he explained to immigrant parents who wanted their children to speak English that they could learn both English and Spanish. He said that in El Paso schools, Asian, black, and Anglo children fill bilingual classrooms. The gift of languages opened doors to foreign countries and jobs, as Álvarez personally knew.

Like Álvarez, Sigifredo Muñoz — public relations secretary of the Jalpa, Zacatecas, United Club — realized that despite his early, private school education in México, he had little chance of landing a good-paying job. He learned English, graduated from Arlington Heights High School and found a job with a national real estate agency. He said his work and bilingual skills allowed him to show immigrants how to buy homes and put down roots in this country.

Muñoz said a common, grand illusion among Mexicans in the US was the dream of earning enough to return and retire in comfort. Even if México raised the standard of living, offered lucrative jobs, and eliminated corruption, few of the estimated eleven million undocumented immigrants would return, he said.

Álvarez and Muñoz spoke of the euphoria of freedom that filled them each time they crossed the border into México. They found joy revelling in their first culture, speaking Spanish, renewing friendships, and comforting their families. After a few weeks, they returned to the US border and were again filled with excitement as they crossed over.

"México is our past, but the US is our future," Álvarez said.[13]

Each passing day in this country riveted in their mind the realization that their destiny was wedded to this country. One of the anthems of the immigrant rights movements in this country was: *Aquí estamos y no nos vamos* – here we are, and we aren't leaving. They accept anti-immigration hostility as the price they pay for a chance to live free of the humiliation of poverty, for their families' respect in earning the good life. Álvarez, Muñoz, and thousands of others from the Mexican state of Zacatecas formed their statewide clubs to help those they left behind as well as improve their lives in this country. They participated with the Mexican government in matching money projects that create jobs, build roads, repair churches, beautify cemeteries, and raise scholarships. For every dollar that the Zacatecan clubs contributed, the local, state, and federal Mexican governments contributed three dollars.

They hoped that their relief dollars would help México build an infrastructure that will slow the immigration push. At the same time, the clubs pool their resources to help Zacatejanos improve their lives here. Their club offered assistance to local Mexican immigrants to secure passports and identification.

On March 17, 2007, the Fort Worth clubs hosted a state convention of the Zacatecan Clubs with Amalia García Medina, the first female governor of Zacatecas, as guest speaker. México was changing, but Álvarez, Muñoz, and millions of other Mexicans couldn't wait. They sent money and wished their native country a bright future. In the meantime, they crossed the border, found jobs and placed their hopes in the Stars and Stripes.

Mexican immigrants bring a work ethos not easily matched by other ethnic groups, regardless of their generational status in the country. Mark Guarino wrote in his article "Anti-Illegal Immigration Bill Stokes Backlash in Alabama Fields" in the *Christian Science Monitor* on October 22, 2011, that after Alabama implemented the harshest anti-immigration laws in this country in October 2011, farmers complained that they couldn't find enough US-born workers to replace the immigrants. And those who did go into the fields generally didn't last long, complaining of the hard work and low pay. Who exactly are these working, Mexican dynamos?

In the predawn hours, working Mexicans swarm my new neighborhood in their battered pickups and vans and don't leave until sun down. Wearing torn T-shirts, faded pants, and tattered shoes, they brick $100,000-plus homes that they'll never be invited into unless to clean after their Anglo owners move in. Sweat shimmers on their dark brown skin as they deftly swing the trowel over the bricks like Mayan sculptors shaping stone monuments to their gods millennia ago.

To ease the lash of the Texas sun, they play *rancheras* that sing of love, beautiful women, and the lack of winning the two. Spanish words fill the development, and for a moment when I look up into the blue, I'm reminded of the barrio of my youth. Some work silently in a row, digging trenches for the buried pipes that will wash away our bodies' wastes. Others carry shingles to roofers whose rapid hammering sets symmetrical rows with seemingly effortless ease.

Most of the workers are young, mustachioed, handsome men who've come to this country to work in the *Norteamericano's* land. They've come to earn money, not as *narcotraficantes* or welfare recipients but as laborers in the kind of work that we warn our children they'll end up doing if they don't go to college or learn better English.

When I worked in a local hospital, I'd translate for emergency-room physicians as they treated Mexican laborers with broken legs, severed fingers, crushed feet, or cracked backs. Lying on sterile, white-papered gurneys, the injured Mexicans—their hair and bodies covered in the dirt, stones, and splinters of the work site—bled and moaned in the common language of misery. When I translated the physician's clinical questions, their grimacing faces would relax momentarily from hearing Spanish and would ask for release from the pain. I'd give them more than the medical terms, slipping words of hope and comfort and asking about family, friends, and home. They'd answer with surprising politeness, considering their discomfort.

Most were from the heartland of México, here to do our dirty work for family and survival. Some had left wives and children to earn money to send back. Others were single men who had parlayed their own free-trade agreement with this country. Risking capture from ICE agents and abuse from underworld railroad conductors, they found the lure of jobs and "good money" too great to be worried about sovereign borders.

When I come from my air-conditioned office and step out of my shiny car to my manicured lawn, I see them covered in dirt, wheeling more bricks up to the exposed frames of the unfinished houses. We exchange friendly *holas*, a smile, a nod. As I enter my new home, I turn and watch with some guilt their dusty, sweaty faces. My eyes hurt from the glare of a computer screen, theirs from the sting of the sun and sweat.

I think of my grandparents who came from México, one of them without papers, as laborers and gave me the opportunity to learn English and go to school. Three of them never learned to speak English well, and the bilingual one was illiterate. They were working Mexicans as well.

Photo 10. Nicho Sáenz

Courtesy of the Delsa M. Pérez Collection, Genealogy, History, and Archives Unit, Fort Worth Library.

Nicho Sáenz on accordion with son Leo Sáenz on *bajo sexto* guitar celebrating Nicho Sáenz Proclamation Day from the City of Fort Worth, September 3, 2006, at the Ranch in the Stockyards.

They picked cotton, built dams, worked salt mines, sheared sheep, hauled hay. Their homes frequently were tents on the side of the road at the edge of fields. They never complained about a hard life, racism, discrimination, or politics. Instead, my grandparents taught us to work hard with the skills one learned, to feed the family, to raise the children and to pray to the Virgin Mary for intercession and strength. They called us pet names; I got tagged as Cochise, since the others were *güeros*, light-skinned, and I looked more like an American Indian. We first learned Spanish, the tongue of first-generation Mexican immigrants, and later

English when we went to our school classes; otherwise, we wouldn't be able to speak and learn from them.

The cycle continues with this new generation of working Mexicans. They will marry, have children, and raise them as US citizens. Texas A&M demographers predict that the brown tide will swell and surpass Texas Anglos in numbers by the year 2030. The future is right outside our doors, alongside the highways, in our housing developments, in our schools, in the kitchens and laundry rooms of our finest hotels.

Working Mexicans will keep coming every morning, playing their *rancheras* about love, women, and luck until all the houses in this new development are completed. After they pick up their tools and leave and the Anglo owners move in, I will continue to hear their music in the air and hope to live long enough to see their children or grandchildren buy the homes their fathers built.

In addition to *rancheras*, Chicanos also love music that rouses the blood and incites listeners to sing, clap, and dance. Mariachi bands evoke *gritos* or shouts from the common man at weddings and festivals. *Conjuntos* or small musical groups invite communal dancing reminiscent of Aztec days.

The arrival of a Mexican youth orchestra at Fort Worth Bass Hall brought Mexican Americans to a concert hall not frequented by many from the barrio. But it was a joy to see Mexican youths surmount borders in the name of art and beauty. When the curtain rose on October 26, 2006, the audience saw the many faces of México in the child musicians of the *Orquesta Sinfónica Infantil de México.*

Children from mountain villages with home-made musical instruments handed down from fathers and grandfathers, children from major cities and fishing towns traveled thousands of miles to play melodies that transcend borders, politics and language. Like children worldwide, the *niños* expressed their hopes, dreams, and dignity in song. At a time when news clamors of international and local ethnic conflicts, we need to see and hear the best talents of other countries to remind us that we share a love for the arts.

Their fine music melted away stereotypes and negative images of México and the United States. We developed a cultural bridge with our southern neighbor by exchanging talents, teachers, and trust. The Mexican children were ambassadors of goodwill, clearing the air of harsh talk and replacing it with a rhapsody in green, white, and red.

Like American youth, these Mexican children enjoyed the attention they received from adults who marveled at their artistry. Through video performances and personal meetings, Maestro Sergio Ramírez handpicked the children, ages eight to eighteen, who represented every Mexican state. After rehearsing in Cuernavaca, Ramírez led them on performance tours throughout their country.

Ginger Head Gearheart, founder and executive director of the Kennedy Center Imagination Celebration Fort Worth, recognized their talent and helped to organize the orchestra's 2004 US tour. She had traveled to Monterrey, México, to enlist composer Arturo Rodríguez to write a symphony called the Mars Project. Through this fortuitous visit, she developed professional relationships with Mexican artists and persuaded them to partner with her to develop a Mexican version of Imagination Celebration.

Her charm, energy, and creativity proved infectious as the Mexicans developed Talentum, an arts organization for children. In exchange, Mexican trainers have visited Fort Worth schoolteachers to instruct them on Mexican customs, culture, fauna, geography, and arts. It was a natural leap to invite the Mexican national youth orchestra to visit Fort Worth. Gearheart's art diplomacy planted seeds of goodwill with the Mexican people and government in contrast with the rancorous debate that swept both countries.

In their second tour of the youth orchestra, we had an opportunity to step back from the heated arguments and to witness the joy of talented children playing beautiful music. We had a chance to see the intent faces of Mexican schoolchildren performing for love of country, honor, and music.

Steve Murrin, "mayor" of the Fort Worth Stockyards, agreed to host a welcoming party for the delegation of 200 musicians and chaperones at his West Fork Ranch. The Mexican entourage enjoyed cowboy culture, ranches, barbecue, and malls. In 2004, the orchestra performed at Will Rogers Auditorium, the Morton Meyerson Symphony Center, and the Latino Cultural Center in Dallas. In 2006, they performed only in Fort Worth at Will Rogers and Bass Hall. Gearheart extended an invitation to area school districts to contact her office for ticket information, permitting thousands of students to attend the performances.

Gearheart described Fort Worth students sitting at first slumped in their chairs at the performances. She recalled speaking to one African-American youth who seemed uninterested in the music. When the orchestra began playing the rhythmic beats of Afro-Latino music, he gradually sat straight up with a smile. After speaking with the musicians, the student developed an interest in performing and learned to play the cello. Gearheart had the foresight to know the importance of exposing children, regardless of income, to as much art as possible to develop their talents and sensitivity to others. After twenty-two years of bringing the arts to youth through this organization, she retired in 2011. The creative agency changed their name to Imagination Fort Worth in February 2015 and continued Gearheart's vision of celebrating the imagination.

It would be naïve to think that the world's conflicts could be resolved in a symphony score. However, an exchange of talent and art could assist in developing creative relationships that increase our understanding of our common goals and interests.

For one night we transcended differences and found the beauty in the children's faces of México.

Chapter 7

White Privilege

This Mexican transformation for even a short time may be near impossible to discard for those holding white superiority attitudes. This piece stirred the ire of several readers. I find the race question a taboo subject often resulting in hurt feelings, miscommunication, and guilt. Given the pride that many white Southerners have for the Confederacy and the Alamo, any talk about racial oppression roils them to heated defensiveness. History is still with us in today's stringent racial divisions. The 2012 Republican and Democratic Conventions offered stark contrasts of the racial make up of the delegates. What would Abraham Lincoln have said to see his party's nearly all white delegation?

Robert Jensen's book, *The Heart of Whiteness: Confronting Race, Racism and White Privilege*, courageously exposes the minds and hearts of whites benefiting from what he calls a "white-supremacist society." Jensen was not a minority radical spouting Anglo-blue-eyed-devil rhetoric and a call for racial conflict. He described himself as "white as white gets in the United States of America. I am a white-bred, white-bread white boy."[14] He was also an associate professor of journalism at the University of Texas in Austin.

His book addresses white middle-class citizens who deny or ignore the existence of white privilege and disparities in economic, social, and educational levels between whites and ethnic minorities.

Jensen acknowledged that the overt white supremacist activities in America's past — the antics of Klansmen and decades of Jim Crow laws —diminished considerably during the twentieth century. However, he asserted that most whites have never accepted, or have ignored, the historical reality that white supremacy was founded on the killing of millions of Indians, the seizure of their lands, the enslavement of millions of Africans, and wars of expansion into the Third World.

Jensen asked that whites look into their hearts. Like Marlow in Joseph Conrad's *Heart of Darkness*, whites should brave a journey of self-discovery to confront their fears of blacks and Mexican Americans and overcome the evils of racist attitudes and institutions. Otherwise, how can the United States take the high moral ground with dictators and terrorists?

As a personal example, Jensen said that he worked and studied hard to rise from his North Dakota lower-middle-class background to earn his doctorate in journalism and land a job at a prestigious university. He knew that, along the way, he received a significant boost from the fact that he grew up in an almost all-white city, attended all-white schools, had white bosses, and never believed that his failures were because he was white.

He recognized that merit was only part of the reason for his success; his white status in a society that valued whites over ethnic minorities gave him the edge. It was this advantage that he asked his fellow whites to examine and work to eliminate.

Jensen acknowledged that dismantling racism would mean a loss of power, material wealth, and status for whites. An underlying white fear is that with a growing Chicano population and political strength, Mexican Americans will gain governmental and social control. Then a white minority might find that it might receive the same treatment it has doled out over the years.

In a brutally honest story, he talked about a panel presentation he made with Les Payne, a Pulitzer Prize-winner and associate managing editor at *Newsday*. Payne was more experienced, had won more awards, written more serious pieces and spoke publicly better than Jensen. Yet as he sat next to the black journalist, Jensen felt superior. When Payne explained to the audience that he had to struggle to overcome feelings of inferiority from his Southern upbringing to succeed in school and professional life, Jensen felt despair. He had thought that he was one of the "good" whites. He realized that despite his political activism and writings on behalf of racial equality, he hadn't shaken his feelings of superiority.

This attitude of white superiority in history, language, and action forced Payne and other ethnic minorities to feel and act inferior. Jensen's — and other whites' — personal recognition of this ideology is the first step to the white superiority cure. Jensen admitted that he was an angry man who wished more middle-class whites would become indignant. They need to howl at an ideology that forced them to exchange their political souls for material affluence. But not all have sold out.

The League of Women Voters' initiative to persuade the John Peter Smith Health Network board in Fort Worth, Texas, to extend non-emergency healthcare to the undocumented was a noble example of middle-class whites fighting for justice. No doubt they risked the loss of support from white, politically conservative organizations by taking up this cause, but they accepted their moral responsibility to ensure that a healthcare system with a $37.6 million surplus provides care to all sick people in Tarrant County.

As Jensen concluded, the White People's Burden was to civilize themselves and their institutions.

If we are to compete successfully in the global markets, then America must draw on the genius of all of its people. At my last job at Tarrant

County Juvenile Services, I tried in vain to motivate the senior managers to instill staff training on cultural and linguistic competency. I had done extensive research in the field, written essays about it, and knew personally the results of insensitive cultural treatment. The senior managers listened with blank looks, engaged in desultory discussions, and never committed to the effort. After I was demoted from the senior management rank for bogus financial reasons, the cultural competency efforts were revitalized. Although I was asked to participate in the development, I was eventually asked not to take a role in the planning committee because of my outspokenness. It seemed that some whites were offended by my directness in explaining that they enjoyed white privilege as a result of historical, institutional racist practices. An elected official in Tarrant County shared that others in the organization treated this office holder with actions reflective of colonialism.

Fortunately, whites like Luke Visconti understand the importance of direct, frank dialogue about race in the work setting. Readers of DiversityInc.com enjoyed a regular dose of Luke Visconti's column, "Ask the White Guy." As co-founder of DiversityInc, he made no excuses for the column title or answering sensitive questions about workplace diversity.

Visconti said he was aware that there were large groups — ethnic minorities, women, the disabled and gays — competing on unlevel playing fields. Visconti exhorted corporations that seek success to find and keep the best talent from a larger pool of candidates.

It worked: The top fifty companies in DiversityInc's 2006 diversity rankings showed superior financial performance. Over a ten-year period, they outperformed the Nasdaq by 28.2 percent, the Standard & Poor's 500 by 24.8 percent and the Dow Jones Industrial Average by 22.4 percent. Verizon Communications/Wireless, Consolidated Edison of New York, and the Coca-Cola Company topped the DiversityInc 2006 ranking.[15]

In 2015, the top ten companies for diversity were Novartis Pharmaceuticals Corporation, Kaiser Permanente, PricewaterhouseCoopers, EY,

Sodexo, MasterCard, AT&T, Prudential Financial, Johnson & Johnson, and Procter & Gamble.[16]

If we believe that talent is distributed among all social groups equally, then it follows that education, mentoring, opportunity, and inclusion will foster the skills in minorities, women, gays and the disabled to excel.

The star performers don't necessarily look or sound like the traditional white male executive or manager.

Visconti acknowledged that for some whites, diversity can be disconcerting. He said most whites don't even think about race on a regular basis. Why should they? "Being white means you never have to think about race; you never consider that your application to college will be treated differently; that the police officer stopping you isn't out for anything more than how fast you were going; that your boss didn't really mean to insult you to your core when he said 'You're so articulate' or dismiss your entire being by saying 'I don't care if you're Black, Yellow, Brown, Green or Polka-Dot,'" he said.[17]

But some minorities who struggle to live up to an unwritten expectation that they need to perform better than most on the job worry about it. The unspoken fear is that peers and subordinates might believe that the only reason that they landed a managerial job was because of the need to fill an affirmative action quota or to stave off accusations of discrimination. Some grow weary of the photo ops and tagging along to business meetings to smile and nod. Others grow tired of hearing how smart they sound, yet wield no real power. And if they don't make it – well, that proves that they just don't have the right stuff.

As the white workforce ages and a youthful minority workforce grows, especially among Mexican Americans, progressive organizations must examine their inclusion strategies. Customers and employees speaking a variety of languages, with different tastes and cultures, require organizations to reassess their work cultures.

Politicians, conservatives and Horacio Alger Chicanos can bemoan the changes in US culture, but businesses should take a hard look at how they respond to diversity if they hope to compete in a global economy where foreign rivals learn English, Spanish, and any other language and customs to take American customers' bucks.

Is it really any surprise that Toyota will soon surpass General Motors in world car sales? Why was it startling to see Chicano actors speaking Spanish in a Super Bowl commercial in February 2006 advertising the Toyota Camry Hybrid?

Douglas M. West, former senior vice president and chief administrative officer for Toyota Motor Sales USA, said, "at Toyota, our work toward creating a culture of inclusion is in harmony with and supports our vision to become the most successful and respected car company in America."[18] *Se habla dinero* at Toyota.

I look forward to a Chicano entrepreneur driving a Toyota and writing a column called "Ask the Brown Guy."

Another way to spread inclusion is to have our media moguls showcase more Mexican Americans on the wide screen. The paucity of Chicano roles distorts the image of American culture and leaves Chicanos wondering when they became invisible.

Minorities in *Minority Report*, a Steven Spielberg movie set in Washington D.C. in 2054, are African-Americans who mutter a few lines and are props for Tom Cruise, the tragic-hero, in his quest to prevent crimes foretold. In a city currently bursting with African-Americans and Mexican Americans, Spielberg invited us to imagine the future capital populated by witty, hip whites who've invented whiz-bang cars and planes, thought projectors and eye-popping technology. The few minorities of the future were foils for brilliant white scientists, G-men, cops, and genetically engineered seers.

Spielberg portrayed Cruise, Brad Pitt, and Tom Hanks as "everyman" characters whom Americans can easily like and therefore pay to sit watching for hours in the dark. White men admired and white women swooned, but I venture that Latinos preferred a Nick Gonzales, Michael Peña, or Andy García to outfight, outclass, and outwit their foes and fates.

Not until the latest Star Wars saga did George Lucas decide to include a Latino, Jimmy Smits, as a minor, costumed character, in his opus of the dark vs. light. Animals, mechanical sharks, dinosaurs, aliens, androids, cartoons, and the Muppets have had more screen and screech time than Chicano/Chicana actors.

In the City of Angels by the Pacific, populated by ethnic minorities who outnumber whites, movie moguls cast an America of the whites, for the whites and by the whites. They spun reels of unrealistic pathos and bathos in which the stars are clever, Aryan-looking men and women and the few Mexican Americans are cooks, cons, crazies, or cowards.

Frances Negrón-Muntaner and others from Columbia University's Center for the Study of Ethnicity and Race published their study "The Latino Media Gap: A Report on the State of Latinos in US Media" in June 2014. Despite the increase in the US Latino population, their presence in the movies and television as actors, writers, directors, producers and CEOs was decreasing. Their findings included: Latino men have disappeared as leading actors while Latina actors have increased their presence slightly; Stereotypes restrict opportunities and perceptions; Latino presence in TV programming and movies is limited; Latino news anchors and producers is low. Negrón-Muntaner wrote "The current data suggests persistent and unchecked job discrimination in a major US industry. The relegation of Latinos similarly deprives media consumers of innovative perspectives at a moment of rapid industry and demographic change." [19]

From a moral viewpoint, perhaps we needed a separate ethnic rating system to prepare the viewer for the depth of ethnic mendacity: "W" for white actors in power roles surrounded by sycophantic minorities; "AA" for movies depicting Ebonics-speaking African-American actors, with whites as cruel oppressors (beware of blaxploitation themes); "L" for Latino actors in Spanglish-speaking roles, mainly associated with drug-dealing, gang-banging, and prisons; "A" for Asian films in which the characters are martial arts experts, extremely polite and wise; "AI" for American Indians, noble warriors of the past with an affinity for white men's scalps, who in the modern era live on reservations and can't handle the firewater.

According to survey research by the Tomás Rivera Policy Institute involving 4,000 Latino actors, all members of the Screen Actors Guild, 73 percent thought a Latino surname was a disadvantage.[20]

Thirty percent responding to the survey said that they were expected to speak poor English or to speak with an accent. Two-thirds said that they lost roles because they didn't fit the Chicano stereotype of a mestizo.[21] Ironically, Mexican casting directors seemed to prefer blond, fair-skinned Latinas in their novelas, or soap operas.

When confronted with the near-invisibility of Chicanos in starring roles, producers and directors respond that economics, not racism, dictated the movies and actors selected. After all, the fair faces of Robert Redford, Julia Roberts, Nicole Kidman, and Russell Crowe generated millions in revenue.

L.A. Chicano activists of a grassroots organization known as the Premiere Weekend Club countered with their own research showing that movies with positive portrayals of Mexican Americans were profitable. Motion pictures like *La Bamba, McFarland, USA, Spare Parts, Like Water For Chocolate, Mi Familia, El Mariachi, EL Norte, Stand and Deliver,* and *Born in East L.A.* earned millions for investors.[22]

They reported that, based on data from the Motion Picture Association of America, Latinos generated about 15 percent of domestic box office monies, or more than $1 billion in revenue.[23] As the Chicano population swells, so do the movie-attending audiences and revenue. From a strictly economic viewpoint, it's risky business for producers to bypass the Chicano movie market.

Spielberg should have listened to his film's central message: The future may be technologically dazzling, but primal passions still shape our destiny. Before making another movie, Spielberg should exchange his irises for Chicano eyes, walk Olvera Street or East Los Angeles and meet the real people of the future. If so, he'll envision a silver screen of Latino actors performing to the artistic heights of the great performers of the past: Anthony Quinn, Ramón Novarro, Rita Moreno, Dolores Del Río, Katy Jurado, Rita Hayward, and Mario Moreno (Cantinflas).

From a man in brown, that's my minority report.

Chapter 8

Cultural Competency

To eliminate the disease of racism and restore a healthy society, whites should steel their hearts and minds for political change and accept their darker brothers and sisters. They should also learn to live in a world that has become increasingly diverse. The future will reward those who learn to travel well between cultural worlds.

I worked seventeen years in hospitals as a medical social worker and director of medical social work departments. The medical culture, steeped in protocol and technology, required strict attention to detail and timely communication with patients and the healthcare team. But what if the patients and their families spoke only Spanish and the team spoke only English? Enter the bilingual social worker to save the day. Even better, enter the bilingual nurse or doctor who spoke Spanish and understood the culture. In the helping professions, nurturing cultural competency is the prescribed medicine for healthy outcomes.

An article in the *Fort Worth Star-Telegram,* July 24, 2006, "PAs Learn Spanish for Accuracy," highlighted physician assistant students reaching into their medicine bags for a cultural tonic. For healthcare professionals, the benefits of learning Spanish were obvious: an understanding of the presenting health problem, patient compliance with instructions, a reduction in patient fear, and improved doctor-patient relationship. The overall results were healthier and happier patients.

For a healthy society to thrive in increasingly diverse communities, good medicine consists of daily doses of cultural competency exercises: the strength to work and play in a culture other than the one in which you were born. Language mastery alone is insufficient to reach across the divide.

The culturally competent revel in grasping the history, traditions, tastes, and values of others. They shed the attitude of "My culture is superior to yours" and assume "I wish to learn your ways" humility.

Whether for financial profit, educational goals, safe neighborhoods, improved inter-ethnic relations, political gain, or healthy people, intimate understanding of other communities enriches. Cultural competency stretches the wrinkles out of our old cultural faces and gives us a youthful look at others. It forces the imagination to accept that there never was and never will be just one American culture. Shed the weighty melting-pot icon, replace it with a charm bracelet of dangling cultures, and wear it proudly.

The beauty of a multi-cultural America is the opportunity to resurrect into a different culture without leaving for a distant country or dying. The new worlds are at Fort Worth's North Side, Como, Stop Six, Diamond Hill, and East Arlington and celebrated at the Gran Fiesta, Juneteenth, and Double Ten festivities.

Save that Cancún vacation money and instead mix with Mexicans at their Mexican Independence Day celebration's downtown parade, or ride a cultural diversity float and hand out friendship beads. Learn that immigrants want the same American Dream and will gladly master English if given the time and chance. Put away the language tapes and find a Spanish-speaking associate with whom to speak *El Español.*

English-plus is the literacy movement to learn English and other languages spoken by millions in America. There's no need for official-language laws in a land where people speak in tones of respect and acceptance.

The spiritual-minded can learn the "Our Father" in *El Español*, sing Spanish hymns or read the *Biblia*. Attend services in Vietnamese or Spanish and learn that the Word is common to all. Lest we forget, Christianity's founder and his apostles were from the Middle East, didn't speak English, and had to travel long distances to spread the Good News.

Cultural competency works both ways. Mexican Americans, too, must stretch their cultural muscles to earn an education and compete in the market. They should read the classics of British and US authors, understand the reasons for European immigration to the Americas and the challenges they faced after Ellis Island. As there is diversity among Latinos, they must learn there that Anglos come from and live diverse heritages.

The culturally competent stretch their circle of friends and acquaintances beyond the comfort zone of the like-minded, same-language crowd. They read books of other cultures, ask about their family and immigration stories, learn about their heroes, and observe how they interact with one another. They learn that other cultures love and pine for their families as much as families of the dominant culture love and miss their sons and daughters far from home. They learn that sons and daughters of other cultures have fought and died in American wars — some non-citizens and barely speaking English. The blue-chip jobs of the future will go to cultural brokers, the individuals who bridge cultural differences and languages. Parents wishing to give their children an edge in the job market and promote their ease in a culturally diverse society should encourage their children's cultural competency. Start foreign-language mastery early, encourage talk about differences and similarities in cultures, display different cultural artifacts and welcome others into the home.

Photo 11. Día De Los Muertos Celebration, Fort Worth, Texas

Courtesy of the Delsa M. Pérez Collection, Genealogy, History, and Archives Unit, Fort Worth Library.
Jennifer L. Bayer on left and Laura L. Flores on right, at Rose Marine Theater, October 2006.

Parents should check their cultural biases and encourage their children to hold positive attitudes about diversity. Model the comfort with other cultures that you wish your children to display. Encourage them to study and cherish their own cultural roots. Celebrate *Dia de Los Muertos*, Chinese New Year and Juneteenth and teach them that America was populated by millions of Indians before the Europeans arrived.

Give them the courage to live in a mixed America.

Photo 12. *Ofrenda* display

Courtesy of the Delsa P. Pérez Collection, Genealogy, History, and Archives Unit, Fort Worth Library.
Día De Los Muertos celebration at Rose Marine Theater, 2006

We must also teach the Anglo-dominated healthcare professionals to expand their understanding of Mexican American culture. Medicine is science-based but they treat humans not chemical formulas and test tubes. Medical schools must do a better job of preparing doctors to engage Chicano patients.

Mexican American children in the United States are proportionally sicker than their white and black peers, according to a study published in the July 3, 2002, *Journal of the American Medical Association.*[24]

"In 1999, 20 percent of Mexican American youth reported considering suicide, compared with 15 percent of black and 18 percent of white youth," said Dr. Glenn Flores, one of the researchers involved in "The Health of Mexican American Children" report. "In particular, Latina adolescents (19 percent) were significantly more likely than white (9 percent) and black (8 percent) adolescent girls to have attempted suicide. Mexican American boys are the most overweight and Latina girls the second most overweight racial/ethnic groups of US children."[25] This condition makes them more likely to develop Type II diabetes and other diseases.

Mexican American children are more likely than black and white children to breathe and live close to air pollutants, hazardous waste sites, pesticides, lead, and mercury. They're at greater risk for premature death, asthma, lead poisoning, cancer, and developmental problems. Of the 1 million children who accompany their farm worker parents, 94 percent are Mexican Americans. As in the times of legendary farm-worker crusader César Chávez, migrant children still face risks of tuberculosis, infectious diseases from parasites, and sexually transmitted diseases.

These findings came at time when the US Census showed that Latino children are the largest minority group under the age of eighteen, comprising 11.6 million, or 16 percent, of the youth population. The health risks that Chicano children face are staggering. They are 13 percent more likely than white children to contract tuberculosis. Chicano children from ages two to four years are more likely to have tooth decay than white or black children. Sixty percent of twelve- to seventeen-year-old

Mexican Americans have had their dental problems treated, compared to 87 percent of white teens.[26]

Among recommendations to overcome healthcare barriers, Flores and colleagues called for the healthcare industry to tackle language and cultural competency issues.[27] Corporate and not-for-profit hospitals, private physicians, allied healthcare providers, and insurance carriers must come to grips with the demographic reality that their patient loads are becoming increasingly Mexican American.

Blaming the culture for the woes of its children was over. Flores recommended "that we abandon the traditional 'deficit' view of Mexican American culture ... and adopt a more balanced perspective that emphasizes appreciation and understanding of the salutary components of Mexican American culture."[28]

A major complaint that Mexican American parents have with their healthcare providers is that they couldn't communicate clearly with them. The researchers reported that there were insufficient numbers of trained medical interpreters available. Physicians resorted to pulling housekeeping staff or drafting the child-patient to interpret. These actions often result in miscommunication and clinical errors, along with forcing the child into an uncomfortable role and violating the patient's privacy.

The obvious solution is for the healthcare staff to learn Spanish as quickly as possible. This isn't a time to assume English-only or who-let-them-into-this-country political posturing. Older physicians and nurses may find the linguistic challenge too difficult; however, medical, dental, and nursing students should recognize that they will serve a population that generally doesn't sound or look like their professors, laboratory peers, or professional role models. To live out the Hippocratic Oath of "do no harm," learn Spanish and do *lo muy bueno* (much good).

A second solution is for more bilingual, bicultural, science-oriented Chicanos and Chicanas to enter health-care professions. As Flores points out, there has been a decrease of minority medical school students, partly as a result of anti-affirmative-action laws. Nevertheless, the demand for bilingual, culturally competent healthcare workers is so urgent that the Mexican American community should use financial and emotional support to encourage Chicanos and Chicanas to pursue medical careers.

While learning *Español*, medical students should close the Gray's Anatomy, leave the sterile laboratory environment and walk the streets of the closest Chicano community. Seek out community/political leaders, parish priests, *curanderos* (folk-healers), funeral directors, children and their parents to learn Mexican American culture.

If healthcare providers are to become culturally competent — to understand a culture's worldview of life, death, disease, pain, sex, marriage, gender roles, arts, language, family — then they must discard the scrubs and stethoscope, leave for a while the ethnocentric cocoon of biomedical rationality, suspend judgment and listen to the stories of Mexican Americans struggling to live their lives free of fear, pain and desperation.

To treat the Chicano child, doctor, heal thyself.

Chapter 9

Letters

Mexican American dance, song, literature, and paintings reflect the beauty, dreams, and aspirations of a colorful, passionate people. A well-rounded view of Chicanos must examine their arts to appreciate their resiliency in the face of oppressive treatment and their hopes that the future brings amorous, financial, and spiritual riches.

Psychological and demographic research by scholars may provide standard deviations, projections, and chi-square results to satisfy statisticians, government grants, and politicians. Deeper awareness of the Chicano/a's experience requires a poet's voice. I measure the Chicano/a's heart with riffs of rhythmic words—not by an Access database. In their humility, Mexican Americans haven't made it easy to penetrate their worlds. For a people who will soon become the Texas majority and deserve pulpits and power, some Chicanos still speak with whispers and insincerity lest they offend.

But they do offend—they insult their own people with their cultural self-deprecation and avoidance of eyes and speaking of truth. They languish like assimilated shadows—muted, distorted, following, falling in step.

Some Texas Mexican Americans act like adults still wearing notes pinned to their clothes by their teachers. We forget too easily the importance of speaking up, talking back, and causing a scene to be noticed and heard. Now that Chicanos have mastered politeness, they are free to commence the politics of poetics. They are free to give up a little respectability and quit trying so hard to "speaky da" English without an accent.

Some Texas Chicano/a poets remembered, wrote, rhymed, and took the stage with their well-crafted words to prove that Spanish accents are suave, to blast their Tex-Mex pyrotechnic words into the air, to stomp the ground and trumpet the awakening of their literary might.

Unlike Chicano convicts who take up pen to tattoo their bodies with the *Virgen de Guadalupe* or diablos, some—like the late Raúl Salinas, the poet laureate of Austin's East Side—wrote poetry to free their minds from the cells of self-hate and despair. A dark-complexioned, American Indian-featured Salinas sang his songs like a post-conquest Aztec priest who asks his gods in caves to explain what horrible sins he committed to merit punishment so severely by the bearded, white strangers.

When does the Mexican-Anglo cultural war end and when do we celebrate all of Texas' voices? Yes, Davy Crockett, Jim Bowie, and William Travis were killed, but so were hundreds of Mexican heroes who fought to defend their country's sovereignty.

Chicano/a poets like Salinas, Tammy Gómez, Pat Mora, Sandra Cisneros, Carmen Tafolla, Tonantzin Canestaro-García, and Jacinto Cardona carry on a literary tradition present in Tejas since the early nineteenth century. Their beautiful Tex-Mex voices flow between Chicano and Anglo cultural worlds, sailing with ease to and from English and Spanish. True to their mixed blood, they write mestizo poems—a blending of their Chicano voice with the dominant Anglo poetic forms.

They are Chicano Dantes, guiding us through levels of America's barrio hell, purgatory, and glory. Chicano/a poets sing of pachucos in their zoot suits, low-riders cruising in their cars, confused Chicano/a students struggling with assimilation far away from home, the joy of eating and naming the diverse types of *pan dulce* (sweet bread), the beauty of the San Antonio River and the El Paso desert. Latina feminists took the stage, removed cultural muzzles, pranced and spoke boldly about their desires, anger, and deception.

Photo 13. Marine Theater

Courtesy of the Delsa M. Pérez Collection, Genealogy, History, and Archives Unit, Fort Worth Library.
Marine Theater on Northside Fort Worth Main Street, January, 2001.

Chicano/a poets visited the Rose Marine Theater and performed before a mixed audience of young and old, Anglos and Mexican Americans. They watched Ray Santisteban's *Voices from Texas* video and heard Mexican American poets read and talk about their writing. Monolinguals missed the subtle humor when poets vaulted from English to Spanish and then Spanish to English. It was as if they were almost deaf and required a hearing aid only found in bilingual homes. This excellent film should be required viewing in all high school and college American literature classes.

Fort Worth's Tammy Gómez's recital of her poem "On Language" is an acerbic look at her overachieving attempts to prove that she "could toe the line with daughters of white professional men."[29] She celebrated her Americanism at the cost of losing her native language and ethnic identity.

Raúl Salinas, in his Austin *Resistencia* Bookstore, told Chicano poets: "Here's a safe space. Come try your poetry out and we'll be able to leave our mark and tell the story of our people for what we are, the worth that we have."[30]

Other Tejano writers celebrated Chicano literary past and present in anthologies. The book *Hecho En Tejas* was a bold attempt to glean the best over centuries of Chicano writings. The book captured the struggles on the Mexican frontier of Coahuila y Texas to the modern day challenges of urban life. Dagoberto Gilb, editor of *Hecho En Tejas: An Anthology of Texas Mexican Literature*, said smart America was ready for a Tejano ghost story.

On a Fort Worth cable-TV book review session that I hosted, Gilb said that the book showcases the best writings penned by Tejanos since the Spaniards' arrival. Gilb called Álvar Nuñez Cabeza de Vaca — who wrote a chronicle of his time as a Texas Indian captive in the sixteenth century — the first Chicano. From there, the anthology progressed chronologically in a grand historical and cultural reflection of the dreams, fears, politics, and passions of the times. Through a collection of corridos, ballads, essays, short stories, poetry, letters, and novel excerpts, readers learn Tejano culture and wit. In the book's introduction, Gilb explained that he is raising the ghosts of Tejano writers, escorting them on stage to state in their own words the dreams, fears, politics, and passions that compelled them to write.

"The publication of *Hecho en Tejas* is hereby a formal announcement: We have been here, we are still here. I want this book to overwhelm the ignorance," he said. This anthology shattered stereotypes, offered insightful historical and cultural reflections, and showcased Tejanos writers, some very much alive and mostly of the twentieth century. Not only were Tejano settlers ranching, roping, and riding – they were writing. Tejanos and Tejanas not only used their hands to build houses, cars, and roads, but they wrote poems, songs, and stories. The book was meant for Chicano students as well as their parents and grandparents, lest they forget and lose their cultural, linguistic, and historical gifts. Ironically, the book highlighting Chicano writers came at a time that Chicano high dropout rates and low reading levels plague the community.

Gilb hoped that high schools and colleges would use the anthology in their curriculums to show that many Chicanos have written well over the years and their students could view them as role models for their own literary aspirations. With the brief biographies of the writers next to their works, students could see that writers learn their art through education and practice.

Hecho En Tejas may stimulate English teachers to expand their Chicano literature offerings beyond Sandra Cisneros and Rudolfo Anaya. Although excellent writers, they represent a small sampling of Chicano literature. It's as if schools offered solely Ernest Hemingway and William Faulkner as the breadth of American letters.

At a time when many large, urban school districts such as Fort Worth and Arlington are minority-majority, Anglo, black, and Chicano students should learn to appreciate the culturally rich and diverse Texas heritage. Let's substitute the taco-eating, serape-wearing, bandito images for the hard-working, literate Tejano icons who fought, ranched, and prayed for a better life.

Tammy Gómez, whose works appeared in the anthology, said at the book review session that Mexican Americans could start reading anywhere in the book and recall their own story. She said a reader told her that her eighty-three-year-old father recalled a corrido in the book and sang it. With about 100 writers highlighted (many of them women), she said, the anthology reflected a shattering of obstacles for Latinas who confronted not only racial but also gender hurdles.

Tonantzin Canestaro-García, a young poet based in Houston, said in the cable TV interview that although she couldn't speak Spanish, "I still love my culture and it's a place where I can go and still feel part of it even though I don't write in Spanish. I think this will open doors for students like me." Her comments confirmed research that, over generations, Chicanos tended to lose their ability to speak Spanish and preferred English. Canestaro-García's poetry offered English-dominant Chicano youth examples of shedding shame and revelling in their Chicano heritage. The anthology also offered samples of poems in which the author moved from Spanish to English and back to emphasize cultural and linguistic sophistication.

Living in America doesn't require crossing a William Travis sword-drawn cultural line in the dirt. Instead, the anthology – written mostly in English – dramatized that Tejanos could learn to keep their cultural identity, Spanish, and heritage as they mastered English and worked in the mainstream culture. Tejano ghosts spoke through their writings in *Hecho En Tejas.* They asked that we listen, read, write, and live Tejano smart.

Spanish-speaking Latinos often hold up the works of Gabriel García Márquez and Carlos Fuentes as examples of world-class literary writers. However, even Márquez had to concede that in his opinion the poetry of Pablo Neruda earned him the title of best writer of the twentieth century in any language. Pablo Neruda's *Veinte poemas de amor y una canción desperada,* or *Twenty Love Poems and a Song of Despair,* provide twenty exquisite reasons to jump for the Velázquez Dictionary or to learn Spanish. Neruda wrote the poems at age twenty and catapulted to the South American literary scene with his rich imagery, sensuous use of Spanish and universal appeal to bittersweet amor. His Latin fervor simmered on each page, imbuing readers with an ardor savored by true lovers of life locked in embrace. In his words, "*Es tan corto el amor, y es tan largo el olvido*"— love is so short, and forgetting is so long.[31]

Neruda won the Nobel Prize in Literature in 1971, two years before his death, and the centennial of his birth was celebrated around the world on July 12, 2004. Mountain climbers organized to read "The Heights of Macchu Picchu" from the tallest mountains in South America and from Asia's Mount Everest. In response to a petition, the International Astronomical Union in 2008 named a Mercury crater after Neruda. Neruda explored the world of the seemingly ordinary in his odes. A chestnut "holds in its structure unblemished delight and edible rose." A book is a "minuscule forest, leaf after leaf your paper smells of the elements." A watch "went on cutting time with its little saw." Wine "stirs the Spring, joy grows like a plant, walls, boulders, fall, abysses close up, song is born."

For readers of Spanish and English, the bilingual editions are a linguistic joy to shuttle across the page from left to right, from the original to the approximate. Those raised with Spanish as their mother tongue find the familiar vowel endings and rhythmic flow a natural poetic timbre. Pride fills Spanish speakers upon hearing Neruda's words match and exceed the elegance of well-crafted English, French, German, Italian, or Chinese.

To commemorate the wonder of Neruda, the Latino Arts Association of Fort Worth in July 2004 presented *Siempre, Neruda*, a multimedia celebration of his poetry. Under the artistic direction of local poet Tammy Gómez, Neruda came to life in the Rose Marine Theater as a boy. Young Actor Alejandro Herrera portrayed Neruda writing poetry in spite of his father's disapproval. The great poet was born Neftalí Ricardo Reyes Basualto. He assumed his nom de plume of Pablo Neruda at fourteen in homage to Jan Neruda, a Czech poet, and to avoid his father's wrath.

Carlos Ayala played the adult Neruda reciting his poetry by the sea and making his banquet speech at Stockholm, Sweden, upon receiving his Nobel Prize. To represent the global appeal of Neruda, three local poets took turns reciting "Ode to the Book (II)" in their native tongues: Spanish, Italian, and Kannada, a language spoken in southern India. Neruda traveled as Chilean consul to México, Burma, Ceylon, and Java (now Sri Lanka and Indonesia, respectively), Singapore, Argentina, France, and Spain. In his travels, he grew increasingly discontented by the oppression of the masses. While in Spain, he wrote fiery poems against the fascists during the Spanish Civil War, and on his return to Chile he joined the Communists.

After a warrant for his arrest was issued because of his political activities, he lived in exile in Europe and visited the Soviet Union. During this time, Neruda resumed writing love poems to his third wife, Matilde Urrutia. Using Neruda's life and poems, Gómez viewed Neruda as a model of the cosmopolitan writer who transcended borders. "We must ignore those messages that would have us mistrust one another . . . we have an opportunity because this is the melting pot to meet people who are our own neighbors," she said. "It is interesting to reflect on his work and feel hope and a sense of righteous indignation rightfully placed – to do what we must do to speak out against injustice."[32]

On the night celebrating Neruda, tango partners Jairelbhi and George Furlong danced to drums, violin, and the poet's words. The sensuous image of two lovers gliding across the stage to "Poor Creatures" drew cheers.

The translation reads:

> And they say terrible things
> about a man and a woman
> who, after lots of vacillations
> and lots of deliberations
> do something incomparable,
> fall together into one bed.

The Spanish sizzles.

Chapter 10

Sports

Watching the Texas Rangers and St. Louis Cardinals in the 2011 World Series Games always raised fans' excitement. This was especially true for residents of Arlington, Texas—my residence and the location of the Texas Rangers baseball team. Despite going to the World Series twice in a row and losing twice in a row, the Rangers stirred our hearts. Latinos in North Texas were especially overjoyed to see Nelson Cruz, Adrián Beltré, Elvis Andrus, and Yorvit Torrealba play marvelously for the Rangers. Latinos have infused baseball with a dynamism not seen since the days of Babe Ruth and Lou Gehrig. Baseball has transformed to *béisbol* and we're all joyous for the change.

Latino cheers for Roberto Clemente, Luis Aparicio, and Juan Marichal still resonate. For Latino players, *beisbol* is the field of American Dreams. The diamond is literally the level playing ground where their bats, gloves, and speed shine.

Despite slim chances, Latino players hone their throwing, hitting, and running skills and try out in droves to play ball. Encouraged by American scouts and the lure of money, Caribbean players compete to get into the big leagues. Most don't succeed and return to struggle on their tropical islands or stay undocumented in the United States. Instead of swinging a bat and running bases, they end up swinging a mop and running errands.

Photo 14. Yovani Gallardo

Courtesy of Emerico Pérez, Emerico Photography.
Yovani Gallardo, Texas Ranger pitcher, receiving award from pony league team mates at Yovani Gallardo day at LaGrave Field, Fort Worth, Texas April 2015.

The American pastime's heroes are the Latino swingers who have taken the sport by storm: Iván Rodríguez, Sammy Sosa, Rafael Palmeiro, Alex Rodríguez, Juan González, Rubén Sierra, Julio Franco, and Pedro Martínez. These power players helped their teams win playoff berths and World Series rings. Their style of play harks back to their indigenous ancestors who played ceremonial ball games. Sometimes they lost their lives in the heat of the game: Baseball is in their blood. Some research has suggested that Latino athletes are more aggressive than Anglo players. A study by Miguel Humara found that Latino aggression was related more to their lower socioeconomic status than their ethnicity, however. He found that when researchers controlled for social status, Latinos were not any more aggressive than Anglo or black teammates.[33] For many professional Latino ballplayers, raised in impoverished, developing countries such as the Dominican Republic, baseball offered a socially acceptable expression for the aggression they saw in their daily lives.

But the odds are stacked against them. According to sociologist W.M. Leonard, the odds of making it to the big game are slim: For Anglos they're 4 in 100,000; for blacks, 2 in 100,000; and for Latinos, 3 in 1 million. Thus, for Latino athletes, the fierce competition, impoverished upbringing, and poor educational alternatives drive them to catch, hit, and throw that baseball with fury.[34]

Sometimes that aggression to win at any costs has tempted Latino ballplayers to cheat. Allegations by José Canseco, the 1988 American League Most Valuable Player, that several top Latino and Anglo ballplayers used steroids were disappointing. Canseco—"The Chemist"—claimed he helped juice up Mark McGwire and witnessed others shooting up.[35]

Sammy Sosa's excuse that he accidentally used a corked bat in a game against the Tampa Bay Rays still rings hollow. In smashing that bat and revealing its core, he broke the hearts of many fans.

Despite Latinos' proven talent, bias still haunts Latino players. In 1999, Houston Astros owner Drayton McLane stirred an uproar when he said that it was "hard to reach Hispanics because the game of baseball is strategy and skill and it's complicated, and that's why more Hispanics don't go to Astros games." When confronted about this statement, he gave a lame, taken-out-of-context defense.[36]

McLane must have forgotten or didn't know that Estéban Enrique Bellán had played major-league ball in the nineteenth century. Before Jackie Robinson broke the color barrier in baseball in 1947, other Cuban players in the twentieth century such as Adolfo Luque and Roberto Estalella hurdled the baseball bar.[37]

Marcos Benton, a writer for the *Sacramento Bee*, wrote on October 4, 2011, that every MLB team has hired Latino ballplayers for a song. In 1997, the Oakland Athletics signed Miguel Tejada for $2,000; in 1995, the A's signed Ben Grieve for $1.2 million. The Texas Rangers signed Sosa in 1986 for $3,500.

Still, Latino hustle spices the game. The magnificent hitting, fielding, and pitching of Red Sox Manny Ramírez, David Ortiz, Pedro Martínez, and Orlando Cabrera helped to break the eighty-six-year-old Curse of the Bambino. The win was certainly a team effort, but one wondered if it required the talents of Latino ghost busters.

Of the 2011 forty-man Texas Rangers Baseball Team who went to the World Series, thirteen were Latinos. This matches the growing trend in Major League Baseball where Latinos comprise 27 percent of the players.[38]

They leave shantytowns and dirt lots in hopes to play in palatial ballparks, reaching star status and earning million of dollars. Some barely speak English; others talk with heavy accents. But on the field, they allow their bats and gloves to celebrate eloquently *béisbol.*

SUMMARY

Chicano culture is rich and dynamic, heavily influenced by Mexican, indigenous, and the greater American mores, customs, and institutions. The culturally resilient child is able to traverse between the culture of his parents and the Anglo-dominated world. At times, some youth, especially Chicana teens, find the cultural demands too stressful, leading to suicidal thoughts and attempts.

Efforts must be made to strengthen *La Familia*, to focus on the importance of fathers in playing a supportive role in the tradition of *hombres nobles.* Chicanos have the advantage of being able to draw on the best of Mexican culture, such as its family orientation and literary and musical traditions, and to avoid any regression to female oppression.

Non-Chicanos can develop cultural competency by learning Spanish and their customs, history, and challenges. An understanding of white privilege and its insidious influence in our thinking and institutions will help to eliminate superiority attitudes and behaviors. Latino ballplayers have demonstrated that on level playing fields, they excel and excite all fans. In the future, Chicanos must enter all fields of dreams and demonstrate our capacity to create, lead, and win.

SECTION 3

RAZA RISING

My first exposure to politics was Richard J. Daley's Machine in Chicago. Daley ran the city in the old-time, big city boss-rule fashion as captured in Mike Royko's book *Boss.* I recall Squeegie, our neighborhood Democrat precinct captain, calling out to my father in the street, "Hey, Joe. You're going to vote, right?" My father said he would. "Make sure you vote right," Squeegie said, making the subtle distinction. And so it went throughout the city: Daley's neighborhood capos worked the Italian, Polish, Jewish, Irish, Puerto Rican, and Mexican sectors to ensure the Democrats stayed in power. On the surface, Chicago seemed to run smoothly with this system. Workers dyed the Chicago River that ran throughout the city green on St. Patrick's Day. Irish politicos ran the city with ethnic alliances and patronage.

My first awakening to the political reality of the day was the turbulent 1968 Democratic Convention in Chicago. Anti-war movement activists occupied Grant Park and protested for the end of the Vietnam War. Although I didn't venture downtown, I watched with rapt attention to the national and local news coverage of the rioting that took place as the protestors and police clashed. I remember watching Daley talking tough to newsmen that he wouldn't allow hippies to disrupt the convention.

The mayor basically said this was his city and he wouldn't allow outside agitators to take over his parks and streets.

When rioting erupted in the predominantly black neighborhoods, Daley again took swift, tough action and sent the police to quell the disturbance. I can recall seeing from my house the red glow in the night air from the fires that raged in the adjacent black communities. Police cars raced through our neighborhood like soldiers heading to the battlefront. Of all the diverse groups that comprised Chicago's ethnic world, the blacks were the most excluded and feared. The political power to control social protests and the marginalized communities' struggle to overthrow oppressive political systems rose to my young reality.

When I moved to Texas, in 1969, the Democrats were still in control of the state. Few Chicanos held public office but I remember House Representative Henry B. González, partly because of our shared surnames but also because of his boisterous Chicano voice in Congress. When La Raza Unida Party exploded on the political scene in the 1970s, I realized for the first time the possibility that Chicanos could actually control the government through disciplined organization and voter mobilization.

A third party movement fired by young Chicano activists inspired me through the Association of Mexican American Students, to invite José Ángel Gutiérrez, co-founder of the Party, to the University of Texas at Arlington campus to speak to the students. Our pride swelled in the boldness of his talk and his witty, acerbic disrespect of the Anglo political system. Although La Raza Unida Party would eventually dissolve, the few years they campaigned energized many activists to participate in politics or at least to vote.

In the twenty-first century, dramatic demographic changes throughout the country resulted in Chicanos outnumbering blacks and moving into states that hadn't seen significant Chicano numbers before. Chicanos are mobilizing again to take political power. Redistricting political battles in 2011 and 2012 have demonstrated that Anglos will resist the political shift to Chicanos with all their financial and legal resources. This resistance to a transfer of power is symptomatic of the reluctance of Anglos to trust that Chicanos can run the government and the loss of status, money, and control. Reverend Kyev Tatum and Bryan Muhammad, two Fort Worth, Texas, African American community activists, have reminded me of the Frederick Douglass quote, "Power concedes nothing without demand. It never did and it never will."[1]

I find the political struggle exciting as Chicanos mobilize to wrest political might. For an astute observer, there is plenty to write about as the political drama unfolds. One such example was the hotly contested race for the 33rd Congressional District, a heavily minority region with 17 percent black, 3 percent white, and 63 percent Latino population. Created in 2011, this district offered a golden opportunity to elect the first Latino congressional representative from North Texas since the inception of the Union. Eleven candidates ran in the Democratic primary, five Latinos, three blacks, two whites, and one Middle Easterner. The district was configured so that it spread over Dallas and Tarrant Counties. Therefore, the assumption was that the elected candidate needed to draw votes from both counties. The race in reality came down to Marc Veasey, former Texas state house representative from Fort Worth, and Domingo García, long-time community advocate, attorney, Dallas City Council member, and state representative. Veasey, who eventually won the primary with 36 percent and the general election with 72.5 percent of the vote, was able to solidify the Tarrant County black community behind him, and gain endorsements from the *Fort Worth Star-Telegram*, the *Dallas Morning News*, and several prominent Latinos from Dallas. On the other hand, Domingo García, who received 24.9 percent of the primary vote and financed his own campaign, could not muster sufficient Dallas nor Fort Worth Chicano votes. Despite his prominent billboard signs in Fort Worth during the election campaign, rallies, and grass roots get-out-the vote campaign and money, García was unable to energize large numbers of Chicanos nor draw in non-Chicanos to vote for him in the run off.

The *Dallas Morning News* endorsement of May 2, 2012, was telling in the establishment's attitude toward García and Veasey. The paper used terms to describe Garíca like "rogue," "authoritarian," "turbulent history," "divisive," and "flawed"; in comparison, they wrote that Veasey was "impressive," "consensus builder," "tested," and "leadership potential." Dallas and Fort Worth Chicanos in sufficient numbers failed to agree that García, regardless of his less-than-saintly persona, had the best chance of winning the election from among all pretenders before the campaigning began. Petty squabbling, historical grudges, downright *envidia* (envy), and unrealistic, personal aspirations required jettisoning to mobilize a united, strong run for congressional office. Chicanos needed to visualize a future when they are congressmen, senators, governors and presidents backed by pragmatic strategies on how to capture the offices. Political intelligence was required, and votes.

This Politics Section addresses the quest for Chicano political ascendency, resistance, and efforts to overcome the barriers. As Republican politicos in 2015 line up to address the tough actions they will implement on immigration reform once they assume the presidency, I offer realistic insights at the complexity of this humanitarian issue. Despite businessman Donald Trump's proclamations of rounding up 11 million undocumented residents, sending them back across the Río Grande and building a secure border wall at México's expense, history reveals that walls to keep people out have failed. I show how community mobilization is effective to impact political change. Finally, in our present crisis of police shootings of blacks and Chicanos, I present a review of our criminal justice system and offer strategies to improve police-community relations.

Chapter 11

Chicano Political Power

If *su voto es su voz*—your vote is your voice—then Chicanos are uncharacteristically quiet. Chicanos bellow *gritos* at Mexican *rancheras*, cheer at Mexican Independence Day parades, and scream on the battlefield, but they whisper at the voting booths. Instead, Chicanos should be roaring their selection as a people on the first Tuesday of November.

Voting is like choral singing: The American democratic opera sounds flat when a large part of the chorus is not projecting its electoral voice.

The US Census Bureau reported that 9.7 million Chicanos voted in the 2008 election, compared with 16.1 million blacks and 100 million Anglos. Forty-nine percent of eligible Chicanos voted, compared with 65 percent of all eligible non-Hispanic Americans.[2]

A key indicator of voting participation is voter registration. The Census Bureau found that in the 2008 elections, 59 percent of Chicano citizens were registered to vote, compared with 69 percent of black and 73 percent of Anglo citizens. Of those Chicanos registered to vote in 2008, 84 percent did.[3] To increase Chicano voter participation, the number of registered Chicano voters needs to grow.

Photo 15. Voter Registration Table

Courtesy of the Delsa M. Pérez Collection, Genealogy, History, and Archives Unit, Fort Worth Library.
Downtown Fort Worth during Immigration March with Tarrant County Courthouse in the background, April 9, 2006.

The Southwest Voter Registration Education Project (SVREP) had the goal of registering 15 million Chicano voters by 2012. Through their "12 N 12" campaign, they hoped to get 12 million Chicanos to vote in the 2012 elections. The project concentrated on registering the young and those with low incomes — groups that traditionally don't vote in large numbers. Census voting data for the November 2012 elections revealed that 11,188,000 Hispanics voted.[4] In states with heavy concentrations of Chicanos like California where the Project hoped to raise four million voters and Texas where their sights were set on 2.3 million voters for the 2012 elections, the increased number of registered Chicano voters could swing the electoral votes to either camp. With increased political activism, fair redistricting, and Chicano population growth, Chicanos could become this country's king makers. Census data showed 3,157,000 and 1,890,000 Hispanics voted in California and Texas respectively in the 2012 elections.[5]

Increased Chicano political activism may change the face of state politics. Gubernatorial candidate Tony Sánchez and senatorial candidate Víctor Morales may have been ahead of their time. But with the Chicano population gallop, it takes little imagination to envision their sons, daughters, grandsons, or granddaughters being sworn into the governor's office officiated by a Latina Texas Supreme Court justice. Their work would not have been in vain.

On the local government scene, energetic Chicano voter mobilization may penetrate into Chicano-less government institutions such as the Tarrant County Commissioners Court or US Congress from Tarrant County. In 2015, Fort Worth and Arlington City Councils had one Chicano representative in each body; Cowtown had two sitting school board members while Arlington had none.[6]

Chicanos learned the service role and they appreciate compliments on their work ethic and party loyalty. But they must master the leadership role. As leaders, Chicanos must vote and confront those who deem them unqualified.

Linda Foley, a veteran Fort Worth political activist, shared that she was pleased to learn that the county elections administrator was trying to place bilingual staffers — both Spanish and Vietnamese speakers — at every voting location. In her experience as an election judge, she observed that the voting process — something that could change with bilingual help—often confused Chicanos. "If you understand where and when you vote, what the ballot looks like, how you mark the ballot... you are more likely to vote," she explained.

Photo 16. Father Stephen Jasso and State Representative Ramón Romero

Courtesy of Emerico Pérez, Emerico Photography.
Celebrating Romero's election at the River Ranch in the Stock Yards, in Fort Worth, Texas, August 2014.

Institutional barriers to voting may contribute to diminished Chicano voter turnouts. Chicano politicians and activists fought the attempts by the Republican-dominated 2010 Texas Legislature to implement new voter identification requirements. Despite research by Justin Levitt of the Brennan Center for Justice that showed that voter fraud was almost non-existent,[7] Texas conservative legislatures passed a bill that required all voters to show an official government-issued photo identification at the polls, effective January 1, 2012. The US Justice Department ruled in March 2012, that the law would impact adversely Chicano voters and therefore the voter ID requirement was blocked. Then Texas Attorney

General Greg Abbott (now governor) filed a lawsuit in Washington D.C. to a three-judge panel to uphold the law.

On August 5, 2015, the US 5th Circuit Court in New Orleans ruled that Texas' law requiring residents to show state-approved IDs in order to vote violated Section 2 of the Voting Rights Act. Governor Greg Abbott said that the state will pursue upholding the "integrity" of voting rights. He said in a press release after the ruling, "In light of ongoing voter fraud, it is imperative that Texas has a voter ID law that prevents cheating at the ballot box. Texas will continue to fight for its voter ID requirement to ensure the integrity of elections in the Lone Star State."[8]

Alejandra Morado, a twenty-one-year-old advertising and public relations major at Texas Wesleyan University, explained to me in a personal interview that she was excited to vote in her first presidential election. She said that her mother, also an American citizen, wasn't politically aware.

"She doesn't vote and doesn't pay attention. We're a lower-class family. Like many other Mexican families, they don't see themselves as involved. They're accustomed to a corrupt Mexican government. They feel they don't make a difference."

Chicanos won't – until they vote.

Sometimes, the right Chicano political leader will electrify the community and bring out the vote. Antonio Villaraigosa represented an excellent example of activated Chicano voting prowess. Shouts of "*Si se puede*"– "yes we can!"– electrified the elated crowd of Villaraigosa supporters as they cheered his historical election as mayor of Los Angeles in May 2005. With his wife, Corina, and Antonio Jr. at his side, he held up their arms in a victor's stance, giving renewed hope to a coalition of Chicanos, blacks, workers, youths, and Jews that he could restore Los Angeles' glory. After having served two terms as mayor from 2005 to 2013, Villaraigosa's legacy left LA safer, cleaner, and smarter. He hired an additional 800 police officers, reducing the crime rate to the lowest level in sixty years.

A strong proponent of a clean and beautiful environment, he had his staff plant 350,000 trees. In a first for an American big city, he oversaw the synchronization of all the traffic lights. This traffic feat reduced travel time and eliminated an estimated metric ton of carbon. To ease the chronically congested traffic, he also expanded the subway and light rail systems. Under his watch, the city quadrupled the use of renewable energy. He created the Partership for LA Schools that pumped fifty million dollars from private donations into raising academic performance scores in some of the lowest performing public schools. He chaired the 2012 Democratic National Convention and served as president of the US Conference of Mayors. Villaraigosa also made the gossip columns when he admitted to having an affair with a Telemundo reporter that resulted in his wife divorcing him after a twenty-year marriage.

Not since 1872, when Cristóbal Aguilar left office, had a Chicano served as mayor of Los Angeles. The past and the future met in downtown LA to triumphant shouts. Villaraigosa's galvanizing personality roused Chicano voters from their slumber. This election enthroned him as the crown prince of Chicano politics. And not since the heyday of San Antonio's Henry Cisneros had a Chicano politico riveted national attention. Charismatic, dapper, and handsome, Villaraigosa personified the growing Chicano political clout and ascendancy. For the Democrats, his victory restored hope that they could regain more Chicano voters lost to the Republican inroads.

It took all of Villaraigosa's coalition-building, fund-raising, organizing, cultural-sensitizing, and bilingual skills to raise the hands of Los Angeles' four million people in victory. He harmonized the diverse aspirations for the good of all Los Angeles residents and polished his role as the new champion of urban renewal. Los Angeles foreshadowed the fate of other major US cities where a growing minority population assumes majority rule. Villaraigosa succeeded in calming the fears of Anglos, blacks, and Asians that he would ignore their interests in favor of Chicano interests. Instead, Villaraigosa convinced the diverse political powers that they had the common goal of improving LA's safety, environment, schools, and economy. Traffic gridlock, crime, healthcare, education, immigration management, housing, and pollution issues affect all Angelenos. Villaraigosa personally confronted and addressed these problems growing up in East LA. As a former teacher and union organizer, state assemblyman and city council member, he had an excellent understanding of how to tackle big city woes. Since stepping down as mayor, he considered a run for senator but decided against it. However, he didn't eliminate the possibility of a campaign run for the governor's office. If elected, Villaraigosa would achieve another Chicano first as the first Mexican American to serve as California governor since the 1800s.

He was an extroverted César Chávez in a suit. A man of humble beginnings, he dressed impeccably – partly in remembrance of his tattered childhood clothes. He struggled, fought, and pushed his way up from the barrios. Born in 1953 as Antonio Villar, the eldest of four children, he faced turmoil as a five-year-old when he witnessed his immigrant father beat his mother in a drunken rage. They divorced soon after, leaving her alone to raise the children on a secretary's pay.

His mother had difficulty curbing young Antonio's rages. She loved to read the classics and poetry to her children; but Antonio seemed determined to live up to the tattoo he sported, "Born to Raise Hell."

Expelled from a Catholic high school for fighting, he attended night high school at his mother's pleading. A teacher who thought him bright and inquisitive took an interest in him and paid the fees for his SAT exams. He graduated from UCLA, where he majored in history, and earned a law degree from the People's College of Law but never passed the bar exam. As an adult, he was charged with assault after punching a man for uttering a racial slur about his mother. He fathered two daughters out of wedlock but retained joint custody. He later married Corina Raigosa, a schoolteacher, and combined her surname with his to create Villaraigosa. They had two children from this marriage.

The people's fascination with Villaraigosa's rocky life stemmed from the fact that it mirrored those of millions of Chicano urban youths. Despite his mother's efforts, the culture of poverty snaked into his young psyche and incited the hostile, rebellious Antonio. At the same time, his survival instincts pushed him to channel his rage into graduating, listening to his mother, and serving his community.

He lived the chant, "*Sí se puede.*"

His detractors pointed to his student activist days at UCLA and labeled him a radical and lackey of the Mexican government.

On election night, Villaraigosa told his supporters, "I will never forget where I came from," as quoted by Michael Blood, Associated Press writer, on May 18, 2005. A new star was born in Los Angeles on a set with a cast of millions called "Resurrection City." This one was a thumbs up, must see.

A review of Mexican Americans' cultural and political roots will help us to understand their growing aspirations for more power and presence on the main stage of the American scene.

José Angel Gutiérrez's passage to political manhood began in 1963 at age nineteen, when he stepped off a bus in front of the Dairy Queen at East Crockett and East Zavala streets in Crystal City, Texas. Raúl Tapia, a local Gulf station owner, drove up beside Gutiérrez and a few fellow junior college classmates, pointed a pistol at them and ordered: "Ángel, *súbete* (get in)!" Gutiérrez's kidnapper drove him to the middle-class Mexican American section of town, mumbling in an alcohol-garbled voice, "You gonna pay."[9]

Gutiérrez, former professor at the University of Texas at Arlington, recalls the events of that day in his memoir, *The Making of a Chicano Militant.* When they entered Tapia's house, Gutiérrez was seated at a table surrounded by Texas Ranger A.Y. Allee, Zavala County Commissioners Jesús Rodriguez, Tom Allee (A.Y.'s cousin), Justice of the Peace Stormy Davis, and Sheriff C.L. Sweeten.

They slapped a pencil in Gutiérrez's hand and for the next four hours tried to coerce Gutiérrez into writing a confession that he had been paid by officials of the Political Association of Spanish-Speaking Organizations (PASO) to register voters and to make speeches urging Mexicans to vote.

"Tell us about your communist training by that PASO bunch. And the union communists," said the cigar-chomping Allee. Gutiérrez refused to write and feared that he would end up like the other Mexican Americans of Zavala County who had "disappeared" at the hands of the Texas Rangers. After the afternoon light dimmed to evening darkness, they released him. They were probably unaware they had unleashed into the night a cold, defiant anger in Crystal City.

The ordeal crystallized for Gutiérrez the idea that if he alone could stand up against the armed, brutal whites and Mexican American sellouts of the county, then an organized, mobilized Mexican American citizenry could seize political control of their local government. In a room of glares, pistols, bravado, and profanity, reeking of alcohol and smoke, he scented another foul odor: fear. They were more afraid of him than he of them.

That night, a raised-fist, Chicano militant was born. It was an ethnic epiphany repeated thousands of times throughout the 1960s and 1970s in America, mostly in the Southwest.

For many Chicanos, César Chávez's bold fight in the field with farm owners so personified the movement that it was simply called *La Causa*—the Cause. They remembered their own annual trips from South Texas to Wisconsin, Illinois, and California to pick the lettuce, grapes, and beets. They gazed at their hands and recalled the sweaty bandanas, bent backs, dirt, and open-air toilets under a beating sun.

In their palms, they read the past, present, and future and saw their family dragging cotton bags row after row while a propeller plane flew overhead showering pesticides. Chicano activists would ball their hands into fists, raise them into the air to crush that vision and shout, "*Basta* (enough)!" The Chicano movement roiled the land.

In New Mexico, Reies Tijerina – or *el Tigre* (Tiger) as he was called by other Chicano militants – founded the *Alianza Federal de Pueblos Libres* (Federal Alliance of Land Grants). This Latino community organization sought, among other issues, the restoration of Spanish land grants to their original owners.

Rodolfo "Corky" Gonzales, an ex-featherweight boxer in Colorado, formed the Crusade for Justice, a civil rights community organization. Once a loyal Democratic supporter who could deliver the Latino vote, he became disenchanted with the party's lack of response to claims of police brutality and its support of the status quo. As an eloquent spokesperson for Chicanos, he radicalized the movement and inspired the writing of "*El Plan Espiritual de Aztlán*" – The Spiritual Plan of Aztlán – at a youth conference in Denver in 1969.

The plan, circulated throughout the Southwest, called for the ascendancy of cultural nationalism with the creation of a separate nation – Aztlán. The manifesto was more romantic musing than an actual plan for a revolution. It did, however, articulate for many Latinos their yearning for self-determination and cultural expression of Chicano power.

In 1967 at a bar in San Antonio, Gutiérrez, Mario Compean, Willie Velásquez, Ignacio Pérez, and Juan Patlan studied and discussed the strengths and weaknesses of the Chicano movement. They researched the black nationalists and farm workers union movements, LULAC, the GI Forum, and Saul Alinsky's confrontation politics. They interviewed Stokely Carmichael, Reies Tijerina, and Martin Luther King Jr.'s staff.

Los Cinco (The Five) formed the Mexican American Youth Organization (MAYO) with the goal of developing natural leaders to spread the Chicano movement in Texas.

MAYO sought opportunities to taunt the white power structure to provoke overreactions and to prove to the Chicano community that white control of Chicano communities was over. In one major incident, Gutiérrez's old nemesis, Texas Ranger A.Y. Allee, was subpoenaed in 1968 by the US Commission on Civil Rights to a hearing in San Antonio on police brutality. Allee refused to attend, claiming that MAYO members had threatened his life.

Gutiérrez dared him to show his face to the commission and the victims of his abuse. Allee responded that if the members of MAYO had any guts "they would face me in my house." Gutiérrez retorted that MAYO would face him "anywhere and on any terms" and called him an animal.

Allee arrived with an escort of Texas Rangers, only to meet hundreds of MAYO members. His entrance and exit through a back door and grilling by the commission elevated MAYO's image to the Chicano community as a cadre of young community defenders. In this growing, confrontational political atmosphere, Gutiérrez pushed for the formation of a third political party at the MAYO national convention in December 1969.

He reasoned that the two major parties cared little for the plight of Chicanos; the Democratic Party particularly had deceived them into thinking they were the people's party.

Gutiérrez said: "Congressmen Henry B. González, Eligio 'Kika' de la Garza, Manuel Luján, Edward Roybal, and US Senator Joseph Montoya all knew our problems but also did little. They didn't even speak out for our special needs, namely the inclusion of Chicanos in the higher echelons of policy-making within the War on Poverty. These politicians were all Democrats, except for Luján, and at this time the white members of the Democratic Party controlled the White House and both houses of Congress. Together, they did nothing; individually, they did nothing. This is abuse of power and abuse of knowledge."

Although some MAYO members opposed the idea, Gutiérrez secured the necessary votes to change MAYO's direction from political educator to political contender with the Raza Unida Party. For the Aztlán plan to shimmer, Gutiérrez yearned to turn Crystal City into the first jewel in the RUP's collection.

Beginning in January 1970, the RUP waged an organized, relentless campaign against the complacent, white-controlled county, city, and school board bodies in Zavala, Dimmit, La Salle, and Hidalgo counties in South Texas.

Once the Crystal City Democratic Party officials became aware of the real political threat, they retaliated with attempts to disqualify a RUP candidate, ran safe Mexican American candidates and dropped 2,000 leaflets from an airplane over the city containing the text of a Gutiérrez speech. In the address, Gutiérrez attacked the Roman Catholic Church, calling himself an atheist and blaspheming. The leaflets contained warnings that an RUP victory would drive away businesses, result in job losses, and promote the teaching of communism in schools.

The people of South Texas decided in the April 1970 county elections that the RUP should win fifteen of the sixteen races in which it ran candidates. Gutiérrez and two other RUP candidates won Crystal City school board seats, and two more RUP candidates won city council seats. In Carrizo Springs, two Chicano candidates backed by the RUP were the first Mexican Americans ever elected to the city council. In Cotulla, the RUP-supported candidates won two city council seats, two school board seats and the mayoralty.

In 1970, the victories by a third party — especially by a Chicano third party — sent political shock waves throughout Texas. Some MAYO members who had been skeptical about the RUP's chances were now willing to join the party. The Democratic Party, awakened to the RUP threat, deployed legal counterattacks and Redbaiting propaganda.

MAYO members, heady with the success in South Texas, attended the first RUP convention in San Antonio on Oct. 31, 1971, and voted to expand the RUP statewide.

Gutiérrez had voted against this action, arguing that MAYO was not politically and financially sophisticated enough to run successful RUP statewide elections. But the taste of victory was too intoxicating, and

MAYO members wanted more. In a sense, Gutiérrez had been too effective in convincing his fellow militants that with wits, drive, and organization, Chicanos could wrest political control from whites.

On February 9, 1972, MAYO leadership held a news conference to introduce Ramsey Muñiz as the RUP gubernatorial candidate, along with several other statewide candidates. A native of Corpus Christi, Muñiz had attended Baylor University, where he excelled in football and earned undergraduate and law degrees. A member of MAYO since 1968, he was the director of the Urban Development Corporation in Waco when he accepted the RUP gubernatorial candidacy.

Muñiz proved to be a political dynamo, stumping across Texas with his wife and child in a 1962 Plymouth to garner the Mexican American vote. Handsome, muscular, quick-witted, personable, and eloquent, he surprised the RUP leadership with his zeal, stamina, and tenacity in promoting the RUP and blasting the Democratic and Republican parties. Muñiz said: "Our connection to the Democratic Party has been nothing more than a cheap marriage ... they have lied to us and betrayed us. ... Now we are divorcing ourselves from the Democratic Party."[10]

After the conservative Democrat Dolph Briscoe beat liberal Democrat Francis “Sissy” Farenthold for the Democratic gubernatorial nomination, Muñiz unsuccessfully sought her endorsement. To her followers, he said: “Liberals have always talked about helping minorities. How much more can they help us than by voting for us? ... What we are saying to the Texas liberals is, ‘how liberal are you?’”[11]

By the election results, obviously not liberal enough. Despite his prediction that he would receive more than a million votes, Muñiz drew just 219,127, or 6.43 percent, while Briscoe won more than 1.6 million votes.

Despite the defeat, Muñiz jumped again at the chance to run for governor in 1974. This time his campaign took a more moderate tone, translating "Raza Unida" to "People Together" and seeking coalitions with liberal whites and African-Americans. This attempt to mainstream the RUP angered many of the RUP veterans, who saw Muñiz deserting Chicano grassroots ties for the comfort of middle-class respectability.

The internal conflict came to a head at that year's RUP state convention in Houston, when Mario Compean threw a glass of water into Muñiz's face. The larger Muñiz swung at him, barely missing while Gutiérrez and other RUP activists quickly separated them. The convention went on successfully, with few aware of the bitter rift between Compean and Muñiz.

Undaunted, Muñiz resumed his campaigning, proclaiming his populist stance of caring for the powerless and bringing education, tax, and insurance reform. He called for the end of the sales tax, free tuition to community colleges and vocational schools, the expansion of bilingual education, and a corporate tax.

He once again challenged Texas liberals to do a realistic assessment of the establishment parties and understand that the RUP offered the best alternative for change. But the election results for RUP were even worse than those of the 1972 races, with Muñiz capturing 190,000 votes — 5.6 percent.

Short of the necessary funding to run statewide campaigns, lacking in experienced leadership and beset by internal conflicts, a lack of positive media coverage and a conservative political climate, the RUP had fought a fight for which it had the hearts and guts but not the cash and clout. Although a national RUP had formed in 1972 at the El Paso national convention, bitter internal fighting between Gutiérrez, Reies López Tijerina, and Corky Gonzales erupted over party leadership. Individually, they were Chicano warriors too full of ego, smarts, and spunk to humble themselves before the leadership of another. They had led the struggle against white political power brokers so passionately that they never learned to make a lasting peace among themselves. The RUP in Texas was never able to recover from its resounding defeat. By 1975, the fervor of the Chicano movement was fizzling, and many decided to defect to the Democratic Party in search of better chances of winning office.

After his defeat in 1974, Muñiz opened a law practice in Corpus Christi. But a mid-'70s drug conviction marred his reputation — and by extension, the RUP's.

An attempt by Compean to revitalize the party with a run for the governor's seat in 1978 failed. The RUP sank into the political sea with the fleet of third parties that had struggled to overcome the two-party rule.

The RUP's victories in South Texas were short-lived. But during the party's contentious life, it showed submissive Chicanos how they could dare to challenge for political control of their own communities; how they could dare to vote as free men and women regardless of cost; how La Raza Unida (the united people) could live and talk boldly; how to dream of Aztlán.

Chicanos must resolve to lead and engage the larger community with their agenda. They must resolve to shed feelings of inferiority and seize the power that comes with their numbers, intelligence, and talents. And at every New Year, they should reflect and take stock of their place in the larger community.

New Year resolutions that I offer Chicanos and non-Chicanos may sting — but they're good with a cold glass of tea.

Chicano resolution número uno is to vote. This act alone by enough Chicanos would revolutionize the political landscape of Fort Worth, Tarrant County, Texas, and the United States. The watchword in cafes, laundries, cantinas, grocery stores, and quinceañeras is not the noun but the verb vote.

Every Hispanic chamber, Pan American Golf Association, Chicano Luncheon, Hispanic Debutante, and Charros meeting should end with an exhortation to vote. Murals, posters, lapel buttons, and airplane-dragging banners should advertise voting.

DJ Pancho Pistolas, KESS La Fabulosa, Univision, and Telemundo should promote ballot casting throughout the year. And on every election day, the people should rise at dawn, singing "I'm a Yankee Doodle Dandy" as they march to the polls and capture political power. Chicanos can perform the miracle of healing the politically deaf by the laying of hands on the ballot.

A second Chicano resolution is stay in school. The Chicano community needs to own up to the problem and steer their youth to study, read day and night, take the hard courses, and work their young brains to a frazzle. Show your love for your children by turning off the novelas and the foul-mouthed wrestling stooges of the World Wrestling Federation (WWF) in order to help them with homework. Expect that they earn good grades and respect the teachers. Parents need to ensure that their children get on that school bus. Otherwise, reserve a seat for the monthly Huntsville, Texas, prison bus trip.

Chicano Resolution Number 3 is to learn to read, write, and speak English beyond "'xcuse me, boss." Although we should cherish and speak Spanish, English is the business, technical, and political language of the world. If Chicanos are to join our community's major players as their growing numbers warrant, they need to enjoy eye contact, my-vocabulary-is-bigger-than-yours dialogues with anyone on this English-dominant planet. Acrobatic English is power.

Chicano Resolution Number 4 is to unite behind genuine leaders. Chicanos must overcome bickering, set aside personal agendas, and support the courageous efforts of community leaders who are willing to risk careers and popularity to confront injustices and champion Chicano issues. No need to wait for a brown messiah to walk on water when our leaders eat, work, and play with us now. Trust your instincts; gaze into the hearts of Chicanos and Chicanas to know those who can lead us out of the shadows. Possess enough humility to allow them to step into the light.

Non-Chicanos may benefit from a few tonic resolutions as well.

The first is to truly accept and celebrate cultural diversity in our community.

Skip the lip service and replace it with action on the jobs, government and social cliques to reveal that in the non-Chicanos' bosoms, they've accepted Chicanos as their equals, bosses, fellow workers, or spouses. Learn and practice new cultural attitudes that open doors and welcome Chicanos into their circles.

The second resolution is to quit trying to pick the Chicano leaders for them. By choosing the safe, happy minority — generally a conservative-talking, propertied businessperson — non-Chicanos deceive themselves into thinking that they've established a communication link with the Chicano community. Instead, they should go into the barrios and ask longtime residents, parish priests, and community activists to name true leaders.

Non-Chicano Resolution Number 3 is to accept the inevitability of a transfer of political power to Tarrant County Chicanos. Like the Berlin Wall crumbling or Nelson Mandela leaving prison or Vicente Fox defeating the *Partido Revolucionario Institucional* (PRI) for the Mexican presidency, the first Chicanos elected as county commissioner, mayors of Fort Worth and Arlington, and congressional representative will see days and nights of confetti-dropping, fire-cracking, piñata-busting fiestas. Resistance to sharing political power fosters unnecessary, interethnic resentment.

A resolution common for both Chicanos and non-Chicanos — and possibly the most important one — is to teach our children that America was founded on the principle "that all men (and women) are created equal." Avoid poisoning their minds with ethnic trash talk and attitudes. By example, teach them to appreciate America's diverse cultures and colors.

This year, let non-Chicanos resolve to accept Chicanos as their political, social, and intellectual equals, and let Chicanos resolve to shed inferiority attitudes and contribute their talents to enrich their communities.

Chapter 12

Immigration Reform

At a news conference on April 4, 2006, on the stage of the historic Rose Marine Theater, an immigrant drama played to a group of Chicano activists, TV cameras, and reporters. Four speakers foreshadowed the March for Justice scheduled to begin at 12:30 p.m. April 9, 2006, at the Tarrant County Courthouse and end at the federal courthouse. Speaking in Spanish and English for the bilingual audience and media, the speakers shared their experiences as immigrants or those of their families. Here was the heart of the immigration conflict. This issue was as hot as chewing a chile because it bites into family ties, personal identity, and political power.

Conservative talk-show jocks, lawmakers, and Anglos howled about how wrong it was for undocumented immigrants to come, uninvited, to receive social services, public education, and healthcare. Even some naturalized Chicanos cried foul to think that even though they played by the rules, those who didn't might also gain legal permission to stay. Their struggle to earn their US identity was precious. They said undocumented immigrants violated the sovereignty of the United States.

Paroxysms of rage swelled at the sight of Chicano youths shouting, "*Viva México*!" and waving the red, white, and green Mexican flag. Vitriolic letters to the editor targeted the flag wavers, telling them to go back to México — even though many were born in the US. The flow of Chicano youths carrying the Mexican flag through downtown Fort Worth dramatized the rapid demographic changes transforming the city, state, and nation.

The speakers at the news conference talked calmly about their personal or families' experiences as immigrants. Memories of the crossing resonated in their voices. They spoke about the need to stop the shouting, walking out of school, and waving the Mexican flag. They called for immigration reform that could reasonably control the borders, bring the undocumented out from the shadows, and develop a path to earned-citizenship.

Fort Worth City Councilman Sal Espino recalled that at eighteen he was the first in his Mexican immigrant family to become a naturalized citizen. He said the average immigrant pays $1,800 more than he or she "costs" in public funds for services such as education or healthcare. Social Security collected $463 billion from the undocumented that they will be ineligible to receive as long as they have undocumented status. Espino pointed out that the buying power of US-born Chicano children was increasing. Arlington City Councilman Robert Rivera spoke about his family's emigration from México several generations ago. His grandfather fought in World War II, and an uncle served in Vietnam. He called for Chicano youths to contribute to the community by staying in school and graduating—and in any future protest marches, to carry only the US flag.

Sebastián Martínez, representative of the Federation of Zacatecan Clubs, told of his journey over the *frontera* — the border. After crossing with his family in 1989 on a tourist visa, he stayed and eventually married a US citizen. He slowly adopted US culture and realized the beauty of drawing the best from two worlds: México, his homeland, and the United States, where he is now a legal resident.

"We eat enchiladas and hamburgers, listen to heavy metal and mariachis," he said. Although he was proud of his son's participation in the protest march, he expected him to stay in school. "It's time to take out the US flags, keep the Mexican flag at home but carry it in our hearts."

José Aguilar, member of the Allied Communities of Tarrant, called for a silent march at the meeting of march organizers. "Let us make no sounds; march quietly with dignity. Bring your kids to show them that with respect we can make changes." Thus on the day of the march, in the midst of hundreds—possibly thousands—of people in downtown Fort Worth, the shuffling feet of immigrants moving in unison toward comprehensive immigration reform will echo.

March planners weren't as enchanted with his second suggestion. Aguilar called for different religions, races, and classes to come together. As a symbolic representation of this unity, he called for carrying flags of the different countries that immigrants represent. The US flag would take the lead followed by the other banners. Fearing misperception, angry backlash, and political defeat, march organizers insisted that no flag but the US flag should fill the march.

Chicanos can assemble and dissent as guaranteed by the First Amendment. But to defeat Senator Bill Frist's Senate immigration bill, S. 2454, the Securing America's Border Act, introduced on March 16, 2006, we needed to learn to play the role of patriots draped in red, white, and blue. This bill failed to provide for a path to permanent residency and further limited due process and judicial review for the undocumented. After considerable debate, the Senate ignored the Frist bill and instead passed S. 2611, the Comprehensive Immigration Reform Act of 2006 on May 25. S. 2611 was more immigrant-friendly, allowing for a path to legal status for the undocumented. Unfortunately, no comprehensive immigration reform legislation was enacted in 2006 because the two houses failed to reach an agreement for the bill to go to a conference committee.

And then we marched with thousands across the country.

Photo 17. Fort Worth Immigration March

Courtesy of Delsa M. Pérez Collection, Genealogy, History, and Archives Unit, Fort Worth Library.

Immigration March Downtown Fort Worth, Main Street, From the Tarrant County Court House, April 9, 2006.

In packed churches across the Metroplex, Chicanos prayed on Palm Sunday morning for the coming of Christ and in the afternoon filled the streets in a crusade for justice. They sought salvation from the undocumented life. Thousands across Fort Worth and Dallas left their blessed palms at home, took up US flags, and joined the biggest demonstrations that this area had seen in years. Dallas police reported 500,000 marchers; Then-Fort Worth Police Chief Ralph Mendoza estimated the Fort Worth demonstrators at 20,000.

Despite the smaller numbers, the Fort Worth marchers' passion for change in immigration laws equaled those of the Dallas crowds. From 10 a.m. onward, waves of immigrant marchers kept coming from all directions toward the Tarrant County Courthouse. To the sounds of patriotic songs such as "Proud To Be an American," "Coming to America" and "God Bless America," thousands massed in joyous expectation.

Photo 18. Immigration Protest March

Courtesy of Emerico Pérez, Emerico Photography.
Immigration Protest Marchers Rallying in Fort Worth, Texas, April 9, 2006.

Speakers encouraged them to keep an upbeat mood, avoid confrontation with counter-demonstrators, and show their loyalty to this country. Aside from Fourth of July parades, few events equaled the patriotic fervor imbuing the event. As is often the case, the most loyal residents were new Americans or those desperately seeking legal status. Organizers with bags encouraged the marchers to pick up any trash on the ground to avoid accusations of messing with Texas.

Young and old, parents and children, bosses and workers, the educated and unschooled gathered shoulder to shoulder in a sea of white shirts and US flags. March organizers with clipboards circulated through the crowds asking people to sign a proclamation written in English and Spanish. Many couldn't vote, so they sought a path to tell the president and Congress that if given a chance to prove their loyalty, they would contribute mightily to this country's greatness. With their signatures, they sought to affirm their declaration of independence from fear and shame.

Two altar boys from All Saints Catholic Church on Fort Worth's north side carried a banner of the *Virgen de Guadalupe* in the streets, reminding some of the marches of César Chávez. When the DJ played "De Colores" and people sang the lyrics that told of the beautiful colors of spring, the fiery spirit of the farmworkers' movement filled the air.

In truth, a new liberation movement was springing up across the country. Hunted and chased, blasted and scorned by angry citizens, immigrants decided to take a stand. Couched in patriotic zeal, marchers carried a fifty-foot US flag down Main Street. Another group carried a Lone Star flag of similar size. Both banners floated along the march to the front of the rally point at the Federal Building. Thousands carried smaller US flags or signs stating that they were here to build, not destroy.

Unlike the Dallas march, the Fort Worth marchers were as silent as at Mass. Participants walked in solemn procession, as instructed, to show their respect and strength. What a change from the raucous rush of Chicano youths shouting and waving Mexican flags the week before. Although the youths had received much criticism in the press and talk shows for their wild display of disagreement with immigration talks, their boldness prompted the adults to take a stand.

Fort Worth and Dallas Chicano youth deserved credit for showing adults how to walk and talk courageously. Chicano politicians who barely spoke about immigration reform suddenly rushed to the microphone to voice their deep concerns. It was fitting that youths led the Fort Worth March for Justice. Hand-picked teen leaders carried the banner, read the proclamations, and shared their views on immigration reform.

Photo 19. Children at Immigration Protest

Courtesy of Emerico Pérez, Emerico Photography.

How much more impressive it would have been if those young lions who led the rush through the streets, climbed the county courthouse steps, spoke to fellow classmates about their ideals, and walked miles from their schools to downtown could have spoken to adults about that day they said "no" to the government.

Photo 20. Christopher Bonilla

15 ¢

EL LATINO

Dedicated to the Spanish-speaking people of Fort Worth

January 1973

The best of luck to Cowtown's Chris Bonilla the state's only Chicano Page in Washington.

Be sure and attend the Stock Show, January 26 thru February 4th.

Courtesy of the Delsa M. Pérez Collection, Genealogy, History, and Archives Unit, Fort Worth Library.

Christopher R. Bonilla, serving as Congressional Page in the US House of Representatives during the 92nd and 93rd sessions of Congress for the Honorable Jim Wright.

Of course, they would have had to leave their Mexican flags at home. But they could have reminded us that a quiet march alone doesn't change laws. Marches, speeches, and giant US flags should inspire us to organize, vote, and lobby the president and Congress. In the spring of our discontent, the youths gave us courage to act.

Led mainly by young Mexican immigrants, grassroots civil rights and legal organizations, sympathetic politicians, and churches, immigration reform movement activists organized throughout the larger American cities, using social media to communicate federal, state, and local immigration policies and proposed laws. Lobbying Congress, they prompted senators and representative to draft and debate various versions of the DREAM Act (Development, Relief, and Education for Alien Minors). The Act would have granted conditional residency after meeting specific requirements and later permanent residency. The Act met stiff opposition from some Republicans who labeled it an amnesty bill, and warned it would become a magnet for other undocumented immigrants. One version of the bill passed the House on December 8, 2010, but failed to pass the Senate. To date, no federal version of the DREAM Act has passed. However, at least twenty states have some version of the DREAM Act whose benefits may include in-state college tuition rates, eligibility for scholarships, and state financial aid.

The immigration reform movement activists efforts yielded success when President Barack Obama signed an executive order on June 15, 2012, titled the Deferred Action for Childhood Arrivals (DACA), delaying the deportation of hundreds of thousands of undocumented youth. On November 20, 2014, President Obama issued another executive order called the Deferred Action for Parental Accountability (DAPA). This act would allow parents of citizens or legal permanent residents to request deferred action and a work permit valid for three years. In addition, he extended the time that DACA-eligible youth could legally work from two to three years. This bold action met with swift resistance from twenty-six governors. A federal judge placed a temporary injunction on the executive action in February 2015, allowing the states time to prepare a suit. The 5th Circuit Court of Appeals upheld the injunction in November 2015. President Obama announced this same month that he asked the US Supreme Court to review the appeals court decision.

The immigration reform movement gained momentum after the marches and propelled this issue to the forefront of Latino political activism in 2015. Their activism drew the attention of Republican presidential candidates such as Donald Trump, Marco Rubio and Ted Cruz, the latter two children of Cuban immigrants. The three took hard-nosed stances against immigration reform, calling for secure borders, universal e-verification of prospective employees' legal status, and sparred among themselves as to who supported a pathway to citizenship. Trump stood out for his proposal to deport the estimated eleven million undocumented US residents and a call for México to build a wall along the border. Latino activism roiled the political stew. Another stew brewing was the question whether the immigration issue had defined accurately for Chicanos and the general public the Latino community's main concerns. Immigrant activists and their allies had dominated the news media focus on an issue that impacted directly a minority of Hispanics. Although Chicano citizens were sympathetic to immigrants, many in their own family had recently immigrated or they were children of immigrants, their concerns also included education, economic, health, and voting issues. Internal political discussions between Mexican immigrants and Chicanos should develop to align mutual goals and strategies. Chicanos learned that activism of the 1960s and 1970s a la *La Raza Unida* Party resulted in political office and power. For the immigration reform movement to succeed, Chicanos and *Mexicanos* must work together.

General public concerns for rising healthcare costs stimulated a closer look at the US healthcare delivery systems. President Barack Obama and Congress sought to address the spiraling costs and accessibility for all Americans with the signing of the Patient Protection and Affordable Care Act on March 23, 2010. Anti-immigrants claim that Mexican immigrants have over-burdened the US healthcare industry causing healthcare costs to rise for all. Some counties and cities have implemented policies limiting the accessibility to healthcare to the undocumented and unfairly holding them responsible for the rising costs. As the country debates President Obama's healthcare plan, a closer look is required on what drives healthcare dollars.

The congressional debate over immigration reform is a war of numbers. If there were a thousand undocumented immigrants, little time would be devoted to the issue. However, an estimated eleven million people live, work, play, and die in this country without permission from the government, according to Federation for Immigration Reform.[12]

While here, they earn money, but they also consume expensive health care services. A standard argument by conservative, get tough-on-the-immigrants organizations such as FAIR is that undocumented immigrants are bankrupting our healthcare system.

According to the group's report, "The Sinking Lifeboat, Uncontrolled Immigration & the US Health Care System":[13]

·33 percent of immigrants have no insurance.

·67 percent of counties responding to a survey claim that immigrants were the predominant users of uncompensated health care.

·16 percent of all immigrants live below the poverty line.

·Among full-time wage earners, 51 percent of immigrants have employment-based coverage.

·Communities with high rates of uninsured residents were more likely to reduce hospital services and divert tax dollars to pay for uncompensated care.

FAIR expected any immigration reform coming out of Washington to include some plan to reimburse the states and counties for uncompensated immigrant care.

"At a time when the country is struggling to provide affordable care to millions of uninsured residents, President Bush's immigration proposal would bring in hundreds of thousands more uninsured — and officially sanction a massive undocumented population already here and already draining health care funds from struggling communities," FAIR said.[14] For now, hospitals such as John Peter Smith in Fort Worth and Parkland Memorial in Dallas were left holding the doctor's bag.

The JPS board decided to deny outpatient treatment to undocumented immigrants in an effort to save money. The Allied Communities of Tarrant, a grassroots organization advocating for immigrant healthcare, has argued that preventive care is less expensive than emergency treatment, so it would make more financial sense to provide outpatient care to all and avoid the high costs that come with catastrophic and emergency room care. A majority of the hospital board was unconvinced of any substantial savings. However, this skirted the main issue: the alleged runaway immigrant healthcare costs.

A study published by six physician-researchers in the August 2005 issue of the *American Journal of Public Health* directly addressed the question of immigrant healthcare costs compared with citizens' healthcare costs. Their study of an analysis of 1998 national survey data of healthcare expenses differs from FAIR's assessment of who's driving US hospitals to the poorhouse. According to the physicians, in 1998:[15]

·Immigrant healthcare costs were $39.5 billion, or 7.9 percent of the total US healthcare costs.

·Average healthcare expenses were $1,139 per immigrant and $2,546 per citizen.

·Uninsured immigrants' expenses were 61 percent lower than those of uninsured US citizens.

·Immigrants younger than 65 had 30 to 75 percent lower expenses than citizens of the same age.

·Immigrant children used the emergency room less often than citizen children, but immigrant children's ER costs were higher.

·Immigrant children in the ER were sicker than citizen children.

The six physicians concluded that "the deficit of care among immigrants is probably not because of less need; immigrants in our study had slightly worse self-reported health than US-born persons."

Cultural and linguistic factors and fear of deportation acted as steep barriers to immigrant healthcare access. FAIR's assessment of the immigrants' lack of insurance and their low income is accurate. However, to conclude that the immigrants are primarily responsible for uncompensated healthcare costs is false.

The six physicians found no relationship between a state's uncompensated expenses and the percentage of immigrants. They added that policies to terminate publicly sponsored healthcare coverage will result in little savings.[16] Based on this research, there was no valid reason to use the immigrant as the whipping boy for spiraling healthcare expenses. US healthcare costs were driven by a combination of economic and social forces, such as technology development, drug costs, malpractice awards, managed care, an aging population, lack of disease management, administrative costs, and third-party payments.

It was easy to blame the undocumented immigrant for high health costs. It was also grossly unfair.

In 2004, a furor rose in Tarrant County, Texas, when a conservative healthcare board decided to make the undocumented ineligible for the JPS Connection. This program had allowed undocumented patients, about three thousand, to receive healthcare services and medicines on a discount payment system depending on household income under the care of JPS physicians. Despite protests by community activists, the board did not budge from their exclusionary policy. The undocumented sick were allowed to receive services but they would have to pay more for it.

Americans first, exclaimed some trustees. Mitch Mitchell, reporter for the *Fort Worth Star-Telegram,* recounted on August 13, 2004, that then-JPS trustees Neal Adams and Erma Johnson-Hadley preferred that sick citizens—not sick undocumented—benefit from taxpayers' healthcare dollars. According to the article, trustee Bernard Rubin, a physician, said, "They (the undocumented) are going to get some of the most expensive care that we deliver." As of 2015, the undocumented were still disconnected from the JPS Connection.

In a land of overweight, chain-smoking, drug-addicted, gun-toting citizens, they tell us that money to fund primary healthcare for the undocumented and their families didn't exist. The rationing of healthcare was upon us. Yet health planners had consistently said that preventative healthcare was more cost-effective than emergency or in-patient care. Then why the reversal in healthcare access policy if money was the primary concern?

Trustees must address some fundamental questions to place this issue in context:

·How many undocumented are present in this country?

Approximately 11.2 million undocumented residents are scattered throughout the United States — 77 percent of them in Nevada, California, Texas, Illinois, New Jersey, Maryland, District of Columbia, New Mexico, Arizona, Georgia, Oregon, and Florida. According to the Pew Hispanic Center, their numbers have seen a slight decrease from the peak of 12 million in 2007 because of a decline in the number of Mexican immigrants.[17] As humans, they will get sick.

·Are they going to leave any time soon?

Unless the federal government is prepared to commit massive financial and personnel resources to track down the undocumented, and unless businesses are willing to stop hiring them, they are here to stay. So far there have been no signs from President Obama that he intends to implement mass deportation. The market economy on which America prides itself is too great a magnet for the undocumented workers and too profitable for businesses.

·Do we desire a healthy society?

Of course we do, notwithstanding the pollution that surrounds us. Carel Bailey Germain, a professor at the University of Connecticut's graduate school of social work, writes that a "healthy society is a humane society that is concerned with the physical, social and emotional health and well-being of all its members."[18]

On August 23, 2004, then-Texas Lt. Gov. David Dewhurst, co-chairman of the Legislative Budget Board, announced the allocation of $1.5 billion to provide "a health care safety net for those who truly need it" as quoted by John Moritz, writer for the *Fort Worth Star-Telegram.* The allocation was intended to offset previous budget cuts.

In spite of pressure from conservative groups, hospital districts in the larger Texas counties, except Tarrant, found it morally sound to treat the undocumented. Dr. Ron Anderson, former CEO of Parkland Memorial Hospital in Dallas, said that denial of healthcare to the undocumented was "morally and ethically wrong," as quoted by Mercedes Olivera, *Dallas Morning News* writer, on August 13, 2004.

·Are the undocumented part of our society?

This is both a factual and a philosophical question. On a factual level, they are. But the denial of local services means that trustees have answered that the undocumented are a demi-people relegated to a shadow world. Like India's untouchables, they are not worthy of treatment as equals to law-abiding citizens.

Instead of shutting hospital doors, trustees should open lively discussions with lawmakers for immigration reforms that promote legalized status. As long as we allow millions of people to be exploited by businesses that don't provide healthcare coverage or pay sufficient wages to allow them to afford health insurance, county hospitals and taxpayers will continue to absorb their health care costs.

·Can we afford a healthy society?

Federal and state governments hold as much responsibility to fund county hospitals as local citizens do. Industrialized countries with smaller gross domestic products than that of the United States have found money in their budgets to provide healthcare. Even impoverished Cuba provides its people with healthcare of a quality that is unmatched by any other Latin American country.

For the physical and moral health of our county, we can't afford untouchables in our midst.

Mexican immigrants also face harrowing journeys to come to the United States and unsafe working conditions. They risk their lives in desperate attempts to work and earn money for families and a chance to live the American Dream.

Plant nineteen white crosses at the Speedy Stop on US Highway 77 in Victoria, Texas, to mark the deaths of migrants lacking water, air, and documents as they fled the Mexican economy despite the skull-and-cross-bones immigration policy of the United States. Eighteen crosses are for the men, women, and children who died from asphyxiation and dehydration in the back of an abandoned trailer. The nineteenth is to mark the murder of compassion and humanity by ravenous coyotes—smugglers of human beings—preying on those desperate for work and for release from their Third World existence in México and Central America.

About 100 people hid in the truck's trailer for what they thought would be a trip to the First World. But they had the *mala suerte* — bad luck — to be under the power of people who cared more about their cash than their lives. Their coyote drivers and a police dispatcher ignored their pleas and screams for water and air. It's as if the smugglers' and migrants' humanity washed away when they crossed the Río Grande.

Thus, their suffering really didn't matter in the hot, dry borderlands where white crosses, shrines, cactus, and bones dot the landscape from Brownsville to San Diego. The deaths expose the underbelly of Mexican society: Years of economic problems force mass migration. Former Mexican President Vicente Fox's policies — as well as those of his corrupt predecessors — failed to meet his promise of job creation and to keep his people home. Instead, the undocumented workers were economic orphans, searching for a clean house, a good life, a decent job.

Theirs is a brutish existence played out millions of times: born into poverty, meager pay, little education, a bleak future, a suffocating death. And in the twilight border zone, the coyotes wait patiently for the orphans to arrive with hope in their hearts and money in their pockets. They lurk, knowing that more will come. It's not too surprising that one of the coyote smuggling suspects was a Jamaican — another immigrant.

Most smugglers are Mexicans ready to beat, rape, cheat, rob, and abandon their human cargo at the first signs of trouble. Raza rhetoric, Aztec pride, a shared history, a common economic struggle mean nothing to Mexican coyotes who feast on the fears and desperation of the job-hungry. The romanticism of Mexican unity crumbles at the crinkle of American bucks.

Besides, what will the victims do—go to the police? For Pete's sake, they were undocumented migrants, the underclass daring to play cat-and-mouse with US border patrols.

But jobs are waiting for those able to run the border gauntlet. Migrants are willing to swim rivers, climb mountains, cross deserts, hide in trucks, and hop trains to reach undetected the jobs that many in the United States will not take. They do America's dirty work — back-breaking, sweaty, smelly, menial. They often have no health insurance, retirement, or vacations. Most lack union representation and avoid complaining of labor injustices for fear of deportation. The risks of death and disrespect pale before the need to earn money for their families in México. Some join the US military with hopes of gaining citizenship, only to return to their Mexican pueblos with American flags draped over their coffins.

And taps is played for the American Dream.

As horrific as the eighteen deaths are, they matched a pattern of migrant deaths tracked by Karl Eschbach, Jacqueline Hagan, and Nestor Rodríguez of the Center for Immigration Research, located at the University of Houston. Reviewing accidental deaths of foreign transients in the United States, they found in their study *Causes and Trends in Migrant Deaths Along the US-México Border, 1985-1998* that migrant deaths by environmental heat or cold sprang from redirected migrant flow to hazardous terrain because of intense border enforcement.[19]

"The answer lies in Washington more than it does along the border," said Rodríguez in a quote by a University of Houston news release dated July 15, 2002. "To the extent that we can legalize some of the migrants who come to work in the US, then I believe we can reduce border deaths." Otherwise, the deaths will continue – and, like the prophet Ezekiel, we will walk among dry bones along the border.

According to a Pew Hispanic Center study, "Latino Labor Report, 2004: More Jobs for New Immigrants but at Lower Wages," by Rakesh Kochhar, the demand for immigrant labor remained high. Kochhar found from the Bureau of Labor Statistics that the US economy created one million jobs for foreign-born Latinos in 2004. Kochhar wrote, "The demand for immigrant labor remains robust and foreign-born workers were a major component of change in the labor market in 2004."[20] He added that the construction industry looked to foreign-born Latinos to meet its labor needs.

President Bush and his economic policy advisers understood this well. They were not about to kill the goose that laid the golden eggs with anti-immigration policies. Instead, the president and the construction industry feathered the economic nest with strict enforcement of Occupational Safety and Health Administration regulations and safety education in

Spanish for Latino workers. If we want Latinos' strong hands and backs to keep this country's economy churning, we must protect them at hazardous work sites.

The US Labor Department and the Mexican Government signed a Letter of Arrangement on June 1, 2010, to collaborate on teaching Mexican workers in the US about safety and injury prevention.[21] The parties agreed to inform workers in Spanish and through multiple mediums, since some workers couldn't read, about their employee rights and responsibilities. Unfortunately, Occupational Safety & Health Administration (OSHA) fatality statistics for 2013 revealed that Hispanic workers had a fatality rate of 3.9 injuries per 100,000 workers as compared to the overall fatality rate of 3.3.[22] In fact, Texas had more Hispanic work-related fatalities than all states, for 2010–2014, except for 2013 when California had two more Hispanic worker deaths than the Lone Star State.[23]

Latino laborers go to work in crowded, beat-up trucks, playing loud salsa music, wearing tattered clothes and crucifixes or medallions of their favorite saints. Work in America is their salvation; sometimes it's their ruin.

Weather-beaten and deeply tanned, they complain little, put up with the heat and grime and take risks. They work hard because they have children, wives, parents, and relatives to feed and clothe. Like their bracero forefathers in the 1940s, 1950s, and 1960s, they dream like most others in this country of nice homes, educated children, weekends off.

After surviving the trek to the United States, they must learn to survive the work hazards. Ezequiel Meza died August 28, 2005, in a job accident, like too many Mexicans in low-skilled, low-paying jobs working with their hands and backs. He labored as a construction worker — the kind of job that people complain immigrants are taking away from citizens. The work is dirty, sweaty, and dangerous. But unskilled, uneducated Mexicans are willing to invest sweat equity because the alternatives of starvation and homelessness are worse. Despite all the rhetoric of

"Undocumented go home!" the data show that the US economy welcomes job-hungry immigrant workers.

On Sunday, August 28, 2005, when many people rested from their jobs and attended church, Meza and his work crew were building an addition to an animal shelter in Mansfield, Texas, when the roof collapsed. Meza lay trapped for more than five hours before rescuers recovered his body. The police said that they couldn't rush in to dig him out for fear of more injuries or deaths. Meza died literally buried in his work.

Unfortunately, Meza's story is not unique. In 2002, The Associated Press issued a report by Justin Pritchard of its analysis of work-related deaths among Mexicans in 1996-2002, "AP Investigation: Mexican Worker Deaths Rise Sharply Even as Overall US Job Safety Improves." The news agency uncovered cases of heads crushed on conveyer belts, fatal heat strokes, cave-ins of trenches, inhalation of toxic fumes, falls from roofs, and other preventable accidents. Spanish-speaking workers weren't informed or failed to heed the warnings, or safety measures weren't enforced, according to the AP investigation.

And things didn't improve over the years. According to the Bureau of Labor Statistics, 5,703 workers died in work-related accidents in 2004 — a 2 percent increase over 2003. The fatality rate was 4.1 per 100,000 workers. The construction industry led in total deaths with 1,224.[24] And Labor Department numbers show that the Latino fatality rate rose from 2000-2007 by 15 percent. A total of 937 Latinos died on the job in 2007; 634 were foreign-born, and 303 were native-born.[25] The Latino worker fatality rate in 2007 was 4.6 per 100,000 workers as compared to 3.9 for blacks and 3.8 for whites.[26]

Perhaps the TV networks should consider a new reality series —"Survivor: Immigrant Work." Two tribes of US citizens could trek across desolate deserts led by abusive "coyotes," or they could hide in trucks. They'd have to elude bandits, border patrol agents, ranchers, and Minutemen and land a job at a North Texas building construction site.

Training would not be required. The contestants would learn the job from bosses who speak a different language. The work would be dangerous, the pay low, the days long. The winner: the tribe member who survives a month. This is the gruesome reality for millions of workers. For Latinos toiling away for years, each day is a trial to survive. Meza's family, sadly, knows this too well on Labor Day.

The reality of the day is that some conservative states and cities have passed strong anti-immigration laws to stop the hiring of undocumented immigrants. Alabama in 2011 passed one of the country's harshest laws making it an offense to hire any undocumented workers. Local police were also authorized to arrest undocumented workers during traffic stops. Schools were required to ask their students for proof of citizenship and report the undocumented to Immigration and Customs Enforcement (ICE).

When the Farmers Branch, Texas, city council had tried to pass similar anti-immigration laws five years earlier, Chicanos mobilized to confront these efforts. Both sides on the immigration issue at Farmers Branch City Hall protested and waved the Stars and Stripes on August 26, 2006. One side saw the stars representing liberty and justice for all; the other saw the stripes as bars to keep the undocumented out. A clash of American visions erupted in North Texas.

Some angry Anglo residents decided to confront those who would sully their vision. While Congress dragged its collective feet on comprehensive immigration reforms, City Councilman Tim O'Hare felt compelled to take legislative matters into his own hands. O'Hare and his followers sought to protect Farmers Branch from the wrong kind of people with a proposed José Crow law. He argued that the undocumented were bad for Farmers Branch's economy and schools. The O'Hare ordinance would have made it illegal to hire the undocumented, to lease to them and to allow their young to play ball in city-sponsored events.

Héctor Flores, past national president of the League of United Latin American Citizens, offered a vision of America that welcomed hard-working, entrepreneurial, taxpaying immigrants. He said US history was replete with contributions that immigrants from all parts of the world have made to this country's greatness. He pointed out that O'Hare's Irish immigrant ancestors were oppressed when they immigrated to the land of the free. But, he said, "The oppressed become the oppressors."[27]

O'Hare's extremist position allowed no room for compromise and negotiation. Pulling the Chicano tiger by the tail only incited the heated reaction of protests and possible lawsuits. It certainly rallied like-minded patriots from the area who welcomed the opportunity to vent their frustration with the Mexican immigrant presence.

Mental health professionals who use the *Diagnostic and Statistical Manual of Mental Disorders 5,* a book categorizing mental disorders, should consider a new entry: Mexicanaphobia. Symptoms include a generalized fear, as demonstrated through ranting and angry outbursts toward people who look Mexican. The closer the Mexicanite comes into view, the more alarmed and hysterical the reaction from the Mexicanaphobic.

As the anti-ordinance protesters marched along the street leading to and from City Hall, one of three Anglo men standing nearby asked where they were going. An older man answered, "They're going to get tacos."[28] Another said that their marching was illegal and hoped they would go home to México. When pressed as to why it was illegal to march, he said because they were all illegal. He obviously didn't know Flores and other marchers were born in this country — but would it have really made a difference to him?

A woman alternately holding her child and a US flag shouted at the Spanish-speaking protesters that she, too, could speak Spanish as a sign of linguistic parity. She said that as a missionary in Spain, she learned to speak fluent *Español.* Her new work called for passing laws that would make English the official language and relegate Spanish to homes. Her husband said that they hoped to pass an ordinance in Granbury, Texas, similar to O'Hare's edict.

As Anglo and Chicano placard-carriers marched in front of City Hall, a counter protester couldn't resist the urge to disrupt their walk. After an hour of speeches on a 100-plus-degree day, Flores was in no mood for an intrusion into their assembly. He motioned for the police to intervene or else. The police pounced on the intruder and escorted the man away from the crowd.

The presence of Anglo teens from Highland Park, Texas, carrying signs in support of the immigrants may have triggered the Mexicanaphobic reaction. Rachael Miller said that her generation is unlike past generations: "We speak freely. ... We have so much going on politically, we have to make decisions. We must view everyone equally and understand that you can't treat a human being like this. We came here because we thought it was right to take a stand against Farmers Branch's choices."[29]

Time for all to take a stand and choose between stars and stripes and between America the beautiful and America the mad.

A novel approach to a discussion of the immigrant issue is to speak with the undocumented immigrants themselves. A disheveled man stood outside the Fort Worth Intermodal Transportation Center hall room where about 100 people had listened to local experts speak about immigration's impact on Tarrant County.

He had hopped a train from the state of Guerrero, México, and traveled to the center on his trek to Chicago. His small stature, worn cap, jacket, and pants would have made him inconspicuous if it weren't for his plea for money to buy food. All that was missing from an informative immigration forum hosted by the League of Women Voters of Tarrant County on February 8, 2007, were the subjects of much debate—the immigrants themselves. If only someone had thought to invite migrants to the forum to explain their quest for jobs in the north. Although the hungry migrant wasn't billed on the forum's flier, and his resume might not have compared to those of other speakers, his presence would have added flesh to the facts presented. He was the missing expert in the shadows.

The migrant's voice might have outraged some in the audience who kept insisting that laws had been broken – case closed. A few called out their views and left early when they didn't like what they heard. But the immigration issue wasn't that simple to the three panelists and the fourth standing in the hall.

Bernard Weinstein, former director of the Center for Economic Development and Research at the University of North Texas, held the floor. Fort Worth school district Trustee Juan Rangel and the Fort Worth office director for the US Department of Housing and Urban Development's fair housing enforcement program Gary Sweeney shared their views on the impact of immigrants on Tarrant County.

But Weinstein's command of the rapidly changing demographics, his assessment on the state's and country's labor needs, and his views on immigration reform drew most of the attention. Weinstein recalled traveling two years earlier through Nogales, Arizona, into México. His interest in the North American Free Trade Agreement took him frequently to the border. He said that the barbed-wire barricades, the ten- to thirty-foot fences, reminded him of the Berlin Wall. "If I were a Mexican national, I would be absolutely offended. We have this economic union, but it's not being accompanied by a migration or human resource policy that accommodates the reality of this North American marketplace," he said.[30]

He claimed that immigration was one of the key economic drivers in this country's economic history and that this was probably truer that day than ever before. According to data from the US Bureau of Labor, Weinstein said, in 1996-2003, people born outside the state filled 60 percent of Texas' job growth. In the face of a restrictive immigration policy, he foresaw a labor shortage. "Sure, the country has to control its border, but at the same time, the country must recognize its need for immigrants. We need immigrants with high- and low-skill levels. We need immigrant labor to keep the economy growing," he said. Weinstein favored former President Bush's guest-worker/road-to-citizenship immigration reform proposal.[31]

He attributed some of the resistance to sensible reform to post-9-11 xenophobia. The world seemed to become more dangerous after the Twin Towers attack. Some citizens allowed their fear of the hungry immigrant in the hall to overwhelm their good sense. They feared the tipping point where mass Mexican immigration became the rule of law. If and when Congress passes such laws, citizens will face the reality that once-undocumented immigrants will become their legal equals.

Another reality that citizens must confront: the state's growing demographic changes. Weinstein said that Texas Anglos became the minority in 2005 in a state of 23 million people. In Tarrant County, the Latino population was growing faster than the black and Anglo population. By 2040, it's estimated, Tarrant County will have 3.5 million residents, and 2.3 million will be Latinos. In 2015, the Migration Policy Institute calculated that 103,000 and 242,000 undocumented mostly Mexican immigrants were living in Tarrant and Dallas Counties, respectively.[32]

Most baby boomers will live long enough to see the dramatic changes. But Generations X, Y, and Z will feel the Chicanoization surge's full impact on society and the economy. The Migration Policy Institute and Weinstein asked us to set aside the immigrant boogeyman and face the fact that sensible immigration reform will help the economy. It's past time to invite the hungry immigrant into the hall.

Republicans appear to have a fascination with walls to keep other hungry migrants from us. In the 2011 and 2015 Republican presidential candidates' debate, most took a hardline stance against immigrants crossing the borders. Herman Cain advocated the stringing of an electrified fence along the Mexican-United States border. This action is only the start of aggressive border construction. Michele Bachmann, like Donald Trump, called for the round up and deportation of all estimated 11 million undocumented immigrants.

US Representative Duncan Hunter proposed a Tortilla Curtain along the US-México border to stop and snare terrorists, undocumented immigrants, and other undesirables. But the California congressman had miscalculated:

One fence alone — even a 1,951-mile barrier from the Pacific to the Gulf of México — would fail because it doesn't go far enough to halt the famished hordes.

History has shown that it takes more than one wall to keep the enemy out. The early versions of the Great Wall of China that snaked across thousands of miles of countryside proved strong for some time but eventually failed; the invading Mongols simply swept around it. If a second wall had been built, deeper moats dug, more archers placed at both walls, Kublai Khan might never have set foot in Beijing.

To keep out Western spies and saboteurs, the East German government built the Berlin Wall. But President Ronald Reagan held the radical notion that the wall was meant to shackle democratic ideals and freedom-loving people. He grew so bold as to go to Berlin and demand that Soviet President Mikhail Gorbachev tear down the wall.

Reagan held the quaint notion that totalitarian governments built walls between countries to keep people in political and economic slavery. He could never accept that the Evil Empire intended only to protect the East Germans from the decadent West. As a member of the Greatest Generation that had fought and defeated Nazis and kamikaze warriors, he couldn't stomach an Iron or Bamboo Curtain. But he might have accepted the brilliance of a Tortilla Curtain once he understood the logic.

As a conservative Republican, Reagan could have seen that to secure US borders, a fence — dug deep and built high, wide, and thick — would hold back the Mexican tsunami and terrorist infiltrators. He might even have helped to construct it, handy as he proved to be with fence building at *Rancho del Cielo.*

An earlier US president, Franklin Delano Roosevelt, understood the need for fences, concertina wire, and watchtowers after the bombing of Pearl Harbor. Roosevelt ordered the US Government to round up and herd Japanese-Americans on the West Coast to internment camps. Corralling them proved successful in foiling any sabotage from the enemy within our midst. (Of course, some 25 years later, the government made politically motivated reparations for allegedly violating those internees' rights.)

Sure, Democrats may squawk about Hunter's dreams of building a Tortilla Curtain. But with the benevolent internment of the Japanese-Americans, the country didn't have to worry about fighting a third front in our backyard. Even former Senator S.I. Hayakawa of California testified before Congress about the "unforeseen benefits" of the internment.

From the ancient Chinese, we should learn that one fence is not enough.

It's estimated that 11 million undocumented immigrants freely roam the country, concentrated mainly in the American Southwest.

A second fence moving up from the Gulf of México along the eastern edge of Texas, rounding up along the Red River and extending west on the northern borders of New Mexico, Arizona, and across California to the Pacific would seal the border jumpers in. Yes, it would cost more money and cause some environmental disruption —especially running the fence across the northern rim of the Grand Canyon — but the security of the country demands bold action.

Once the Tortilla Curtains are constructed, ICE officials could start cordoning off the barrios in the major cities. A fence could be constructed around Fort Worth's north side. Chicano residents could register with the police and be given forgery-proof, indelible tattoos.

Getting caught outside the fence without the made-in-the-USA tattoo — or the almost-as-good "Naturalized but not native"— would mean an immediate, all-expense-paid trip to sunny México (one-way, of course).

Repeat this fencing often enough across the southwestern borders, and soon we could wipe the dust from our faces, knowing that the Mexican undocumented and terrorists are on the other side of the Tortilla Curtain.

Pass the wood, hammer, and nails.

If we are to see beyond walls and concertina, news coverage of the immigration issues requires in-depth, consistent coverage. Americans will have better opportunities to understand fully its complexities. The importance of accurate news about immigration issues was stressed at the League of United Latin American Citizens 78th National Convention I attended in Chicago in July 2007.

John Quiñones, ABC News correspondent, told the LULAC audience how he hired a Mexican human smuggler to get him across the Mexican-US border at Laredo. Working for a Chicago TV station at the time, Quiñones sought to provide an in-depth look at undocumented immigrants' entry into this country. After riding an inner tube across the Río Grande, he said, he was probably the first Mexican to cross without papers and sleep that night in a Hyatt Regency.

Quiñones won an Emmy for his story and soon was hired by ABC. During the convention in Chicago, Quiñones moderated a panel discussion in a workshop on media coverage of immigration issues.

Olga Briseño, director of the Media, Democracy and Policy Initiative at the University of Arizona, said that many educators and reporters who write extensively about immigration have never been to the border.

"It's one thing to talk about immigration, and it's another to live it," she said. "The immigration story is a story about economics; it's about social history. It's not something that a reporter can jump into and jump out. Because this story impacts the Latino community and the country, we must demand that the newsroom cover this story with the depth that it deserves."

Briseño cited a UCLA study of news reporting by Otto Santana, instructor at the UCLA Department of Chicana and Chicano Studies. She found that reporters described immigrants in animalistic, criminal, and foreigner terms such as *herding*, *undocumented*, and *alien*. The stories slant the coverage to imply that Mexicans shouldn't be here, that they're uneducated and inferior, she said. This happens at a time when Chicano youth should be encouraged to pursue education and well-paying jobs.

The panelists cited TV talk-show hosts such as Lou Dobbs who provide inflammatory entertainment but no real, in-depth immigration coverage. Quiñones encouraged LULAC and other civic organizations to confront Dobbs and others who earn their living bashing immigrants. He said we need cable news outlets that counter right-wing commentators. Where are the Chicano talk-show hosts?

Domingo García of Dallas, the national co-chairman of LULAC's civil rights commission, said that he has asked US Representative Nancy Pelosi to reintroduce the "Fairness Doctrine" in Congress to call for balanced coverage of controversial issues. He challenged Spanish news media corporations such as Telemundo and Univision to counter these attacks. Instead of showing telenovelas or R-rated entertainment that does little to change society, they should enter the immigration fray with counter-viewpoints. Esteban Creste, news director for Telemundo Chicago, said that his station covered an unsuccessful attempt by the Illinois Legislature to allow the undocumented to get driver's licenses. The bill failed, not for the lack of news coverage but because grassroots organizations and legislators offered weak political strategies, he said. Since the convention, twelve states and the District of Columbia enacted laws that allowed the undocumented to obtain driver's licenses. The states were California, Colorado, Connecticut, Delaware, Hawaii, Illinois, Maryland, New Mexico, Nevada, Utah, Vermont, and Washington. Despite repeated attempts by Texas State Representative Roberto Alonzo of Dallas, the Texas Legislature had not passed a similar law.[33]

García pointed out that as a result of conservative commentators' encouragement, viewers and listeners flooded congressional representatives' e-mails and phones with their opposition to the reform bill. The only major Latino voice was Eddie "Piolin" Sotelo, the Los Angeles, Spanish-speaking DJ who delivered more than a million petitions for a comprehensive immigration bill.

Briseño said community organizations play a major role in balanced news coverage. After the April 2006 pro-immigration marches, former

President Bush's popularity ratings went down. However, she said Latino presence in the news media has declined between 1996 and 2006. She said Latinos comprised 4.4 percent of employees in newspapers and less than 2 percent in radio. They have a better showing in television because of Telemundo and Univision.

The 4th Estate, an online infographic outlet that reviewed newspaper coverage of the 2012 presidential election, published an article on October 24, 2012, titled, "Newsroom Diversity, a Look at Diversity on the Front Page." After reviewing thirty-eight of "the most influential print media in the US market" for the period of January 1 to October 12, 2012, they found that white reporters wrote 93 percent of the front page articles. The *Dallas Morning News* had the most minority writers represented on the front page with 18.8 percent black and .1 percent Latino. The *New York Times* had 2.5 percent front-page articles written by blacks and .8 percent by Hispanics. On the immigration topic for all surveyed papers, white reporters wrote 94.8 percent of the articles while Latino writers wrote 3.8 percent, and blacks wrote .7 percent. The 4th Estate concluded that Hispanics are largely underrepresented as journalists.[34]

The journalist John Quiñones said that as a son of a poor migrant worker family, he received his professional break when a San Antonio community organization demanded the local news media start hiring people who looked like San Antonians. The group threatened to go to the Federal Communications Commission and challenge their licenses if the stations didn't hire more Chicanos.

"Thank God for them," Quiñones said. "I wouldn't be here."

Chapter 13

Community Mobilization

From the eighteenth-century Boston Tea Party to the twenty-first-century Tea Party movement, American citizens have taken to the streets to protest their opposition to governmental policies. The Occupy Wall Street and similar movements across the country have proclaimed the common man's and woman's anger toward corporate greed. Chicanos, too, have taken part in protest movements, from Vietnam War protest marches in Los Angeles to immigration reform marches across the country. Chicanos have learned the importance of demonstrative protests if we're to be heard above the din of competing voices.

I want my teenaged son to value the dove of peace over the dog of war, and so we march. On sunny afternoons, his fingers fly like fluttering butterflies over the piano keys to the jazz piece, "Body and Soul"; I hope these same hands never point or fire a gun at another human in the dark. I wish them to milk melodies from notes, not bullets from gats. To calm the dog and coo the dove, we marched alongside thousands of peace lovers of all ages and races on a brisk Saturday afternoon in Dallas to protest the US invasion of Iraq, this mad war against foreign madmen.

We were veteran marchers. On Fort Worth's Main Street with hundreds shouting, "*Si se puede*!" (Yes we can), we had marched in honor of César Chávez. Then, most marchers were Chicanos, wearing red T-shirts with Chávez's face emblazoned on them. We waved the United Farm Workers Union black eagle flag and marched for the rights of the common man and the principles of peaceful resolution to conflicts.

In a state that is a consistent leader for the highest number of executions, in a country struggling with violent crime, in a world at constant war, I sought to teach this young man that despite the government's moralistic and patriotic preaching, the culture of death was truly abnormal. And so we march.

I'm afraid that my son's quick reflexes, sinewy body, foot speed, and smarts in football and track may delude him into thinking that he can dodge bullets. Too many minority boys from American barrios and ghettos thought likewise when signing up for the Vietnam War. They were President Johnson's dominoes sent to offset the tumble of Southeast Asian countries to communism.

President George W. Bush sought to convince America and the world that cutting off the head of the Iraqi government would stop the snake of terrorism. More domino boys armed with the latest gizmo guns and goggles were sent to stop another distant, foreign threat. The toppling of the Iraqi government by the US-led invasion left the country in political disarray and allowed for deeply pent-up hostility between Sunnis and Shiites to surface. After the US withdrew most of its troops, the Islamic State in Iraq and Syria (ISIS) fought both the Iraqi and Syrian Governments to establish a caliphate in the region. ISIS terrorists have conducted several attacks in the Middle East and Europe, and threatened to extend their religious war to the US. In 2015, after the bombing of a Russian airliner, simultaneous attacks in Paris and the bombings in Beirut, all resulting in hundreds of civilian deaths, the US went on high alert for possible ISIS terrorist attacks. I wanted my son to learn that, in America, patriotism means sometimes saying "no" to the government. I took up a plastic U.S. flag (made in China) and waved it amid a sea of signs: "No Blood for Oil," "Truth Is the First Casualty of War," "Thou Shall Not Covet Thy Neighbor's Oil," "Is Saddam Worth World War III," "Atheists Oppose Bush's Crusade."

We were pilgrims of peace in a Chaucerian caravan in Dallas, listening to our fellow marchers spin their stories, reading their signs, and hearing them pray to God and Allah. Our destination was the Kennedy Memorial Plaza, where thousands would gather to hear anti-war speeches, music, and a play.

A red-capped Nigerian chanticleer beat a drum, danced, and sang to the marchers that if you kill an Iraqi, you kill an American; if you kill a Muslim, you kill an American. Our American bodies swayed to the music of international peace, a rhapsody in blue, red, white, black, and brown.

Two men carried between them a colorful banner of the Queen of Peace, the *Virgen de Guadalupe.* One said that he had marched before to support the farm workers and to end the Vietnam War. His peace fever had never broken. In times of conflict, he said, the banner of the Virgin was carried for spiritual protection. The other man said that, besides marching, we must bend the knee in prayer to the *Virgen.*

A Palestinian-American mother and daughters, dressed in hijab scarves, talked of Allah's desire for peace in the world. Their Muslim life had become more difficult after 9-11. A young, pretty girl said beneath the white scarf that she's an American, not a terrorist.

An eighty-one-year-old World War II veteran, who had flown bombers over France and Nazi Germany, carried a sign: "Justice or Just Us." In his first peace march, he said that he loved his country but that this war was not the same. He called Bush a cowboy, unable to negotiate.

Hippie Rick recited a peace poem:

> Hope those youths keep singing enough is enough
> The machine still goes on spewing its stuff

For without youths to speak out, there's no other course
Who else will tell them to stop the wars

I pray that my son and all the children of the millions of worldwide peace marchers learn to crow like chanticleers: "No more wars!" And so we march.

César Chávez led many marches and boycotts for *La Causa.* Some Chicanos use Chávez as their model for peaceful, militant movement to ensure social justice. José Aguilar resembled César Chávez in his passion to fight for the dignity of the poor. Like Chávez, he was angry that in the richest country in the world, working men and women lack adequate healthcare.

Aguilar had stood before bosses like the John Peter Smith Hospital (JPS) board to tell them that it was their moral and financial responsibility to treat the undocumented and working poor well. As a volunteer community organizer for the Allied Communities of Tarrant, he spoke to Spanish-speaking immigrants, churchgoers, and the survivors of those who died without receiving adequate medical treatment. He encouraged them to channel their cold anger into focused, meaningful action to convince the board that the sick were people first and a political purse a distant second. He challenged people to convert their sweet talk about justice and ethics into gritty social work.

Chávez was not motivated solely by quixotic idealism. Nor was Aguilar. Witnessing and experiencing hunger, pain, and poverty fueled his desire to press the issue of medical care for the indigent and working poor. And watching, at a young age, others speak up for the poor taught Aguilar that the strong have an obligation to help the weak.

When Aguilar's wife was transferred as a patient from Harris Methodist to JPS, he understood intimately the dramatic struggle for healthcare. Caught in insurance issues, he learned the difficulty of getting JPS to provide follow-up treatment for his wife's cancer. She was stymied by citizenship issues.

His early days taught him that he would need to work hard to find solutions. Aguilar went to work at five years old in Ciudad Juárez, México. He led US tourists to the best restaurants and markets on his bicycle or by running alongside cars. He sold food, shined shoes, and learned his first English words with his US customers: "One dollar." As the oldest of seven children, he knew early that people either work or starve. He also learned the sad effects on a family of an alcoholic father. For a boy to take on the load of helping to feed brothers and sisters, attend school and watch out for a sick father may seem harsh to some. The responsibility forced the boy to become a man-child in a broken-promise land. His paternal grandmother, Teresa López, gave him the fuel to persevere.

Aguilar helped her sell heating and cooking oil to people in her neighborhood. When the issue of raising the cost of the oil surfaced, Aguilar recalled accompanying his grandmother to a business guild meeting. In a room full of men, Aguilar watched the only woman in the room struggle to break the men-only rules. She pushed her way to the front past growling, jostling machos. They shouted to keep her from the microphone. She finally reached the front and raised her voice above the rancor. As she began speaking, the men howled — but she persisted, and they soon quieted and listened. At the end of her remarks, they gave her a clamor of approval.

At the time, Aguilar didn't understand the significance of her courageous act. It wasn't until they left the hall and were walking home that he noticed his grandmother weeping. Grandmother Teresa told him that she was really happy because the businessmen had agreed with her plea to keep the oil price at the same level and not to raise it for the next seven years.

"We won, my son, we won," she said. Although this agreement cut into her profits, she knew that raising prices would force her neighbors to choose between food or clothing, starvation or heating in the winters. She had the power not to force such choices. But first, she had to choose:

speak up or keep quiet. And so Aguilar learned that he had to make a choice: speak up or shut up.

For his willingness to stand and speak for the poor, Aguilar received the Spirit of César Chávez award at the Rose Marine Theater. The award was presented by the César Chávez Holiday Celebration Committee at the Chávez festival on the labor leader's birthday, March 31, 2007.

Like Chávez and Grandmother Teresa, he had taken on the tough tasks of organizing and meeting with the bosses. He had earned the prize, but more importantly, he had won the respect of many for speaking up for the poor.

Grandmother Teresa was just one of many Mexican women who have historically advocated for their communities or fought in wars alongside their husbands and lovers. Like the heroine in the Mexican song "*La Rielera,*" Rosa Rosales personifies the ardent Chicana rousing Chicanos to muster the courage to struggle for social, economic, and political power. Wearing her trademark wide-brimmed hat, Rosales, former national president of the League of United Latin American Citizens, told the audience at the 5th Annual Jim Wright Symposium at Texas Christian University in October 2006 to improve their communities through organizing. She recounted how she overcame shyness, fear of failure, Chicano machismo, and discrimination to learn the art of organizing grassroots support. From housewife and mother of three boys to the national presidency of LULAC, Rosales' life story was that of the emergence of a political tiger.

Photo 21. Jackie Valenciano

Courtesy of the Delsa M. Pérez Collection, Genealogy, History, and Archives Unit, Fort Worth Library.
Valenciano was the first Chicana Congressional Page from Tarrant County. She is pictured here with Jim Wright, former Speaker of the House and Pauline Valenciano, veteran political activist, at Texas Christian University banquet, 2006.

She told the audience she had wept when her husband, Rodolfo Rosales, informed her that he had received a Ford Fellowship to pursue a Ph.D. at the University of Michigan in August 1973. Like many Chicanas, she found it difficult to leave her extended family and her hometown, San Antonio. Rosales was an "A" student in high school, but despite encouragement from a counselor to pursue college, she decided to follow the traditional path of Latinas: work and wed. At her husband's insistence, she pursued a college degree as a thirty-year-old mother.

College opened a whole new world for her. She felt a longing to connect with other Chicana students far from home, and so she sought them out. As a natural organizer, she helped to form the Third World Women Minority Caucus. Through mentoring from a professor at the University of Michigan, the women's caucus learned how to research and present their request to the university president for increased money for minority women programs and scholarships. Rosales' shyness wore off.

After returning to San Antonio, she was impressed with the city's economic growth. But she noticed that Chicanos were still a pool of cheap labor, poor and uneducated. She decided to work for their rights and founded the National Association of Public Employees. As its CEO, she advocated for public employees in San Antonio. She's proud of her role in the union movement and its successes in negotiating for employee benefits. She said that employees don't ask for special favors — instead, they seek respectful and dignified treatment.

After some coaxing from friend Angie García, she joined LULAC, which she'd considered primarily a social club. García convinced Rosales that LULAC was determined to make positive social changes for Chicanos and Chicanas. She was attracted by the power that focused, organized Chicanos can wield when united.

Rosales was proud of LULAC's inclusion of women. But it wasn't always the case. "Women weren't voting members," Rosales remembered. "They were allowed to participate in auxiliaries and make tacos." Latinas organized and demanded equal treatment. Women now make up more than half of the organization and hold several key positions. Rosales said, "They're *mujeres luchadoras*" — women fighters.

She told the attentive audience it took three tries to become LULAC's national president. She recalled the men saying that she was a loose cannon and washed up. She donned her battle hat, organized her support and brought busloads of voters to Milwaukee from across the country to win the presidency in July 2006. She recalled the convention rally cry: "The buses are coming."

Rosales continued to tell the audience that she was tired of talking about the dismal statistics concerning Chicanos' educational and political woes. She had attended enough conferences to know that Chicanos lead in high school dropout rates, illiteracy, and first-year college dropout rates.

"Chicanos are under siege," she said. "We're being attacked. It's time more than ever that we organize. If we're to become the number one minority, then we must have an educated population." She wants more Chicanos to vote.

During her tenure as national president of LULAC (2006-2009), she was most impressed with the work of José González and John Arnold, who had developed effective dropout prevention programs. She asked them to lead a LULAC commission on education and to develop a master plan on improving education for Chicanos. Rosales sought to partner with other Chicano organizations to implement the plan.

She said LULAC offered volunteers a channel for their passion and love for their community. With her commander's hat on, she called for Chicanos and Chicanas to organize, mobilize, and engage their world.

Chapter 14

Criminal Justice

National and local data have shown that African American and Chicano adults and youth are disproportionately arrested and incarcerated. The facile argument raised is that blind justice administers sanctions based on the evidence presented and not on color of the defendants. Closer examination of the justice system reveals blind justice peeking at the accused and meting out justice influenced by the defendant's hue.

Several years ago, Dallas County commissioners agreed to fund the construction of one of the biggest juvenile detention facilities in the state. Quite visible along Interstate 30 as you enter Dallas from the west, it consists of gray, institutional buildings surrounded by a tall chain-link fence topped with barbed wire. The prediction "If you build it, they will come" was becoming all too true.

With the help of a grant from the Annie E. Casey Foundation, Dallas County Juvenile Services administrators have decided to reduce the practice of locking up minority kids and instead create innovative programs and culturally competent alternatives. The program was called the Juvenile Detention Alternative Initiative and was still in operation as of 2015.

Don Smith, then-manager of research and statistics for Dallas County Juvenile Services (DCJD), explained at the Third Annual Latino Youth Issues Conference held April 2007 in Fort Worth that officials had decided not to throw any more money at detaining juveniles. How often do you hear of a county department telling county commissioners not to give them more money to hire staff? That's exactly what the Dallas County Juvenile Department did. DCJD decided to break the chains of the old ways of thinking and doing things. Instead of locking up more kids, staff members sought to release them to the community, working with organizations that understood their culture.

Banking on community partnerships with respected minority agencies with a history of working toward the improvement of the community, they entered into partnership with the League of United Latin American Citizens in Dallas for diversion programs and mentors. Oak Cliff Bible Fellowship agreed to provide temporary placement and pastoral counseling to youth who assaulted their parents. The LULAC and faith-based folks spoke the language, walked the streets, and knew what went on behind closed doors. Troubled minority youths needed to see professional minority role models solving problems in calm, rational ways.

Smith's statistics pointed out the need to move toward the community for help. In 2000-2006, the data showed that the detainee population was 50 percent blacks, 36 percent Latinos, 13 percent Anglos, and 1 percent others. In contrast, the Dallas County youth population was 25 percent blacks, 45 percent Latinos, 25 percent Anglos, and 5 percent others. Clearly, blacks were detained out of proportion to their total population numbers. Smith's research showed that blacks were four times and Latinos one and a half times more likely to be detained than Anglo youths.[35]

Smith said this pattern of disproportionate minority confinement was not unique to Dallas County. He claimed that it was rampant throughout the state and nation and in industrialized countries that contain large minority populations. If there were parity, the kids would be detained in roughly the numbers they existed in the population.

A review of the disposition of the detained youth also showed that blacks and Latinos were offered probation less often and were committed more often to the Texas Youth Commission (TYC) than Anglos. The referrals to the community organization resulted in a discernible decline in the number of youth committed to TYC. Texas Juvenile Justice Department statistics showed that the number of youth committed from Dallas County in fiscal years 2006 to 2013 dropped from 320 to 48.[36]

Smith's research showed that various sociological, familial, cultural, and behavior factors, as well as access to resources and diverse police arrest policies caused the disproportionate number of contacts with minority youth. Where you live sometimes determined whether you were going behind the chain-link fence. He said Garland police preferred field releases for their arrests rather than transporting to the detention center because of the distance. Dallas Area Rapid Transit police arrested kids on their trains and buses because they lacked student identification badges. Smith said that some kids were brought to detention with felony-level charges for shoving another child or stealing a bicycle.

Irving and Grand Prairie, which have large Latino youth populations, tended to have fewer custodial detentions than Dallas because of their diversion programs. Another financial factor was that suburban Anglo kids tended to have insurance and could afford private placements for drug-related offenses, whereas poor minority kids in Dallas County stayed in detention for an average of thirty-two days before they were sent to a drug treatment program.

Some youth certainly needed to be detained for the safety of the community. However, when disproportionate numbers of minority children were detained and sent to TYC, more humane policies and programs were needed.

One answer: less barbed wire and more community collaboration. Another rational option is for the legal system to closely examine hard facts before jumping to conclusions about a case.

Texas tall tales abound when it comes to fighting crime. Notions on how to reduce criminality have held political sway in the Lone Star State too long over scientific studies of "what works." Politicians, who should know better, have pandered to fears that crime runs amok in the streets. The results are counterproductive "get-tough" policies that exacerbate crime, break up families, and cost taxpayers billions.

In a criminal justice policy brief that the Texas LULAC state executive office released in August 2004, researchers showed that since the 1990s, Texas tripled the number of prisons and had a 51 percent higher incarceration rate than any other state.

The Legislature gave the Texas Department of Criminal Justice about $5 billion each biennium. TDCJ spent 90 percent of the money on prison beds and 10 percent on treatment and probation programs.

Part of the reason for the hefty spending was that Texas felony sentences were double the national average. Yet 70 percent of the prison admissions each year were for nonviolent crimes. About half of the prisoners were serving time for drug convictions for possession of less than one gram.

The interest of the League of United Latin American Citizens in Texas crime and punishment stemmed partly from the over-representation of Latinos and blacks in prison. The Justice Policy Institute found that even though 40 percent of Texans in 2003 were black and Latino, 70 percent of the prison population was minority.[37] According to the Texas Department of State Health Services, in 2012, the Texas black and Latino population constituted 50 percent of the entire state's numbers.[38] The Fiscal Year 2012 Statistical Report by the Texas Department of Criminal Justice revealed that 68 percent of the Texas prison population was minority.[39] LULAC projected that at the Latino imprisonment rate at that time, one out of six Latino men born in 2001 will serve prison time.[40]

LULAC cited studies claiming that racial profiling by police departments and drug task forces resulted in more searches of Latinos than whites.

To accommodate the millennium prisoners, LULAC predicted, there will be a need for 2,000 new prison beds each year.[41]

Texas also had the distinction of having the largest on-probation population in the United States, mainly because of its long probation terms for nonviolent offenders. The study found that probation officers had too large a caseload for them to respond adequately to probationers' needs. Although probationers can successfully meet the terms of probation for years, one slip-up may land them back in prison.

The average prison term on a revoked probation was 4.3 years. In 2001, this cost the state $470 million. In 2015, the average sentence length for a person who had been received into prison on a prior probation status, not necessarily as a result of revoked probation, was 4.27 years. According to the Criminal and Juvenile Justice Uniform Cost Report, in 2014 it cost the state $54.89 per day to incarcerate in a state prison. Applying the 2014 costs per day to the 9,584 offenders in prison who had been on probation, in fiscal year 2015, the estimated costs to the state were $8.1 million to incarcerate the prisoners over the 4.27 years.[42]

Despite the money, probation terms, and hard time, Texas crime didn't decrease more than any other state's. Instead, the crime rate was 24 percent higher than the national average, according to 2003 TDCJ data.[43]

Imprisonment of the heads of households also took its toll on the family and community. The LULAC study claimed that the children of imprisoned parents tended to make lower grades, drop out, become delinquent and increase their chances of following their parents into prison. Removing the significant male adult from a child's life left a void difficult for the mom and grandparents to fill. The absence of fathers in a community devalued males and placed increased child-rearing burdens on women.

The report also found that imprisoned parents owed $2.5 billion in unpaid child support. A cycle of intergenerational poverty and crime was set in motion, abetted by tough policies that punish criminals and families. LULAC said that "tough on crime punishments simply do not work on most offenders."[44] In a state looking for quick and easy solutions to crime, "lock-'em-up" blocks our chances to teach nonviolent felons internal restraints and different thinking patterns. The US Department of Justice found that punishment increased criminal behavior; psychological treatment and cognitive skills programs decreased criminal activity the most. The study found that "what works" are job training, drug treatment, and peer and family support. That kind of treatment is meant not to mollycoddle criminals but to provide a way out of self-defeating thoughts and actions.

LULAC traveled across the state to raise awareness in communities that evidence-based alternatives to incarceration for nonviolent offenders saved money, time, families, and communities. It recommended that the Legislature reduce nonviolent, small-quantity drug use from felony to misdemeanor status. Texas legislators should stop the bravado crime-fighter shtick that does little to reduce crime and instead rely on "what works" studies.

Texas needs fewer Robocops and more Joe Fridays. "Just the facts" will do fine.

A factual examination of the frequency that police stop blacks and Chicanos is required to dispel or corroborate the complaint that they are profiled.

Police agencies counter they enforce laws based primarily on the evidence presented to them. Many in the minority community who have personally experienced or witnessed police stops and arrests aren't convinced that the police have abandoned racial profiling. An article "Study Finds Disparity in Police Stops" by *Fort Worth Star-Telegram* reporter John Moritz on February 4, 2004, revealed that African American and Latinos were stopped more often than Anglos by the police.

Robert Starr, first vice president for the local NAACP chapter, was convinced that racial profiling existed in Tarrant County. He recalled that while driving one night in the Westover Hills area near Naval Air Station Joint Reserve Base Fort Worth, a car tailed him. He slowed to let the vehicle pass, but it continued to follow. After he slowed to a crawl, the police switched on their lights and sirens.

The reason given for stopping him was that he was driving too far to the right. Starr laughed at the flimsy excuse; he believed the white officers stopped him because he was an African-American man driving a nice car. He was DWB—driving while black. State Senator Royce West of Dallas thought the police practice of stopping and searching individuals because of their race went on throughout Texas. It humiliated the victim, made a mockery of police authority, and poisoned minority-police relations. As author of a racial profiling bill, SB 1074, he shepherded the bill into law in 2001 and raised "the hope that our rights and liberties will be protected and enforced under the laws of Texas."[45] It required Texas police agencies to maintain annual race statistics on traffic and pedestrian stops and searches. No longer should Latinos be lumped into the white category for statistical purposes.

Suspicions of racial targeting prompted NAACP and LULAC leaders to host a racial profiling conference on February 19, 2004, at Fort Worth Town Center. They welcomed Fort Worth and area police to attend and listen to the minority community's concerns and personal testimony.

LULAC District XXI Director Alberto Govea saw this as an opportunity to educate the community on racial profiling law and their rights. He rejected a report by the Fort Worth Police Department that it received only one complaint of racial profiling in 2002, and that the complaint was considered unfounded.

"If the vast majority of the drivers are Anglos, it would stand to reason that they would be stopped more often instead of less," he said.[46] Govea pointed out that a racial profiling study released February 2004 by the Steward Research Group showed that Fort Worth police stopped blacks two times and Latinos 2.4 times as often as Anglo drivers. The study gathered data through open record requests from 413 Texas agencies.

Researchers concluded that "in the absence of department-level mitigating factors, the statistical racial disparities in stop and search rates suggest a pattern of racial profiling by law enforcement agencies across Texas."[47]

According to David Garrett, Fort Worth Police Department planning manager, minorities may be stopped because they may drive older-model vehicles. For example, tail lights were out or inspection stickers had expired. Minorities were stopped not because of their ethnicity but because they neglected to make the necessary repairs to their cars. "This is an economic factor," Garrett said. "We are not racially profiling."[48]

He added that the Steward study was incorrect in listing the Fort Worth department as one of many agencies that failed to report all required racial profiling data to the state. He said Fort Worth had complied with all the requirements of the law for data submission. Garrett attended the racial profiling conference and listened attentively to the discussion.

Indeed, frank talks should take place between the minority community and the police. Stereotypes—the idea that blacks and Latinos may be more likely to deal drugs or steal, or that white police are out to nab minorities—must give way to reason and facts.

For example, according to the Steward data for Austin, Latino and black motorists were searched more often for contraband than Anglos. Yet the "hit rates"—instances in which contraband actually is found—were highest for Anglos in Austin. Faced with the evidence, further investigation was needed to determine why minorities were more likely to be searched.

The *Austin American-Statesman* reported on November 23, 2015, that researchers from the University of Texas and the University of North Carolina at Chapel Hill reviewed the Texas Department of Public Safety (DPS) traffic stop reports for the period 2003–2014. Their analysis found that white drivers were more often given a warning than minorities. In addition, they found that DPS's statistical monitoring of traffic stops was faulty and gave the incorrect impression that they treated drivers of different races equally. DPS officers were more likely to search black drivers at higher rates than white drivers.[49]

Television station KXAN reported on November 6, 2015, that a review of sixteen million traffic citations from 2010 to 2015 revealed that DPS troopers recorded incorrectly millions of Hispanics as white. The five most common surnames of "whites" that the officers gave citations for this time period were Smith, García, Martínez, Rodríguez, and Hernández. The television investigators suggested that the number of Hispanics stopped may actually be higher than actually reported. Texas Highway Patrol Chief Luis González said: "Implying or insinuating racial profiling without concrete evidence is slanderous and unfairly tarnishes the reputation of the commissioned men and women of the Texas Department of Public Safety, including approximately thirty percent who are Hispanic, who proudly risk their lives every day to protect and serve all residents and travelers in Texas."[50] DPS Director Steven McCraw announced on November 18, 2015, that DPS officers will ask drivers they stop their race and ethnicity to ensure accurate recording. He blamed the inaccurate racial identification data on an in-car computer system.[51] Starr says that after he was stopped, he "didn't act the fool." He advised all blacks, especially young males, to respond politely when detained by police and to keep their hands always visible on the steering wheel—good counsel that adults should model. He said that police were as afraid of young blacks as young blacks were of police. Let's bring this simmering fear into the coolness of calm, honest talks among blacks, browns, and blues.

For a change, let's profile reason.

National and local data show that black and Latino youth were disproportionately arrested and jailed. Research also showed that the school-to-prison pipeline shuttled many minority youth from the mainstream to a marginal life at a time that their population numbers were increasing. The courts and police must examine how to curb black and brown youth from entering and penetrating their jails and courts.

"Where is the justice?" youth advocates asked when they witnessed the disparate treatment of Latino youths in this country's juvenile justice systems. The report "*Dónde Ésta La Justicia?*" by Francisco A. Villarruel and Nancy E. Walker of the Institute for Children, Youth and Families at Michigan State University indicated that, instead of blind justice, Lady Justice meted out law based on a youth's skin color.

If you're brown, the juvenile laws of the land were enforced more harshly than for white youths committing the same crime, according to the report, released in July 2002. Published by the Building Blocks for Youth Initiative — an alliance of children's advocates, researchers, law enforcement professionals, and community organizers — the coalition called for nationwide action to fix a juvenile justice system that was unfriendly to Latinos.

Chicano civil rights and child-advocacy organizations such as the League of United Latin American Citizens (LULAC), the Mexican American Legal Defense and Education Fund (MALDEF), the National Council of La Raza and the Children's Defense Fund have declared June 3, 2003, as *Día de la Juventud* (Day of the Youth) as the first day of national action to sound the alarm of wayward justice.

They want barrio dwellers, lawmakers, youths, taxpayers and jurists to know that:

·Latino youths are over-represented in the justice system.

·Juvenile data collection is inadequate, resulting in undercounting and inaccuracies.

·The juvenile system fails to provide adequate bilingual services to Latino youths and fails to ensure culturally competent staff.

·Consideration of immigration status of a youth may result in incarceration, deportation and permanent separation from families.

·Anti-gang laws result in harsh consequences for Latino youths.

More specifically, Villarruel and Walker found that Latino youths were admitted to state facilities five times more often than whites for violent offenses, two times more often for property offenses, and thirteen times more often for drug offenses. Latino youths also spent 143 days longer than whites in these facilities for violent offenses, forty-five days longer for property offenses, and 262 days longer for drug offenses.[52]

The report said that in Texas in 1997, youths of color (blacks and Latinos) comprised 50 percent of the youth population but accounted for 65 percent in secure detention, 80 percent in secure correction, and 100 percent held in adult jails.

As an example of judicial culture clash, the report recounted the case of a fifteen-year-old boy charged with marijuana possession. At a disposition hearing, the judge spoke to the boy and his caseworker in his chambers and ordered the youth to look at him. The boy kept his eyes downcast, in keeping with the Mexican cultural gesture of respect for authority. The caseworker tried to explain this cultural trait, but the judge refused to listen, talked in harsh tones, and took the boy's behavior as an admission of guilt. He sentenced the youth to two years in a juvenile facility. The judge suffered from cultural myopia.

Some have argued that the over-representation of minorities was simply a result of more minorities committing more offenses than white youths. But the researchers found that over-representation was a complex issue with multiple causes. Socioeconomic factors such as poverty, joblessness, poor healthcare, and housing density, which were more common for minorities, increased the risk of delinquent behavior.

In addition, the report found that increased police presence in "high-crime areas" will bring minority youths to the attention of the law more often than white youths. Racial profiling of minority youths was another factor. A study of probation officer case notes showed that they tended to attribute negative personality and attitudinal traits to minority youths as the cause of their crime and to attribute social environment as the cause of white youth crimes.

Villarruel and Walker observed that "it would be a travesty to conclude that the problem of over-representation and disparate treatment of youth of color in the justice system is not the result, at least in part, of racial bias and discrimination."[53]

Some recommended fixes:

·Members of the Chicano community should organize and educate themselves on the over-representation issues and pressure the justice system to be more accountable to them.

·The community should encourage the juvenile system to provide staff cultural competency training and bilingual interpretation services.

The report called for legislators to hold hearings on how the state collected data on Chicano youths in the justice system and encouraged local justice systems to diversify their staffs, from clerks to judges, to mirror the diversity of their clients.

Perhaps then we can find justice in the raised eyes of Chicano youths.

One effective method to reduce black and brown arrests is to defuse police/minority encounters at the point of street contacts.

Law enforcement veteran Steve Holbert thought police officers should treat minority youths with respect. After more than thirty years as a patrol supervisor, detective, SWAT supervisor, and racial profiling and accident reconstruction expert, he knows that the "trail 'em, arrest 'em and jail 'em" approach led only to embittered youths and poisoned police and community relationships.

Co-author of *The Color of Guilt and Innocence: Racial Profiling and Police Practices in America*, Holbert said minor infractions too often escalated into major incidents as the minority kid and the cop squared off in the "Big Showdown." Speaking before an audience of law enforcement professionals at the Disproportionate Minority Contact conference in September 2006, aimed at examining and finding solutions to disproportionate minority contact, Holbert said people weren't born with stereotypes. But after enough negative encounters, perceptions, and fears, the blues and youths glare at one another across a yawning chasm of distrust and contempt.

Holbert said that police often confronted defiant minority youths with force. It was known in cop circles as flunking the attitude test. According to a Gallup survey that Holbert cited, 75 percent of black youths who were stopped by the police believed the primary reason was their race.

A report by the Steward Research Group in 2004, "Racial Profiling: Texas Traffic Stops and Searches," found that six out of seven law enforcement agencies reported searching blacks and Latinos at higher rates than Anglos. The study also said it found evidence that three out of four law agencies reported stopping blacks and Latinos at higher rates than Anglos.

Holbert cited 2003 crime statistics that although black youths represented 16 percent of the juvenile population, they accounted for 63 percent of juvenile arrests for robbery, 48 percent of juvenile arrests for murder, 40 percent for car thefts, and 38 percent for aggravated assaults. The US Department of Justice data showed that in 2010 when black youth represented 17 percent of the US juvenile population, they accounted for 51 percent of violent crime and 33 percent of property crime arrests. In more detail, their proportion of juvenile arrests was 67 percent for robbery, 56 percent for murder, 42 percent for car thefts, and 41 percent for aggravated assaults.[54]

"All of these arrests have one thing in common: The ultimate outcome was highly dependent on what happened at point of contact," he said. Although the law said that you're innocent until proven guilty, the police carried a powerful tool that youths didn't carry: a pen. The police report that was filed about the contact will follow the youth throughout the judicial process. Holbert notes once the police officer's report is completed, the accused youth will have a difficult time refuting the statements. If you were the judge, whose story would you believe: the kid's or the cop's?[55]

To reduce the disparate contacts between police and youth of color, Holbert recommended efforts to: Control the outside influences that develop harmful stereotypes and unjust fears of those we perceived were different and change or improve the relationship and exchanges that occurred between police and youths so that point of contact doesn't become point of conflict.

The effort should be to turn these contacts into experiences that have long-term positive impact on juveniles and on officers. Police officers are no different from the average citizen when they read or hear reports about youths carrying weapons to school or shooting one another in gang fights. If minority youths are willing to kill a fellow teen, what's to prevent them from opening fire on officers? Police worrying about their safety and wondering whether they will go home to their families can cause them to lose focus on the quality of the encounter.

Still, if officers were to take the time to speak respectfully with youths, allow them to explain their side of the story and get to know the teens on their beats, stereotypes and defiance could vanish. In these instances, familiarity doesn't breed contempt. Seeing beyond gang colors or uniforms builds relationships. It's hard to racially profile a friend.

Holbert claimed that police departments missed the mark in developing good community relations. The burden of reaching out lay with the police. They should not expect youths or their parents to come to the police for counsel. Holbert recommended the police step out of patrol cars and meet the youths and their families before crime strikes.

At the same time, the minority community must ask: Are we projecting an attitude of resentment, fear, and bias because of our own teenage experiences? More important, what teen behavior do we consider acceptable, and what acts are intolerable?

Regardless of the cops' color, they should be allowed to keep the peace, promote safety, and do their job without suffering harm or losing their lives. In short: Replace gangsta bravado and cop swagger with blue knight respect.

SUMMARY

Since Tejano days, Chicanos have run for office, voted, and organized for their political interests. After the arrival of Anglo settlers to Texas, the political winds shifted, leaving Mexican Americans politically puny. With the growth of the Chicano population, the political vanes favor a Mexican American resurgence for political might. The experience of La Raza Unida Party demonstrated that Chicanos can mobilize thousands of voters and win office. Despite these gains, twenty-first-century Chicanos still struggle to get to the polls in significant numbers, face redistricting machinations, and failed to run Mexican American candidates.

Hesitancy to dive boldly into the political fray was evident in the absence of a Chicano presidential candidate in 2015 while two Cuban Americans entered the debate. Both Ted Cruz and Marco Rubio promoted harsh immigration policies and a dismantling of the Patient Protection and Affordable Care Act (PPACA) or Obama Care. Billionaire Donald Trump marched across the nation touting mass deportation of Mexican rapists, drug dealers, and "anchor babies." Despite his outrageous targeting of Mexican immigrants, he led for months in the polls as the most popular Republican candidate.

Disproportionate imprisonment and police stops of Chicanos and blacks call for more intense review of the Texas criminal justice system. Communities must become more involved with the state and local juvenile justice system to understand how minority youth become channeled into the school to prison pipeline. They must learn what works to divert youth to pipelines that lead to a productive life. More scrutiny by the minority community on elected judges and their judicial conduct must take place to ensure lady justice serves us all fairly. Start by examining the number of minority elected judges in comparison to the community composition they serve. Invite the judges to community meetings to explain their legal processes as they discern the guilt or innocence of youth who appear before them.

In light of police-minority communities clashes across the country, more collaboration between Chicanos, blacks, and the police force must occur to enhance safety and peace. As the community should hold its members accountable for their behavior, the police must be held accountable for their interactions with minorities. The police may not be social workers but they should work socially with a diverse community.

Time and population growth are on the side of Chicano politicos. Community leaders like Rosa Rosales and Antonio Villaraigosa challenged Mexican Americans to assume power through community mobilization and organizing. Mexican Americans must move beyond tepid intentions and resolutions to seize political control. Jesus "Chuy" García's formidable run against Rahm Emanuel for Chicago mayor in April 2015 exemplified the growing Mexican American political strength, ability to form political coalitions and the courage to run for office. Chicanos may lose elections in the short run but with more political savvy, mobilization, and votes, they will win offices and ensure the rise of *La Raza.*

SECTION 4

CHICANO ROOTS

I displayed a photo of six historical Chicano figures on an overhead to a room-full of Chicano college students and asked them to identify the people. Some identified César Chávez—no one knew the others. This was an improvement over a previous presentation when I asked Mexican American high school students to tell me what they knew about César Chávez. Several said he was that famous Mexican boxer and held up their fists to demonstrate his punching prowess. I explained I thought they meant Julio César Chávez. The César Chávez I referenced was the founder of the United Farm Workers Union who organized the field workers to fight for their labor rights, better pay, improved working conditions, and respectful treatment.

Photo 22. Dolores Huerta and Sal Espino

Courtesy of Emerico Pérez, Emerico Photography.
Dolores Huerta and Fort Worth City Councilman Sal Espino with students from Dolores Huerta Elementary School of Fort Worth, Texas, May 2014, on the tenth anniversary of the school's opening.

Our schools' curricula lack the cultural awareness that American history goes beyond the Anglo-centric stories often repeated. In the 1960s, St. Philip High School, where I attended, expanded their reading list to include black heroes like Frederick Douglass, Crispus Attucks, Sojourner Truth, and Booker T. Washington. We also read Claude Brown's *Manchild in the Promise Land* and John Howard Griffin's *Black Like Me.* The Black Power movement swept the country as American black leaders exhorted their community to raise their voices and assert their rights against the prevalent racism. I never recalled reading in any of my classes throughout my formal education works by or about Mexican Americans. It was as if

Chicanos had never written a book worthy of inclusion in a high school curriculum or ever existed in the history of America. As my reading habit grew, I felt an awakening of an historical consciousness that sought to know where my people came from. I felt compelled to discover where I fit in the sociological, historical map of our country's history.

My ancestors didn't experience the Mayflower, Bunker Hill, Ellis Island, or southern plantation existence. As I read and studied the history of Chicanos for my historical identity, I discovered the Aztec, Mayan, and Inca civilizations, the Spanish conquest, Tejano frontier life, the Texas Revolution, the Mexican American War, Mexican American soldiers, the Bracero Program, César Chávez, La Raza Unida Party, and other significant Chicano events, authors, and works. But only after reading a photo-book called *Mexican Chicago* by Rita Arias Jirasek and Carlos Tortolero that traced the history of Mexican immigrants working and living in Chicago did my historical identity search crystallize.[1]

The photos of Chicanos walking streets I knew well from my youth transported me to my true roots. To my delight, the book included a photo of a Mexican woman acting as a Mexican Pavilion hostess at the Chicago World's Fair (Century of Progress) in 1934.[2] In addition, the introduction told of José Mariá Velasco, famous nineteenth-century Mexican painter, visiting Chicago as a delegate organizing the Mexican Pavilion at the Chicago World's Columbian Exhibition of 1893.[3] When he went downtown to buy material to hang paintings, he found a Mexican selling tamales for ten cents each. Although I honor my Mexican heritage, it's my Mexican American heritage that rings most true of my identity. I'm an American with a Chicano perspective. I feel more at home in Chicago than any other place in the world. I feel more akin to the history of the United States than to the history of México. I embrace my Mexican heritage but at my historical core, I revel in my Chicano Chicago roots. I definitely look Mexican with my dark, Mexican Indian features but I have a Midwestern tone, talk too much, and sometimes act too brash. When some folks ask me where I'm from, I tell them "I'm a Chicano from Chicago." I'm a Taylor Street and Oakley Boulevard boy with a love for the history of my maternal grandparents emigrating from México, settling on Roosevelt Road, and raising their two daughters and son. This is the city where my father, a Tejano, met my mother and raised a family of four children in a rat-infested flat until we moved to the Italian side of the Near West Side. The United States is where I came to know, accept, and cherish my Mexican American heritage.

This History Chapter pulls back the curtain on selected Chicano historical events and heroes to demonstrate their contributions and sacrifices for this country. I discuss the frontier, Tejano experience, and the Anglo authorities' response to their rise. When America entered wars, Chicano soldiers fought valiantly for their country. Their war experiences are rarely told because of humility and oversight. I look at Chicano heroes who excelled in their professions and activism. Finally, I illustrate the influence of Mexican historical adventure and lore that influence American celebrations and media. The intent is to impress that Chicano history merits wide-spread dissemination in order to complete the American montage.

Chapter 15

Tejanos

A complete understanding of Mexican Americans in the United States requires acceptance of their contribution to the settlement of the Texas frontier. The early Tejanos brought European and Mexican Indian cultures to the Texas plains, forests, and ravines in hopes of expanding New Spain's influence. The introduction of presidios, ranching, the horse, and cattle revolutionized the Indian and Anglo settlers' way of life. With the current rapid growth of the Chicano population throughout the country but especially the Southwest, a renewed interest in this country's Chicano roots has arisen.

History at times is like a wild mustang that needs to be caught and tamed before you can ride. The history of Tejanos — Mexicans living in Texas — in the formation of the state has wandered afar, with little notice by mainstream historians and schoolbooks. The Tejanos' story was elusive until recent historians lassoed a closer look at the life and times of Mexicans in the Coahuila y Texas frontiers.

The attention paid increasingly to this almost forgotten period of Texas history is due to the growing numbers of educated Tejanos in search of ancestral value. It didn't make sense that popular history could celebrate Davy Crockett, Jim Bowie, and William B. Travis and not honor thousands of Mexican settlers who brought the horse, cattle, Christianity, laws, and architecture to the Texas wilds. Civilized life in Texas didn't begin with the arrival of Stephen F. Austin and his Anglo settlers. It had been thriving for 300 years in Tejano settlements along the Río Grande, in the Bexar-Goliad area and in the Nacogdoches region. Before their northern neighbors fought their Civil War, Mexicans abhorred the savagery of slavery and outlawed it in all of the Mexican lands. For slave-owning Anglos interested in raising a cotton cash crop, human bondage was one of several disputes with the Mexican government. Mexicans and Anglos both believed in a Christian God but not on whether to extend the divinity to blacks.

In a tour of the Texas Capitol grounds, Dr. Cayetano Barrera of El Paso was astonished to discover that not one monument commemorated the Tejano legacy. Out-of-state visitors and schoolchildren could walk the grounds and never know of the Mexican settlers' presence.

A decisive man, Barrera contacted state Representative Ismael "Kino" Flores and urged him to motivate the Legislature to correct this omission. Members of the 77th Legislature responded with a resolution that they "hereby approve the construction of a statue or monument on the Capitol grounds that pays tribute to the contributions of Tejanos to the State of Texas."[4] This unfunded approval launched a statewide effort by Barrera, historians, and Tejanos to set the Texas record straight. Activists like seventy-year-old Benny Martinez of Goliad, who rode on horseback from his hometown to Austin to raise funds and awareness for the monument, have called for the light to shine on Tejano history.

On March 29, 2012, a monument to the Spanish/Tejano influence and contributions to Texas culture and history was unveiled on the Texas Capitol grounds. Designed by Armando Hinojosa, the monument showed an armored Spaniard standing on higher ground, hand to brow, as if awed by the vast, open lands stretching out before him. A vaquero riding a mustang herded two distinctive Long Horns cattle. A closer look at the vaquero's clothing revealed the origin of the chaps, western saddles, lassos, and wide-brim hats that deerskin-wearing Anglos soon adopted. On lower ground observers found a huddled family of Tejano settlers. At the base of the monument, a woman fed a sheep while a boy pulled on the horns of a reluctant goat, two animals introduced by the Spaniards to the New World.

In his seminal work, *Tejanos and Texas under the Mexican Flag, 1821-1836,* Andrés Tijerina — a history professor at Texas A&M University at Kingsville — gave a detailed account of the life, culture, and legacy of Tejanos.

He explained that the first Tejanos were a mixture of Tlaxcalans — Native Americans from central México — and Spaniards.[5] As allies of the Spaniards during their conquest of the Aztecs, the Tlascalans quickly learned the Spaniards' horsemanship. On the *frontera*, the Tlascalans, Texas Indians, and Spaniards easily intermarried, producing a mixed race of Tejanos. This mingling contrasted with the Anglo settlers, mostly Southerners, who kept apart, held rigid racial attitudes, and shunned interracial marriages. Across the Mexican northern *frontera*, the *compañia volante* (Tejano flying squadron) rode *mesteñas* (mustangs) to repel marauding Apaches and Comanches, hunt down criminals or arrest undocumented aliens. (You may guess their identity.) Having lived under the dominance of the ferocious Aztecs, they valued the independence that life in Texas offered.

The Tejano push to recognize the historical significance of Mexicans in Texas was evident in a Fort Worth statue in honor of the vaquero. Former Fort Worth City Councilman Jim Lane said in a personal interview with me that from the time he took office representing the North Side, May 1, 1993, he had visions of a vaquero statue on Main Street leading to the Stock Yards. He deliberately zoned a small park at the corner of Main Street and Central Avenue so that when cars and buses stopped as they were heading to the Stock Yards, they would see the statue.

"I wanted dads to explain to their sons that the first cowboys were Mexicans." He said his father Wesley Lane, an American Indian who had taught aeronautics at Trimble Technical High School, told him the most important cowboys were vaqueros. "When I visualized the statue of the vaquero, I thought about Joe Lazo, (long-time Fort Worth resident) a true cowboy. The vaqueros looked like you."

Photo 23. Joe Lazo, Sr.

Courtesy of the Delsa P. Pérez Collection, Genealogy, History, and Archives Unit, Fort Worth Library
Joe Lazo, Sr. riding Pancho in the Mexican Independence parade on Main Street, September 2000.

Jim Lane used his political influence to mobilize the city council to support the statue effort through zoning and finances. He organized a community committee, headed by Justice of the Peace Manuel Valdéz, to make the vision a reality. His zeal to acknowledge Fort Worth's western cowboy roots led to his creation of cattle drive reenactments along the

Trinity River. A stickler for historical accuracy, he insisted drovers consist of Mexican American, African American, woman, and Anglo cowboys.

An unfortunate dispute arose between the committee and the sculptors about the presence of a holstered pistol on the completed statue. Valdéz took issue with the sculptors' decision to place a pistol on the vaquero's hip. He thought it perpetuated the *bandido* stereotype, and the model they had approved had no pistol. The sculptors, Tomas Bustos and David Newton, countered that their historical research validated gun-toting vaqueros to protect them from real *bandidos*, hostile Indians, and wild animals.

As this dispute showed, historical accuracy was still hotly debated and underscored the importance of protecting the images of Tejano ancestors.

An annual, historical roundup is the Fort Worth Stock Show and Rodeo that continues the long tradition of rodeos or roundups started in the early 1600s by the vaqueros in what would become New Mexico. At the time, the vaquero was considered a heroic horseman, capable of roping and riding anything that bucked. These men proved their horsemanship at rodeo contests based on standardized rules and point systems. The prototype vaquero, like his mustang, was brave, hardy, and loyal to his ranch.

Historian Donald Chávez y Gilbert's online book, *Vaqueros: Origins of the First American Cowboys*, gives a fascinating account of the Spanish-Mexican origin of cowboy life and vaqueros' contribution to Anglo and American Indian cultures. When the first Anglo settlers came to Texas in 1823, they found millions of roaming longhorns for the taking. They just had to learn how to round them up.

Although seasoned vaqueros attempted to teach the first-generation Anglo Texans in the 1800s how to rope cattle, many lost their thumbs in the struggle. As soon as they lassoed the steer, they were supposed to *dale vuelta*, or dally (tie the lariat around the saddle horn). Before the Anglo wrangler could get his thumb out from under the rope, the steer pulled on the other end.

The rodeo or roundup was a skill that vaqueros had perfected since their arrival to the Southwest in 1598 in an expedition led by Don Juan de Oñate. The Oñate expedition formed a four-mile-long caravan with 560 men, women, and children, more than eighty wagons and between 7,000 and 13,000 livestock. Calling on centuries-old traditions of Moorish-Spanish horse breeding, riding, saddle making, and branding, the vaqueros rode their hardy mustangs across the wide-open New Mexico and Texas plains.

The American Indian called the horse Big Dog, God Dog, or Seven Dogs because the horse seemed seven times more powerful than their domesticated pets. As soon as they learned to ride Seven Dogs, the Indians increased their range for hunting buffalo and raiding neighboring tribes and Mexican and Anglo settlers. In a twist, the Indians learned the art of jewelry making – now a rich source of their income – from the Spaniards. At the same time, the Spaniards found the Mexican Indians' tamales, tortillas, and chilies irresistible. The ubiquitous presence of "Mexican" restaurants is a tribute to Indian cuisine. In the Moorish-Spanish tradition of cultural exchange, the New World people learned to improve their lives by sharing traditions.

Photo 24. Charra riding up Main Street

Courtesy of the Delsa P. Pérez Collection, Genealogy, History, and Archives Unit, Fort Worth Library.

Charra riding up Fort Worth, Texas, Main Street toward downtown in Fort Worth Stock Show parade, January 2008,

The cultural sharing continued with the arrival of the Anglo settlers into México-Texas. Chávez y Gilbert documented the vaquero influence on cowboy culture in their dance, music, clothing, lingo, ranching, and horsemanship. He wrote: "When Gene Autry died in October 1998, the media touted him as the first singing cowboy. Not so! ... there had already been at least a dozen generations of singing vaqueros who lived and died before him."[6] Anglos who adapted Mexican *corridos* to western ballads quickly adopted the Spanish guitar. Western square dancing had its origin in the Mexican quadrille dance, and the often-heard "do-si-do" sprang from dos-y-dos, or two-by-two.

Although the Anglos and Mexicans fought over Texas independence, the Texians were smart enough to accept the vaquero culture as well suited to ranching life. In this age of mobile phones, laptops, and cars, the vaquero life on the range might seem romantically quaint. Yet their skills of roping and riding, fending off Indian raids on their settlements, chasing down desperados and sharing their skills with Anglo settlers made them real American heroes.

Chicanos also fought for ascendency on the political frontier. Tejano heroes are often obscured in the fog of political and cultural skirmishes that arise in the quest for power. A comparison of the plights of Juan Seguín in the nineteenth century and Tony Sanchez in the twenty-first century proves racial animosity still enters the political arena.

Juan Seguín, Tejano defender of the Álamo, and Tony Sánchez, Tejano defender of the Democratic Party, were casualties of a cultural war waged since the days of Texians and Santa Anna. The image of a true Texan was the victor's prize.

Both prominent Tejanos, who acted as cultural bridges between the powerful white and Tejano communities of their times, were rejected and turned away from political office. As in the 1800s, so in the 2000s — Texians and Texans found the surrounding Méxicanismo a threat to a Texas myth that the land was best governed by the children of the victors of San Jacinto. They forget that Tejanos' ashes were mixed in the Álamo defenders' remains that Seguín buried with honors in San Antonio a year after the fall.

Despite the gallantry of Seguín and other Tejanos at the Álamo and San Jacinto, the newly arrived whites of San Antonio labeled their Tejano mayor a traitor, forcing him to flee to México. Fearful of more Mexican invasions, Texians of the 1800s failed to see much difference between Mexicanos and Tejanos. They forgot — or never knew or cared — that Tejanos had ranched and settled in Tejas generations before the arrival of whites and their slaves.

A billionaire Mexican American banker, Sánchez lunched with other bank presidents, oilmen, university chancellors, and former Texas governors. He contributed to Democratic and Republican political causes in his business' best interest. He fit better the Republican, business-world candidate image than did former Governor Rick Perry. Yet when it came to draw the line on the ballot, the whites felt more comfortable with Perry. Perhaps it was Sánchez's Spanish-lashing of the Anglo-sycophant Dan Morales in their historic debate, or his open friendships and business dealings with border Mexican governors that sowed the suspicions of disloyalty.

Voters had seen the oft-repeated television ad proclaiming that Sánchez's Tesoro Savings and Loan Assoication had laundered Mexican drug-gang blood money. How else could a border Chicano earn so much cash? Perry's camp painted a lurid picture to imply that a vote for Sánchez meant a vote for the bagman of ruthless Mexican killers of American undercover narcotic agents, along with a few good Chicanos.

Texans, like their Texian forefathers, struggled to accept that sterling Texans include the descendants of Seguín, and freed-man Greenbury Logan, and the mixed-race great-great-great-grandchildren of Quanah Parker and his Comanches. Our children's school history books, until recently, haven't written about Seguín, José Navarro, or Lorenzo de Zavala.

Without early exposure to the contributions of other cultures to the development of Texas, the historical significance of the Seguíns and Sánchezes are marginalized and viewed with curiosity rather than seriousness. Their value to a Texas future becomes warped by a Texas that continues to forget the original Texans.

Both Anglo and Chicano children found it hard to believe that Tejanos were heroes of the Texas independence movement or that a Tejano could become governor of Texas. Their parents dreamed of a Texas white Christmas and awoke on New Year's Day to an increasingly polychromatic world of different languages, physical features, and tastes. As they toasted the future, old Tejano acquaintances are oft-forgot.

Some Texas schools, with urging from the Mexican American community, sought to remember all who fought and died at the Álamo. After some debate, an essay contest and years of Chicano parental pressure, Arlington school district trustees agreed to name their newest high school after Juan Seguín. At the dedication ceremony on November 10, 2002, a Seguín descendant, Albert Seguín Gonzales, recounted a short history of his forefather and his decision to throw his lot with the independence movement. Principal Ed Farmer told the audience that we had forgotten how many diverse people it took to develop Texas.[7] Former Arlington Mayor Elzie Odom read a proclamation declaring the day as Juan Seguín Day in Arlington. The highlight was a gift to the school by descendants of a Juan Seguín portrait in military attire. The real prize went to the students who may learn every day, as they gaze on Seguín's image, that Texas heroes, senators, soldiers, and future governors have been and can be Tejanos—true Texans.

Texas Rangers lore, often portrayed in books and movies as fighters for law and order and protectors of the weak and innocent, has transformed them into large-than-life heroes. Why, even a major league baseball team in Arlington, Texas, was named after them. A closer look at the Texas Rangers myth revealed another contrasting, sordid image. We learned Texas myths die slow and hard on the frontier.

Next to the fallen defenders of the Álamo, Texas Rangers are the epitome of Texan toughness and courage. "One Riot, One Ranger" was their motto. But in 1915, it took several Model T-riding Rangers to shoot off their horses unarmed Mexican Americans—Jesús Bazán, sixty-seven, and his son-in-law Antonio Longoria. The killings were meant as a warning to Mexicans not to cross the Rangers.

Bazán and Longoria were well respected in the Tejano community. Longoria was a state-certified schoolteacher and US postmaster for Hidalgo County.

Like most children raised on the Lone Ranger lore, cowboy comic books and Roy Rogers westerns, Kirby Warnock, director and writer of the documentary *Border Bandits*, which aired May 16, 2005, on KERA/Channel 13, found it hard to believe that Texas Rangers killed so ruthlessly.[8] But his grandfather Roland Warnock recorded what he saw as a nineteen-year-old cowboy for his grandson's oral history project at Baylor University. In haunting words, the elder Warnock was shown talking about the troubles — when legalized terrorism raged on the border.

In his history classes, the younger Warnock learned from his professors that our Texas forefathers didn't descend from heaven but were people with failings. He didn't realize how far from heaven some Rangers had fallen until he dove into the details of the border killings. Their killings were "murder by proxy" as Texas historian Walter Prescott Webb called these all-too-common border deaths. The Texas Rangers of the early twentieth century were determined to bring banditry under control. The roiling Mexican Revolution spilled over the border, with bandits stealing cattle and horses for the Mexican armies, which the US Army was unable to stop.

Texas historians estimated that 5,000 Mexican men, women, and children were tortured, lynched, and shot at the hands of Mexican-hunting Rangers. The documentary narrator says that the US Army regulars would shout "Halt!" and then shoot —the Rangers would shoot and then shout, "Halt!" One postcard of the era featured in the documentary showed Rangers standing around dead Mexicans stacked in piles. Another displayed Rangers sitting on horses with one end of their ropes tethered to their saddle horns and the other end lassoed around Mexican bodies.

Webb captured the sentiment of the times in his book *The Texas Rangers* when he wrote: "It may be said that there is a cruel streak in the Mexican nature ... this cruelty may be a heritage from the Spanish of the Inquisition; doubtless should be attributed partly to the Indian blood."[9] According to Tejano writer Américo Paredes, a common Anglo myth was that the Mexican must be treated cruelly because by nature that is what he understands.[10]

Most myths are created to glorify heroes, teach lessons, set good examples, and bind communities. But myths that proclaim the dominance of one people over another are divisive and sinister. Manifest Destiny was a popular nineteenth-century myth used to justify the stealing of land from the American Indian. In Texas, the myth of Anglo superiority over the Mexicans is rooted in the struggle for Texas independence and has been hoisted to rationalize taking land owned by the Mexicans since the days of Spanish land grants.

In the 1910s, Texas Rangers like Henry Ransom entered the borderlands with encouragement from Governor James Ferguson. The governor said: "I sent him down there to clean it up. If he has to kill every one of them to do it, that's OK with me. I'll pardon him when I get the chance."[11] The Rangers took him at his word.

In an interview with *The Brownsville Herald*, Warnock said that he didn't want to be considered as a Texan Michael Moore: "I own a Suburban, seven guns, I drink beer and I go hunting." His intent with the documentary was not to disparage the Rangers. Instead, he meant to tell a story that his grandfather witnessed. (Roland Warnock also disclosed that Texas Ranger W.W. Sterling and Sterling's brother shot and killed Warnock's father.)

An historical marker rests at Sterling's grave in Corpus Christi. For the sake of improved Chicano-Anglo relations, as an act of apology to the

5,000 slain Mexicans and Chicanos, another marker needs to be driven into his grave to commemorate the death of the Texas Ranger myth.

Chapter 16

Chicanos at War

From the American Revolution to the Afghanistan engagement, Chicanos have fought alongside Anglos and Blacks in their country's wars. A review of Chicanos' military service will forge a deeper understanding of their claim to first class citizenship status. The Félix Longoria story dramatizes the treatment that many Mexican American soldiers faced after returning from fighting for their country.

Beatrice Longoria longed for her husband, Private Félix Longoria, to come home from the war. She yearned to see again his broad, handsome face, his dark hair and eyes, his winsome smile highlighted by a thin mustache. He had left her and their four-year-old daughter in Three Rivers, Texas, when his country called him and thousands of other young men during World War II to make the world safe for democracy. Men like thirty-two-year-old US Representative Lyndon B. Johnson enlisted in the Navy the day after the Pearl Harbor attack in December 1941. In the book *LBJ and Mexican Americans*, Julie Pycior wrote that, after Johnson flew as an observer in a single bombing mission in the Pacific, General Douglas MacArthur awarded him the Silver Star.[12] Friends in Congress were important to the politically astute. Heeding the summons of President Franklin Delano Roosevelt in July 1942 for all congressmen in active duty to return to Washington, LBJ did so.[13]

Photo 25. Sgt. Gabriel Pérez

Courtesy of Emerico Pérez, Emerico Photography.
Sergeant Pérez is pictured at Fort Leatherneck, Afghanistan, pointing to Latin Express CDs, a Fort Worth-based band.

Thousands of miles away in North Africa, Dr. Hector García and his infantry unit were slugging it out with Field Marshal Erwin Rommel's Afrika Korps. García later landed in Italy, fighting and serving in the Army Medical Corps to treat the wounded and dying GIs. For his combat and medical services, he received the Bronze Star with six battle stars.

On June 16, 1945, seven months after Longoria kissed his wife and child farewell, he volunteered to hunt for retreating Japanese in the Cagayan Valley of Luzon in the Philippines. MacArthur had lived up to his promise to return. It was time to repay the humiliation of the American and Filipino defeat in 1941 and their horrible treatment in the Bataan Death March. (According to Pycior, a quarter of the American prisoners on the march were Chicanos).

But the Japanese fought with tenacity, forcing the Americans to pay dearly for every foot of land they took back. Advancing through woods, the patrol approached suspected Japanese positions. An enemy rifleman spotted the Americans and opened fire. Men fell, others jumped for cover and returned fire. Longoria's breath and soul were torn swiftly away on a Philippines mountainside, shot dead in the first volley.

Beatrice Longoria and her in-laws wished for Félix's body to come home to Three Rivers, the town that his father, Guadalupe Longoria, had helped found. After petitioning the Army, the family received the good news in 1948 that the military agreed to send the body stateside to the cemetery of the family's choosing.

Then the bad news followed, and the unfinished battle for democracy in America resumed.

Tom Kennedy, proprietor of Rice Funeral Home, owned the only cemetery in Three Rivers. As in life, dead white and brown Texans were separated by Southern customs. A barbed-wire fence demarcated the Mexican and white cemetery sections. The reason given for the segregation was that, at the time, the cemetery was getting too crowded to include Mexican graves. Lest the bones of browns taint the hallowed grounds holding the bones of whites, the segregation of the dead was a common practice in Texas. Robert Caro wrote in his book *Master of the Senate* that Kennedy refused Beatrice Longoria's request to hold a wake in his funeral home because "the whites won't like it."[14] Instead, he recommended that she do what all the other Mexican American families in Three Rivers did until then: have the wake at her home.

Texas in 1949 was the land of Mexican-hunting Texas Rangers, King Ranch cacique overseers, racist business owners, poll taxes, Mexican and white schools, Mexican and white sides of town, Mexican and white churches, *patrón* farm bosses and cheap Mexican labor.

If a white woman and a Mexican man fell in love, better the Mexican leave town than risk violence. Chicanos were loathed, commonly called greasers, pepper-bellies, beaners, meskins. They were guests on land that their forefathers once owned but now were barely tolerated by the new owners. It was also the time of returning Mexican American veterans like Dr. Hector García. While convalescing from a kidney infection contracted from his long hours as an emergency room physician, he decided that it was time for Mexican American GIs to assert their American rights.

For those veterans who had defeated the armies of the fascists, liberated Paris, Rome, and Manila, freed surviving Jews at Dachau and other concentration camps, the specter of a master race in Texas tore at the heart of the reason that America had fought a world war on two fronts and lost so many American lives.

On March 26, 1948, 700 Mexican American men gathered at Lamar High School in Corpus Christi to hear García explain the need to form a veterans' organization to fight for the same educational, health, and financial benefits for Mexican American GIs that white GIs received. Although local American Legions and Veterans of Foreign Wars organizations helped white veterans, these institutions didn't welcome Mexican Americans.

That night, the American GI Forum was formed — so called to emphasize that although the membership was primarily Mexican American, they were just as American and patriotic as whites. Sara Moreno, Beatrice's sister and president of the American GI Forum's girls' club, knew firsthand García's bravery, intelligence, and organizing skills. When she heard of the funeral home director's refusal, she asked García to intervene.

Henry A.J. Ramos recounts in his book *The American GI Forum* a telephone conversation between García and Kennedy:

"Well, you see, it's this way. This is a small town, and you know how it is. I'm sure you understand. I am the only funeral home here, and I just have to do what the white people want. The white people just won't like it."[15]

"But, Mr. Kennedy, this man is a veteran, a soldier who was killed in action and he is worthy of our greatest honors. Doesn't that make a difference?"

"No, that doesn't make a difference. You know how the Latin people get drunk and lay around all the time. The last time the Latin Americans used the home they had fights and got drunk and raised lots of noise, and it didn't look so good. We have not let them use it (the chapel) and we don't intend to let them start now. I don't dislike Mexican people, but I have to run my business ... you understand, the whites here won't like it."

In the past, such humiliation was accepted in resigned silence, as another misfortune of being born Chicano. But there came a confluence of political, moral, and historical river currents that moved a people to stand silent no longer, to release the passion for decency, justice, and morality, to overcome fears of confrontation and reaction. The war had taught García and other veterans that appeasement of Nazis, racists, and their institutions perpetuated a culture of hatred. Combat veterans had seen death many times and knew that the sweetness of life comes not from its length but from the daily sip of the nectar of courage.

That day, García called George Groh, a reporter for the *Corpus Christi Caller-Times*, and told him of the incident. Groh confirmed Kennedy's stance when the funeral director said to him, "We never have made a practice of letting Mexicans use the chapel and we don't want to start now."[16]

García also sent seventeen protest telegrams to members of the media, the Legislature, and the Texas congressional delegation. He called for a protest meeting of the Corpus Christi American GI Forum chapter for the next night.

In the morning, newspapers across the country, including *The New York Times*, carried stories of the Three Rivers incident. Nationally syndicated radio commentator Walter Winchell told his listening audience, "The state of Texas which looms so large on the map, looks mighty small tonight."[17]

According to Caro's *Master of the Senate*, Johnson was so moved by García's telegram and the plight of Longoria's family that he said, speaking of the national cemetery near the District of Columbia, "By God, we'll bury him in Arlington."[18]

That night at the American GI Forum protest meeting, García took the stage and read a telegram that he had just received from Johnson:

"I deeply regret to learn that the prejudice of some individuals extends beyond this life. ... However, I have today made arrangements to have Félix Longoria buried with full military honors in Arlington National Cemetery here at Washington where the honored dead of our nation's wars rest. Or, if his family prefers to have his body interred nearer his home, he can be reburied at Fort Sam Houston National Military Cemetery at San Antonio. There will be no cost. ... This injustice and prejudice is deplorable. I am happy to have a part in seeing that this Texas hero is laid to rest with the honor and dignity his service deserves."[19] With such national support, the stock of the American GI Forum rose, and the Three Rivers white community and the Texas Legislature found itself on the defensive. Exposed in all their racist ugliness to the world, they pursued various deceptive machinations to paint the Longoria family as the culprits and Johnson as a political meddler pandering to the Mexican American vote.

In the words of an editorial in the *Three Rivers News*, "No town in South Texas has better relations with Americans of Mexican descent... hasty action by Senator Johnson was largely responsible for the unfavorable publicity."[20]

Caro wrote that funeral director Kennedy released a statement that explained that he "discouraged" the wake at the funeral home because he had heard that Beatrice Longoria and her in-laws were feuding about her alleged dating of another man and feared a disturbance at the funeral home. However, he was now willing to overlook that and welcomed the use of his funeral home by the Longorias.

The town's chamber of commerce president, the mayor, and the city secretary went to Guadalupe Longoria's home to persuade him to sign a typed statement stating that he and the family wished his son to be buried at Three Rivers but his son's wife kept them out of the funeral arrangements.

Guadalupe Longoria refused to sign. Instead, he released another statement: "If any embarrassment has been caused by this case to anyone, I am sorry, but after all, I did not create a feeling of prejudice which seems to exist in many places in Texas . . . I think we would only be fooling ourselves to try to leave the impression that people of Mexican descent are treated the same as anyone else [in] Texas."[21]

The Legislature formed a five-man committee in 1949 to investigate the alleged discrimination. After listening to testimony, four of the committee members concluded that there was no evidence of racist practices by the funeral director. At the same time that the hearings were taking place in the Three Rivers Rotary Club building, the white owner of a barbershop next door told a Mexican American veteran who asked for a haircut, "We don't serve Mexicans here."[22]

The fifth committee member, Frank Oltorf, wrote a minority report so convincing that it persuaded one of the four to withdraw his name from the majority report. The Legislature never incorporated the report into the records and took no action.[23]

The Longoria-Three Rivers incident galvanized the Mexican American civil rights movement in Texas. It dramatized to the world that the fight for democracy never really ended with the defeat of the Axis. Indeed, the fight goes on today in the subtle and sometimes not-so-subtle racism seen and heard in workplaces, schools, churches, private clubs, and neighborhoods across America.

The fight is not one of bullets but of hardened hearts, entrenched customs, attitudes and beliefs involving people of diverse cultures, class, and color. Today we perceive that our country's greatest threats are from foreign enemies bent on destroying our way of life. In reality, the greatest subverters of democracy are fears of our growing diversity. As long as we harbor and act on these fears, there will be a continual need for civil rights groups like the American GI Forum, LULAC, and the National Council of La Raza to challenge those who despise Chicanos, question their patriotism, and ignore their historical contributions to this country's greatness.

On a cold February 16, 1949, at Arlington National Cemetery, rain fell on the families gathered around eighteen graves of American servicemen who had been killed in action. Listening to the playing of Taps and a rifle volley salute were Beatrice Longoria, her daughter, and other relatives; Senator Johnson and his wife; General Harry H. Vaughan, President Truman's military aide; several congressmen; and Mexican diplomats.

A teary Beatrice Longoria accepted the American flag that draped her husband's coffin. She had finally brought her soldier home to the land of the free and the brave.

There were many Longorias who died in the Pacific and European theaters of war during War World II. Yet, the ample evidence of their participation is often neglected in current history books or documentaries.

Ken Burns' 1990 documentary *The Civil War* hurled him onto the national stage as one of this country's premier documentary filmmakers. His exhaustive research brought the Civil War era to life through still photos of the times, moving narration, and period music.

Several Chicano scholars, journalists, and politicos shook their head in disappointment that Burns didn't live up to his past with his film project on another war. He failed to use a single photo or spend any time telling the Latino experience in his fourteen-hour documentary about World War II, *The War.*

Sad to say, the glaring failing didn't surprise: The omission of Latinos from American's military history had happened before. Historians, like most people, were influenced by cultural biases of their time and before. Burns, no doubt, had seen war correspondent videos, movies, and books about the band of brothers that stormed across Europe and the Far East. These works tended to glorify the Audie Murphys but neglected to mention the José Lópezes, both Texas recipients of the Medal of Honor for gallantry under fire. Of the two, whom do you remember?

Burns ignored or forgot the works of Chicano chroniclers such as *Among the Valiant* by Raúl Morin or the *US Latino and Latina WWII Oral History Project* directed by Maggie Rivas-Rodriguez, associate professor of journalism at the University of Texas at Austin. It's hard to imagine that he wasn't aware that an estimated 500,000 Latinos took part in the war and that eleven received the Medal of Honor. For baby boomer Chicanos who have prominently displayed World War II photos of their dads, uncles, and grandfathers, preserved military uniforms, stored battle ribbons and medals or folded flags given at the burial of their kin, the omission was offensive. Mexican Americans, to a fault, tend not to boast of their war exploits or sacrifices for their country. They accept their military service as the price of American freedom. But we who benefit should not forget.

Photo 26. Seaman 1st Class Fernándo González

Courtesy of the Fernándo González personal collection.
Seaman 1st Class Fernándo González, second from left on back row, with fellow sailors on USS *Sands* destroyer, 1944. [24]

A press release about *The War* by the Public Broadcasting Service said that the documentary "explores the history and horror of the Second World War from an American perspective by following the fortunes of so-called ordinary men and women who get caught up in the greatest cataclysm in human history."[25]

Photo 27. Private Joseph Gonzales in Germany, 1945

Author's personal collection.

A true American perspective about ordinary people should have included García, Valderas, Sánchez, and Reyes. From Southwestern towns, ranches, and cities, Chicanos set aside their second-class citizenship status to join up, suit up, and jump out of planes over occupied Europe or storm Pacific islands. Their blood flowed as quickly as that of any first-class American who was captured, wounded, or killed in action. This omission could almost be understandable if the film had been created in the 1950s, when Chicanos were politically almost nonexistent, or if Burns' other films lacked depth and detail. But this film, described as "in the can," was made in the millennium when Latinos ascended to become this country's largest minority group. In the six years needed to make the film, Burns neglected to shed the cultural blinders that make Latinos invisible in US history.

On February 16, 2007, the National Association of Hispanic Journalists wrote Paula Kerger, PBS CEO, to say: "Many of us remember the pride in our elders' voices as they recalled their roles in ensuring an Allied victory. ... So it escapes us how Ken Burns could have made a seven-part series that does not mention the contributions of Latinos."[26]

The obvious answer: Burns wasn't as brilliant as PBS and supporters make him out to be. Like other directors who have risen to fame on the crest of outstanding work, Burns has developed a reputation that made him nearly invulnerable to accusations of unfinished work. Yet a World War II documentary that failed to show Chicanos sending their sons to hell, living a second-class status while supporting the war effort, and burying their dead soldier boys in the Mexican side of cemeteries, was incomplete and insulting. The original release date was September 16, 2007, Mexican Independence Day and the second day of Hispanic Heritage Month. After much protest, the film producers changed the release date to September 23, 2007. In addition, Burns added twenty-eight minutes of footage of interviews of two Latinos and one American Indian veterans.

Chicanos didn't ask for special treatment—they just asked for equal respect in recalling *The War.*

They earned it.

Chicanos again responded to the call to arms and joined up for their trip to the Iraqi front. Researchers discovered that in an all-volunteer military, the soldiers' ranks primarily consist of the lower classes. The Iraq war was no different and Chicanos found themselves doing much of the fighting and dying.

Photo 28. Marine Sergeant Gabriel Pérez of Fort Worth, Texas with Iraqi soldiers in Iraq, 2008

Courtesy of Emerico Pérez, Emerico Photography.

Retired General Tommy Franks told thousands at a Get Motivated seminar in March 2005 in Dallas that every American generation experienced war. "We can wish war would go away; it's not going to happen," he said.[27] With indoor fireworks and flames shooting up, the patriotic crowd clapped and cheered the old warrior's fervor. Earlier, former New York Mayor Rudy Giuliani had told the audience that courage was a matter of mastering our fears and then acting.

And so we did, invading Iraq on March 20, 2003. In Operation Iraqi Freedom, 4,424 American soldiers and civilians died as of November 20, 2015, to give the Iraqis the right to vote and dip their finger in purple ink. [28]

If Americans were so inclined about fighting terrorists and spreading democracy, it became paramount to examine who exactly was paying for our patriotism with their lives. Chicano soldiers fought and died courageously throughout all of America's wars, as chronicled in such books as *Among the Valiant* by Raúl Morin. Recent research findings that Chicanos died at disproportionate rates at the opening of the Iraq invasion should come as little surprise.

According to Brian Gifford, sociologist from the University of California at Berkeley, Latino soldiers found themselves in the thick of the fighting. Gifford, reviewing military casualties during 2003-2004 combat, found: "If any group of minority service members faces an elevated risk of casualties, it is Hispanics under high-intensity combat conditions. . . When US tactics dictate a more active, aggressive role in finding and attacking enemy targets, Hispanics incur casualties in excess of their participation in ground combat units."[29]

His research found that at the beginning of the war, Latinos comprised 11 percent of Army and Marine combat personnel and less than 9 percent of all active duty personnel. However, they accounted for 16 percent of US military deaths during the opening of the war.[30] For first- and second-generation Latinos, many of them immigrants with low educational levels and limited English, gun-slinging was their specialty. Like their rural white comrades, they found the military to be their ticket to education and world travel. Juan Castillo and Bill Bishop reported in the *Austin American-Statesman* on February 27, 2005, that of the fifty-six immigrant soldiers who received posthumous citizenship, thirty-one were from Spanish-speaking countries and eighteen from México. In comparison, Gifford found that Anglos were under-represented in combat deaths in the initial phase of the war.

Although Anglos made up 65 percent of all active-duty soldiers, they comprised 60.9 percent of the deaths in the invasion. He attributed this disparity to their officer corps protection and rear echelon support duties. But fortunes changed after President Bush declared, "Mission accomplished."

During the occupation phase, Iraqi insurgents resorted to roadside bombings, urban warfare, and mortar and suicide attacks all along the American supply lines and rear command centers. Seventy percent of soldiers killed in this phase were Anglo.

According to Gifford, it was a myth that minorities suffered an inordinate number of casualties after the initial invasion. However, an *Austin American-Statesman* statistics consultant, Robert Cushing, found that Texas Chicano soldiers died at 60 percent higher rates than the country's military-age population.

Castillo and Bishop reported: "Of the 142 Texans killed in Iraq as of February 19, 2005, 54 —or 38 percent—were Hispanic, although Hispanics account for only 32 percent of military-age Texans."

Unlike the general population, Latinos had enough of the Iraq War. A majority of Latinos wanted American troops to withdraw from Iraq, according to survey results released in February 2005 by the Pew Hispanic Center.[31] The survey showed that 55 percent disapproved of Bush's handling of the war. In comparison, the general public responded that 52 percent disapproved. When asked whether the US made the right or wrong decision in using military force against Iraq, 51 percent of the Latino responders said the wrong decision, while 46 percent of the general public responded the same. Chicanos wised up to the fact that there were safer ways to prove your patriotism than going to war.

Sociologist David Segal found that social class determined who fought. In an all-volunteer military, the top 25 percent of the economic strata were no-shows. There were too many country Johnnies and barrio Juanitos toting guns in Iraq. If our goal were to spread democracy, we should encourage the bluebloods to master their fears and join the ranks of America's freedom fighters.

Although in 2011 President Obama pulled out most of the American troops, my guess was that the war would have come to a speedier end if more of the upper class's sons and daughters had toted a gun in Iraq.

Chapter 17

Chicano Heroes

In the summer of 2011, the Texas Board of Education wrangled about the inclusion of Thurgood Marshall and César Chávez in the school history books. Conservative members resisted their inclusion, stating that their contributions didn't rise to the level of Thomas Jefferson and other traditional American heroes. Public pressure and moderate and liberal school board members prevailed in the final decision to include these heroic, historical figures. Chicano students need to learn about outstanding Mexican Americans who struggled mightily to overcome personal and social barriers to reach the peak of their chosen fields. All students may then understand that great Americans come in all colors.

On the cool morning of March 17, 1966, César Chávez, cane in hand, told about seventy farm workers waiting for him, "*Nos vamos.*" The words "We go" launched the most pivotal march in the struggle of *La Causa*, The Cause. Farm workers took turns carrying the banner of the *Virgen de Guadalupe* along the 350-mile Easter march from Delano, California, to Sacramento – the state capital.

Photo 29. Dolores Huerta collage with Fort Worth César Chávez marchers in the background, May 2014.

Courtesy of Emerico Pérez, Emerico Photography.

The march was symbolic of Chávez's painful ordeal to rally farm workers to confront corporate growers' guns, dogs, and goons for better wages, working, and living conditions. Chávez's turn-the-other-cheek practice belied his fierce determination to see the fight in the field to the end.

Growers physically beat him and his union members and even killed several. Police unlawfully arrested strikers during their protests and on one occasion slapped chains on Chávez. But they never shackled his passionate desire for decency, justice, and freedom. He witnessed many hard-working, hungry families, weathered and aged too soon from stoop labor, living in shacks. He resented the lack of water and restrooms and the spraying of pesticides over fields while men, women, and children toiled. He was riled at low wages and the lack of pensions, benefits, and healthcare in a country espousing, "In God We Trust."

Like David, he was compelled to go into the field to face the Goliath growers. US Attorney General Robert Kennedy observed that Chávez was "one of the heroic figures of our time."[32]

Chávez challenged farm workers in the Delano grape strike to wipe the dust from their faces, rise from their knees, keep their eyes on the *Virgen* and follow him to justice. After six months of national boycotts and strikes against several corporate grape growers in the Coachella Valley, the National Farm Workers Association still was unable to wrest concessions. As farm workers' morale flagged and the young union faced possible defeat, Chávez drew on Mexican history and religion to persuade campesinos to sacrifice and keep faith with *La Causa.* Mixing religion, politics, and drama, Chávez tagged the march *"Peregrinación, penitencia, revolución."* In a solicitation letter to supporters, he explained that he adopted the centuries-old Spanish tradition of Lenten processions.

"The penitential procession is also in the blood of the Mexican American ... they hope by the march to set themselves at peace with the Lord so that the justice of their cause will be purified of all lesser motivation," he wrote.[33]

He explained that Mexicans traveled long distances to pray before the image of the *Virgen* at the Basilica de Guadalupe in México City. On the last mile, he said, some believers walked on knees. He added: "The revolutions of México were primarily uprisings of the poor, fighting for bread and for dignity. The Mexican American is also a child of the revolution."[34]

The primary difference between the Mexican and Chávez "revolutions" was his insistence on nonviolent resistance. Drawing heavily from the teachings of Martin Luther King Jr. and Mohandas Gandhi, Chávez told farm workers that no union victory could justify the loss of a grower's or farm worker's life.

Runners preceded the marchers to rally the farm workers along the route. In town after town, the residents welcomed them, offering food and shelter. *El Teatro Campesino*, a farm workers theater group, dramatized their struggle with satiric jabs at the growers and corrupt police. In the evenings, they sang *La Causa's* theme song, "*De Colores*." The marchers would gather for morning Mass, raise the *Virgen* banner and set off. As they trudged on, their ranks swelled until 10,000 people marched into Sacramento on Easter, April 10, 1966.

Governor Pat Brown was away vacationing with Frank Sinatra when Chávez stepped up to the microphone on the Capitol steps before a sea of signs and banners. To the shouts of "*Viva la Huelga, Viva La Causa, Viva Chávez*!" he told the marchers that Schenley Industries, a grower, had agreed to sign a contract with the NFWA. To commemorate the fortieth anniversary of the march in 2006 and to encourage civic engagement, the César Chávez Foundation called for nationwide observances around his birthday, March 31.

Since 2001, Tarrant County residents have honored the *peregrinación* with a march and rally in downtown Fort Worth. More than 4,000 Tarrant County government employees tipped their collective hat with a paid, Chávez holiday on the last Monday in March.

Again, *nos vamos* on César's *Marcha de la Virgen.*

Another Chicano hero often overlooked in American history books is Rodolfo "Corky" Gonzales, the fiery ex-boxer from Colorado.

The Mexican American activist heavyweight died April 12, 2005. Gonzales, seventy-six — prizefighter, migrant worker, La Raza Unida organizer, and poet — said his final *adios* to his family and followers.

Throughout the 1960s—in high schools, colleges, pool halls, cantinas, and gyms, using mimeographed paper, books, and barrio newspapers—

Chicanos recited or listened to his epic poem "I Am Joaquín" as a paean to their pride.[35] It was the spring of the Chicano movement. The Coloradan was the prince of Brown Power America and a counterpoint to the assimilation rush into the Great Society:

> I am Joaquín.
> I must fight And win this struggle for my sons,
> and they know from me Who I am.
> Part of the blood that runs deep in me
> Could not be vanquished by the Moors[36]

As the Moors couldn't conquer his Spaniard ancestors in the Old World, neither would he allow racist practices to oppress his people. Gonzales was overshadowed by the fame of United Farm Workers organizer César Chávez and La Raza Unida party founder José Ángel Gutiérrez. Mexican American youths may not be aware of his drive and courage in protesting police brutality, inadequate housing, educational failure, and the Vietnam War. If so, their Chicano history lessons were incomplete.

Born June 18, 1928, in Denver, Gonzales was the youngest of five brothers and three sisters. His father emigrated from México and raised him on tales of the Mexican Revolution, history, and pride. The stories helped instill an indomitable spirit in the Gonzales family to persevere through the hardships of the Depression, migrant work throughout New Mexico and Colorado and many schools. His mother died when he was two. At sixteen, he graduated from a Denver high school.

In the ring, he won Golden Glove championships as a featherweight and earned a professional boxing record of 65-1-9. At one point, *Ring Magazine* ranked him No. 3 in the world. The Colorado Sports Hall of Fame inducted him in 1988.

Gonzales began his political activist career in 1955 as the first Chicano district captain for the Democratic Party in Denver. He later acted as the coordinator of the Viva Kennedy campaign in Colorado.

His zeal to effect social change brought him into conflict with his Democratic Party bosses. Moderation, conciliation, and compromise were not suited to his pugnacious temperament. He just couldn't stomach the go-it-safe course that the Democrats and especially moderate Mexican Americans followed when he witnessed the rampant poverty, police mistreatment, and educational failures around him.

He was like Joaquín: "I rode with Pancho Villa, crude and warm./ A tornado at full strength, nourished and inspired by the passions and the fire of all his earth, people."

During the 1960s, the media portrayed race relations primarily as a black-Anglo issue. Eloquent speakers such as Martin Luther King Jr., Malcolm X, Eldridge Cleaver, and Angela Davis captured the television lens and print news coverage.

Under the media radar, Gonzales and other movement leaders were pushing the brown community to mobilize. He and other Chicano organizers respected and learned from the black civil rights movement. But they knew that the success of their struggle for economic and social justice rested on Chicano shoulders. Gonzales represented the eloquent, angry Chicano who identified with a bloody, glorious past but was now caught in a daily struggle for economic survival. Like other Chicano leaders, he boycotted, picketed, marched, organized, and exhorted his people to master their fears and seize their destinies. The vital question to him and others was how much to sacrifice one's ethnic identity for a full stomach. It's a question still asked and answered daily by many Chicanos.

In 1966, he founded his Crusade for Justice — a grass roots, civil rights, and cultural movement. He gained national prominence for his youth conferences and a call for a return to Aztlán, the ancient homeland of the Aztecs in the Southwestern United States. Gonzales envisioned a retaking of the land once possessed by the Mexicans. With the rise in the Mexican American population throughout the Southwest and a greater acceptance of multiculturalism, the retaking may be more of a reality in a cultural sense.

Gonzales offered his people an option to the grin-and-bear-it assimilation process. He inspired Chicanos to say loudly and proudly, "I am Joaquín."

Along with community activists, Mexican Americans have written passionately about their struggles to enter the American mainstream. Rubén Salazar, a writer for the *Los Angeles Times*, gained prominence for his insightful perspective of the Chicano movement of the 1960s.

On August 29, 1970, journalist Rubén Salazar was too close to the action he was covering. As news director for the Spanish-language TV station KMEX and a columnist for the *Los Angeles Times*, he and his crew were reporting on the National Chicano Moratorium March against the Vietnam War. They witnessed 500 baton-swinging, tear-gas-throwing police confront 30,000 peaceful marchers at Laguna Park in East Los Angeles. The ensuing riot left hundreds injured and three dead, including Salazar. A sheriff's tear-gas projectile struck him in the head.

Chicano activists immediately elevated Salazar as a martyr to their cause, a move he probably would have thought nonsense. He considered himself first a journalist whose job was to cover the news accurately and fairly. Chicano leaders, including the militant Brown Berets, praised his columns as a true reflection of the socioeconomic plight of the Chicano community. His writing skills and insight into Chicano culture pleased editors and activists alike — a feat hard to achieve for minority journalists.

In 1968, Chicano students walked out of their Los Angeles high schools protesting inferior education, discriminatory treatment, and the lack of a culturally relevant curriculum. The Chicano Movement was building steam throughout the Southwest as activists such as César Chávez, José Ángel Gutiérrez, and Corky Gonzales rallied support for their causes. It was hard to ignore thousands of Chicanos marching, boycotting, rallying, and politicking.

Editors at the *Los Angeles Times* realized that their benign neglect of the largest minority group in their city was intolerable and assigned

Salazar as their point man to get the stories. A political moderate who resented the term "Chicano journalist," Salazar at first was reluctant to take on the assignment. But as he interviewed Brown Berets leaders and other activists, attended Chicano conferences, investigated police brutality cases, and read statistics about the disproportionate numbers of Chicano soldiers killed in Vietnam, he developed a deeper understanding of *La Causa.* Fortunately for the paper's readers, his ability to translate this understanding into well-written columns helped raise the awareness of Angelenos beyond the slogans of *Si Se Puede*, Brown Power and *Viva La Raza.* (In 1974, the future mayor of Los Angeles, Antonio Villaraigosa, was honing his protest, organizing, and public speaking skills at UCLA.)

In a February 6, 1970, column titled "Who Is a Chicano? And What Is It the Chicanos Want?" Salazar wrote, "A Chicano is a Mexican American with a non-Anglo image of himself. He resents being told Columbus 'discovered' America when the Chicano's ancestors, the Mayans and Aztecs, founded highly sophisticated civilizations centuries before Spain financed the Italian explorer's trip to the 'New World'."[37]

He went on to say that despite the Chicanos' large numbers, they were politically impotent in Los Angeles. Thus in 1970 — as in 2015— Latinos, Chicanos, Mexican Americans or whatever your preferred labels were politically shooting blanks. Salazar was unafraid to state the obvious. He concluded his column with "Chicanos, then, are merely fighting to become 'Americans.' Yes, but with a Chicano outlook."[38]

The major reason for the Chicano political weakness in the early twenty-first century was their lack of voting power. As long as Chicanos stayed away from the polls, politicians had little reason to fear that the "sleeping giant" would stir from his *siesta.* During the 2015 presidential candidates' campaigning, virulent anti-immigration ranting stirred some outbursts from immigrant activists that the candidates did the community a favor by raising the Mexicans' and Chicanos' anger. Unfortunately, the undocumented weren't able to vote legally and not enough Chicano citizens cast ballots. Grass roots immigrant organizations and their allies conducted national campaigns to pressure Congress to pass an Immigration Reform Bill to no avail. Not until millions of lower and middle class Chicano citizens who vote take on this fight could this bill pass. Facing well-organized opposition such as Tea Party members who vote and Chicano politicos who understood the Realpolitik that their tenure depended on appeasing their white constituency and sponsors, Chicanos' and Mexicans' interests were marginalized. Eventually the sheer growth of the Chicano population to a tipping point where a critical mass of voters outweighed the opposition would Chicanos acquire political might. The power question then arose: Were Chicanos willing to wait for their young to experience a political epiphany and vote or would they have the *ganas* to do the hard work of uniting, organizing and mobilizing behind authentic leaders? It was time to kick the snoring, slumbering giant out of bed.

Salazar addressed the undocumented immigration issue in an April 24, 1970, column "The 'Wetback' Problem Has More Than Just One Side." (Editorial standards have since changed, frowning on the use of the w-word.) He wrote, "A wetback lives in constant fear. Fear that he will be discovered. Fear of what might happen to him once *la migra* finds him. Fear that he will not be paid before being deported. The wetback employers know no such fear. There is no law against hiring wetbacks. There is only law against being a wetback."[39]

Rumblings from Washington and 2015 presidential candidates foretold major crackdowns on those hiring the undocumented. In 1970, Salazar wrote, "It is obvious that the United States and México must talk and plan on the highest level to forestall an even more serious wetback explosion in the future."[40]

Man, was he right.

The media of the 1940s and 1950s weren't accustomed to brash-talking Mexican American sports figures with talent to back up their words. Richard "Pancho" González, tennis great, took his verbal licks as well gave them out. A fiery temper, killer serve, and feline swiftness propelled

González to the top ranks of tennis from 1948 to 1969. At six-foot-three, he towered over most of his opponents with his natural skills and competitiveness.

Spike TV featured the documentary *Pancho González: The Latino Legend of Tennis*, on September 16, 2006, profiling the man and his struggle to become one of tennis' greatest champions. Through actual tennis footage, re-enactments, and interviews with professional players, celebrities, former wives, and kin, González prowls the court again. The documentary and interviews and correspondence with his brother before his death painted a picture of González' climb to tennis fame.

His name captures the enigma of his tennis world bad-boy persona. When an Anglo tennis acquaintance called out for "Pancho" in front of his house, González' mother, Carmen, told the man no Panchos lived in her home. She felt insulted that someone would use an ethnic slur for her first-born, Richard.

Carmen quickly identified her son's keen competitiveness and athletic skills. At ten, his keen hand-eye accuracy won him the Los Angeles marble-shooting championship. With her seamstress money, she bought Richard a tennis racket. She hoped that he would learn to compete like the gentlemen in México whom she recalled watching play tennis. González became enamored with the game, sleeping with his racket and practicing at a local public court. He ignored his father's discouragement and, despite a lack of formal lessons, entered and won city tournaments.

The tennis establishment felt uncomfortable with González' raw talent and consistent thrashing of their favorite, Herbie Flam. Before deciding who would represent Southern California at the under-fifteen nationals, the Southern California Tennis Association (SCTA) gave González an ultimatum: Go to school or be banned from competition. González, who had dropped out of five schools, preferred to play tennis. The SCTA gave Flam the nod to go to the nationals.

González allowed "Pancho" to stick as a name, but told his family to call him Richard. It was as if he taunted the tennis-club set to tag him what they wished; in the end he would uncoil, swing, and smash until they called him "Champ."

At the Los Angeles Tennis Club, frequented by Hollywood celebrities and the social set, González was mistaken for the help. He quickly dispelled their wrong impressions when he picked up a wooden racket and served at 120 miles per hour. González understood that to break into the tennis world and overcome class hostility, a kid from the Los Angeles barrios had to become good — world-class good. He developed a graceful, attacking game and honed a warrior's edge. In 1949, at age twenty-one, he held the clay, grass, and indoors national championship titles.

Along with glory came boos. His temper would flare during matches, lashing out at audiences, referees, and opponents. Instead of making him lose concentration, his rage would focus his game. A Chicano tough in a gentleman's sport roiled the press and fans. The media accused him of eating, drinking, and eating too many tacos, according to his brother Ralph. A radio show about bad boy González dramatized a pool hall knife fight that explained the scar that marred his good looks. The González family was outraged. The truth was that he had fallen in a scooter accident as a boy.

The Mexican Consulate offered the Mexican American champion $50,000 a year to give up his US citizenship to become a Mexican citizen, playing on the Mexican national team. González turned down the offer, stating he would never forsake his US citizenship for any amount of money.

González beat the best of his era: Ken Rosewall, Jack Kramer, and Ted Schroeder. In later years, past his prime, he beat rising young players such as Jimmy Connors, John Newcombe, Stan Smith, and Arthur Ashe. At forty-one, he played Charlie Pasarell, twenty-five, at Wimbledon's Centre Court. In five hours and twelve minutes, over two days, they played the longest match in the history of Wimbledon up to that point. When

González stumbled and fell, Pasarell commented he hoped González would call it quits. But the old warrior kept fighting back, answering serves and volleys as if he had gotten drunk at the fountain of youth. González beat the kid.

His former wife Madelyn Darrow recalled the English crowd shouting at his victory "Pancho, Pancho, Pancho."

Legacy calls him the champion.

Another Pancho realized the public relations benefits from mass media to further his interests. Pancho Villa embraced the movies to promote his revolutionary army and México.

From the safety of rooftops and across the Río Grande, Americans watched Pancho Villa's army storm buildings full of armed *federales*. When an American film crew crossed the river in 1914 to capture Villa and his *Dorados* (golden horsemen), reality rolled into a celluloid, tragicomic view of the general and the Mexican Revolution.

In a Dallas preview of an HBO movie aired September 7, 2003, *And Starring Pancho Villa as Himself* (with Antonio Banderas in the lead role), about 200 moviegoers were treated to a sympathetic look at a complex man who still stirs Mexican and American passions.

A shrewd revolutionary, Villa had grasped that $25,000 for the film rights could buy much needed guns and bullets for his *División del Norte*. He also sought American and Mexican public support for his uprising against dictator Victoriano Huerta. As a propagandist, Villa knew that the lens was mightier than the sword. The result was an unusual contract signed by Villa and the Mutual Film Corporation to film in the midst of battles.

Villa agreed to fight only during the daylight needed for the camera (although he didn't always honor this part of the contract) and to stage battles for dramatic effect. Thus we have one of the first cases of the American media meddling in international affairs for profit. In an ironic HBO scene, William Randolph Hearst's newspapers blast the film company for its role in the fighting. It's ironic because it was Hearst's newspaper company that in 1898 concocted the Spanish conspiracy behind the explosion of the battleship *Maine* in Cuba that fanned the Spanish-American War.

Before Villa's infamous but successful raid on the Army garrison in Columbus, New Mexico, that killed seventeen Americans in 1916, D.W. Griffith wagered that Americans were ready for their first action film. Griffith expected actual battlefield coverage to sell more movie tickets than the fake gunfights in his other films. As long as Mexicans were killing Mexicans, an American audience would find the fighting scenes to be exotic matinee entertainment.

Like American TV cameramen and photographers of the Vietnam War who captured the jungle and street fighting between Americans and the North Vietnamese, and indirectly stirred anti-war sentiments, the Mutual Film Corporation's film crew dodged bullets and shells to film Mexican glory and horror.

Villa's humor, charm, and genius impressed the young producer, a Harvard graduate who sported his school's emblem and motto on his tie. The Ivy Leaguer found a Mexican Veritas — truth — in the cactus land that forced him and his crew to cringe often.

The HBO film portrays Villa as a man of contradictions. In one scene, he's patting children and giving them candy. In another, he instructs two boys to run a foot race, and the faster one is ordered into battle. As Villa comforts the mother of a dead revolutionary, the film crew tries too late to capture the scene. But they do record Villa shooting the wife of a clerk who attacks him after his men mistakenly execute her husband. In another scene, the boy who lost the race watches alone the reels of the fighting and sees his friend, rifle in hand, running into battle. The next moment, a bullet tears into the boy's chest and drops him to the ground. The loser of the race slows the reel and replays the moments of his friend's last foot race as if the film could bring him back.

At the first American film screening of Villa and the fighting, the audience laughed derisively at the posturing general, complained of his rag-tag army's dress and suggested outfitting them with better costumes. They lacked the historical perspective to appreciate the priceless film coverage they were viewing.

Although some Mexicans voiced their displeasure that a Spaniard played Villa in the HBO film (he detested them), Banderas masterfully captured Villa's wit, courage, and brutality. The actor said he prepared for the role by modulating his native Spanish to include a Mexican accent. In one scene, Villa tells the American producer that the Spaniards brought religion and the whip to the Mexicans.

For millions today on both sides of the Río Grande, Villa was México: wild, passionate, clever, charming, defiant. When the HBO movie credits rolled, a man in the audience shouted, "*Viva Villa*!"

The civilized should not forget their heroes and life lessons lest they wander clueless about the gifts their forefathers and mothers have given them. Remembrances of times past help them to cherish their freedoms.

At a career fair in 2008, more than eighty Chicano high school students were ambushed with a quiz on Mexican American heroes. They had intended to spend a Saturday talking with doctors, educators, nurses, engineers, lawyers, and other professionals about career paths. They rotated in groups of twenty to hear the panelists tell how they chose their vocations, what they enjoyed most about their work and what a typical day on the job looked like.

But in the education panel group, a panelist fired off: Who was Dolores Huerta? Juan Seguín? Rodolfo "Corky" Gonzales? César Chávez? Ché Guevara? José Ángel Gutiérrez?

Despite the celebration of Hispanic Heritage Month, September 15–October 16, most of the students were quiet — too quiet. One student identified Chávez as a farm worker advocate; another recalled that Seguín was at the Álamo. A student with the last name of Guevara knew that the

Argentinean was a communist revolutionary but couldn't recall where. A few of them remembered reading Gonzales ' celebratory poem "I Am Joaquín"; they said nothing of his civil rights work. None answered that Gutiérrez founded La Raza Unida Party in Crystal City, Texas. For the rest, the blank looks earned no points.

Was it a matter of not knowing, not caring, or not possessing historical consciousness? One of the panelists remarked that an elementary school in Fort Worth was named after the farm worker union organizer Huerta. How is it that they didn't know anything about her? Although not a true test or one that a reasonable person could conclude would prove that these Chicano students possessed a shallow understanding of their people's history, concerns did rise.

A certain degree of responsibility for the students' knowing these historical figures was vested with the schools. But it was also the students' assignment to seek out books about their cultural past. They're taught about the bravery of the Founding Fathers against the British monarchy, of the defenders of the Álamo against the Mexican government, of the victory of the Allied forces over Germany and Japan. They must also know the history of the first cowboys in Texas — the vaqueros, of the first mestizo settlements and universities in the Americas, of the separate graveyards for Chicano servicemen killed in combat fighting for their country, of Dr. Hector García and the rise of the American GI Forum.

The common danger of not knowing your people's history was repeating the mistakes of the past. A more troubling issue was thinking that the opportunity to go to high school and college was always there. The students may think that walking through the front doors of department stores or sitting at restaurant tables was always open to their families.

For those who lived through the struggles, history was much more than an intellectual pursuit. A bilingual education administrator panelist talked about her family of nine brothers and sisters. She told the students that as an elementary school student, she was paddled for speaking Spanish. In high school, she remembered, the other students received advice from the school counselor about how to get into college. When she asked for the same advice, the counselor said that was not possible because she wasn't going to college – she was poor and Mexican. She defied the counselor and the exclusion that she represented. She said that her father told her that the proudest moments of his life were the college graduations of all nine of his children.

A Texas Christian University (TCU) education professor told the students that in her native Colombia, high school students were required to perform community service. As a teen, she was assigned to teach English to uneducated factory workers. She found the work so fulfilling that she decided to pursue an education career and earned her doctorate.

Teachers can link the past and present by inviting long-term residents of North Texas to give an oral history of what it was like to live in the region. Allow the students to hear about life as a minority thirty or forty years ago. Despite the years, the emotions still resonate.

The reason to look back with an unblinking eye is not to dig up skeletons or rekindle ethnic hatreds. Links to the past will imprint on the students the struggles and sacrifices many people endured for their opportunity to excel in the classroom.

Photo 30. Stock Show Parade Vaqueros

Courtesy of the Delsa M. Pérez Collection, Genealogy, History, and Archives Unit, Fort Worth Library.

The vaqueros are riding on Main Street in downtown Fort Worth with the Tarrant County Courthouse in the background, January, 2008.

Chapter 18

Mexican Indigenous Roots

Thanksgiving and Christmas, two of the most popular holidays of the year, have Mexican indigenous roots often overlooked. Mayan and Aztec civilizations still fascinate twenty-first-century men and women for their art, religion, architecture, math, and conquests.

In the holiday season, modern lovers of Mexican cuisine should pay tribute to the Aztecs for tamales, tortillas, peppers, and chocolate. Less commonly known is their cultivation of a popular holiday plant they called *Cuetlaxochitl*.

After the Spanish conquest, the Mexicans named the brightly colored plant *Flor de Noche Buena*, or Christmas Eve Flower. Botanists call the plant *Euphorbia pulcherrima* — the "very beautiful" Euphorbia. We now know this popular, festive greenery as the poinsettia.[41]

Photo 31. *Matachines*

Courtesy of the Delsa P. Pérez Collection, Genealogy, History, and Archives Unit, Fort Worth Library
Matachines are processing with the *Virgen de Guadalupe* at the Fort Worth Convention Center, December 1998,

The Kansas State University Research and Extension web site provides a detailed history of the poinsettia's Aztec origin, its Spaniard adoption, and its discovery by North Americans. Congress became so enamored with the Mexican plant that it decreed December 12 as National Poinsettia Day. But the ancient Mexicans had long honored the brightly colored plant.

According to Pierre et Janine Soisson in *Life of the Aztecs*, the warlike Aztecs were also lovers of flowers, poetry, and the arts. As represented in the eagle and snake on the Mexican flag, the Aztecs believed in a duality of life. Surrounded by beautiful wildlife and plants, snow-capped volcanoes, constant wars, and gods' cravings for human hearts, they nurtured plants on their floating gardens and called their fights the flowery wars.

For the Aztecs, flowers represented the fragility and sweetness of life. *Cuetlaxochitl's* beauty symbolized purity. From its pagan roots, the brightly colored plant blossomed into a striking Christian symbol. Its Aztec origins don't diminish the poinsettia's charm but instead show the ability of North American society to absorb the best foods, arts, and plants of foreign cultures.

Long before Hernán Cortez, Pilgrims, Santa Claus, and the Nativity story came to the Americas, Aztecs honored their gods and decorated their homes with roses, mimosas, *Cuetlaxochitl,* and other native plants. Emperor Moctezuma would have the decorative bush, sometimes growing to ten feet tall, brought in caravans from Taxco to his gardens. The Aztecs valued the plant not only for its beauty but also for a purple dye that they extracted from its leaves. *Cuetlaxochitl's* milky white sap was treated as a tonic to combat fevers. Contrary to popular lore, poinsettia leaves are not toxic. Ohio State University conducted a study that found no basis for the claim that the poinsettia is poisonous if eaten. However, the plants should be admired and not enjoyed as a salad.

Cortez and his soldiers were impressed with the beauty of Moctezuma's floating city; but a heathen people's love of flowers and the arts couldn't stop the Spaniards from conquest.

According to the University of Vermont's Department of Plant and Soil Science, seventeenth-century Franciscan priests were the first to give Christian meanings to the plants when they were carried in Nativity processions. A Mexican legend sprang up about the plant's divine message. The popular story told about a poor Mexican girl who searched for a gift to give the baby Jesus at a Nativity scene. She fretted that she had no riches to buy a present worthy of the Christ child. Her older brother told her that her offering would take value from the love she gave despite its humble appearance. She gathered weeds alongside a road, arranged them into a bouquet and placed them at the feet of the baby Christ. Her weeds suddenly burst into a flaming red-leaf blossom. The worshippers who witnessed the scene called it a miracle, and the plant became known as the *Flor de Noche Buena.*

The Paul Ecke Ranch web site explains that the first US ambassador to México (1825–1829), Joel Poinsett, became equally enamored with the brilliant plant. A botanist with greenhouses back home in Greenville, South Carolina, he traveled the Mexican countryside admiring the varieties of Mexican greenery.[42] In 1826, when he sighted *Euphorbia pulcherrima*, he took cuttings and sent them to his greenhouse. Poinsett grew the plants and gave them to friends and botanical gardens. After showings at exhibitions, they were shipped around the country and to Europe. In 1920, Southern California horticulturist Paul Ecke promoted the plants as a Christmas favorite. Today, all fifty states grow the plant, and 90 percent of the world's poinsettias are exported from the United States.

Kansas State explained that William Prescott, historian and horticulturist, was asked to come up with a user-friendly name for *Euphorbia pulcherrima.* He had written a book called *The Conquest of México* in which he covered Poinsett's discovery of the plant. He named it the poinsettia. To commemorate the death of Poinsett, Congress declared December 12 National Poinsettia Day.

Conquerors can change names and symbols, but Aztec legacy lives on in Christian churches and homes in the bright red leaves of *Cuetlaxochitl.*

Another version of the origin of the Thanksgiving traditional celebration takes a different look at when and where the custom began.

Since Abraham Lincoln declared the last Thursday of November as the official Thanksgiving holiday, Americans have celebrated the feast to commemorate the Pilgrims' grateful sharing of food with their Indian neighbors at the Plymouth settlement in 1621. Lincoln hoped that the holiday would spur patriotism during the dark days of the Civil War. The traditional history lesson taught to children wearing paper bags, face paint, and feathers is that the Pilgrims wished to show their gratitude to

God and their Indian neighbors for helping them survive their struggles in the New World. Few in numbers and surrounded by the Wampanoag people, they learned from the Indians how to hew out a living in the wilderness.

Historians have also written that the Indian-Pilgrim relationship was far from idyllic and eventually would degenerate into King Philip's War, the deaths and enslavement of Indians, and the seizure of their lands. That's similar to an earlier event in another part of the New World.

Historians Don Adams and Teresa Kendrick, writing from Chapala, Jalisco, México, argued that the first European Thanksgiving celebration actually occurred April 30, 1598, at the south bank of the Río Bravo (now the Río Grande). Their account described how near modern-day El Paso, Don Juan Pérez de Oñate y Salazar and his expedition of more than 500 people and 7,000 head of livestock celebrated their arrival in *El Nuevo México* with a feast of fish and waterfowl.[43]

The 560 explorers consisted of Franciscan monks, Spaniards, Canary Islanders, Italians, Greeks, Cubans, Portuguese, Africans, mestizos, a volunteer from Flanders, and Indian slaves. After eighty-six days of trekking 800 miles through the uncharted, barren wilderness and sand dunes of northern México and battling frequent bouts of thirst, they arrived at the wide Río Bravo. A captive Indian had drawn a detailed map for the lost expedition on how to reach the river. A tribe of Indians that the Spaniards called "Mansos" showed the expedition where to ford the river and presented them with fish. Grateful that they could drink water and enter the land of the mythical "Seven Cities of Cibola," they celebrated by giving thanks to God and king. Don Oñate's talk about gold, land, title, and Indian slaves seemed more real now as they ate their feast.

Oñate ordered his men to build a church big enough to accommodate all of the expedition. After Mass, they baptized the visiting Mansos and watched a play written especially for this occasion by a captain of the expedition. During the celebration, Don Oñate, following Spanish protocol for all conquerors of *Nueva España*, pronounced *La Toma*, or the taking of this land. He said:

"In the Name of the most Holy Trinity ... I wish to take possession of the land today ... in the voice and name of the most Christian King, our lord, ... I take and seize one, two and three times ... without excepting anything and without limitation, with the meadows, glens, and their pastures and watering places .... the leaf on the mountain to the rock in the river and sands of it. ..."

To a fanfare of trumpet and a volley of musket fire, he affixed the royal standard and a cross to a tree. Thus, with nails driven into a tree, Nuevo México became the possession of Spain's King Felipe II. The expedition would search extensively for the golden cities, kill Indians, and establish Spanish cities such as Santa Fe. They brought with them a rich Spanish culture and introduced Christianity, cattle, the horse, and the cowboy way of life.

As in New England, the Indians of New Mexico paid a heavy price for sharing food with foreigners who crossed an ocean and a river. While we celebrate our Thanksgiving feast, we expect the Indians to be grateful that a national football team is named after their stereotypical hue in exchange for the leaf of the mountain, the rock in the river, and the sands of it.

Chicano activists look to Aztec, Mayan, and Mexican Indian cultures to remind them of their former indigenous greatness. A recreation of the Mayan world in an action-packed film by movie director Mel Gibson stirred pride in many Chicanos.

Mel Gibson risked his artistic neck on a movie about an unfamiliar, native world corrupted by its lust for violence, power, and greed. *Apocalypto* was a cutting-edge film affirming Gibson's genius for movie-making entertainment. Like a red-streaked Mayan pyramid rising from the midst of a jungle, *Apocalypto* was a bloody, beautiful film that hurled the audience into a struggle of survival between good and evil. The parallel to our times, as we destroy our environment, invade countries, torture prisoners, and treat neighbors as prey, is obvious.

A mainstream film that starred mostly unknown Mexican and American Indian actors in a Mayan world, this film used an ancient Mayan tongue with English subtitles and portrayed gory violence worthy of a *Mad Max*. As Chicano and American Indian audiences desperately searched for swarthy heroes, Gibson filled the screen with handsome, lithe, muscular Indian and Latino actors. Their emotive expressions, laughs, and cries transcended any cultural divide. It was hard to reconcile Gibson's anti-Semitic rant with his sympathetic portrayal of the pre-Columbian world.

Two movie companies rejected the idea of making a picture of an unknown people, history, and setting for a North American audience. The Walt Disney Company had faith that Gibson's artistry, despite his personal flaws, could captivate and earn millions.

That well-placed faith paid off as *Apocalypto's* box office sales on the first weekend of $14.1 million release lifted it to the No. 1 earning film. The total earnings for the film were $27.9 million. Disney had proven to its stockholders that its concept of American family entertainment had expanded well beyond the mouse and duck. (Watch the kids when the Magic Kingdom opens Mayaland.)

The director of *Braveheart* and *The Passion of the Christ* had proven once again with *Apocalypto* that he was the master of the historical epic. Like a great novelist who uses a broad, historical canvas, Gibson humanized his grand stories with sympathetic characters, cruel villains, raw emotions, and fast-paced action. The day and night chase scenes through thick foliage and trees, over waterfalls and through quicksand were among the best ever made.

The natives' tattoos, decorative ear and nose plugs, ritual scars, hair shavings, jewelry, headdresses and paint took the audience captive. The viewers were as tethered and awed as the prisoners when they are taken into the Mayan city filled with chalk-white-covered artisans, a slave market, priestesses, and looming pyramids. The only regret was that Gibson didn't allow time to see the entire jungle city. The sight of sacrificial victims tumbling down the long staircases wickedly alarmed us of our own fate.

But Gibson fans knew that this was coming. As with *Braveheart* and *Passion*, Gibson chose a violent setting to tell his story of corruption, bravery, and new beginnings. His juxtaposition of likeable, peace-loving people with cruel, power-hungry foes proved to be a winning stage.

At the beginning of the film, Flint Sky told his son, Jaguar Paw, not to speak about the fear they saw in other Mayans traveling through their land lest he contaminate their tribe. They must be brave, he said, even in the face of death. Flint Sky soon proved his words when the enemy sliced open his throat in front of his captured son. Gibson knew we like to believe that good guys will suffer at first but will triumph over evil in the end through strength, cleverness, and courage.

Critics have complained about the movie's beheadings, sacrifices, maiming, and killings. Some described Gibson as a sick, angry man who pretended to be a director. But any student of Mayan and Aztec history and culture was familiar with much more violent practices by the Indians in appeasing their gods. In the sixteenth century, Hernán Cortez and his conquistadors were horrified at the ritualistic killings. Their righteous anger led them to slaughter Mayan and Aztec men, women, and children with their swords, crossbows, cannons, and lances. Those who refused to convert to Christianity were burned at the stake or garroted.

In *Apocalypto*, Gibson had drawn back the jungle curtain to show us a violent world where good can win over evil. Like Flint Sky, he urges us to be brave and outrun and outwit the savages who share this world.

The question arises: Who are the savages, and who are the civilized?

SUMMARY

The United States of Mexican America has thrown this country into a tailspin on how to respond to the accelerated change in the American face and language. The brave new world of the future will require a cultural change that many will find difficult to accept.

It was easy to be an American in the twentieth century when the country was overwhelmingly Anglo.

It was easy to be patriotic when fans sang "The Star-Spangled Banner" at baseball games that allowed no "colored" players. It was easy for the Italians, Germans, Irish, and other white European immigrants to dissolve into the mythical American stew. But it was never easy in the twentieth century for the minority to be Americans. It was never easy to think highly of yourself when Al Jolson or Judy Garland sang and danced wearing black face, or when the KKK marched down Pennsylvania Avenue in Washington holding the Stars and Stripes.

It was never easy for Chicano zoot suiters in Los Angeles in 1943 when American sailors and Marines went on a ten-day riot, hunting down Mexican Americans. The incident is now called the Zoot Suit Riots. It was never easy for West Coast Japanese-Americans to be herded into internment camps while their sons went off to fight the Germans.

The discomfort persists in the new century, but now the Anglo feels the social pinch. I've taught the history lessons of this book several times to mostly white professionals seeking continuing education hours at a university setting. At the start of the class, I displayed the photos of five deceased and living historical Latinos who've made outstanding social or artistic contributions to this country. The classes normally identified correctly two photos. When I displayed six African American historical figures, the classes always named every photo. I then asked how they discerned the identities of the blacks but not the browns, the largest ethnic minority in the US. I received an uncomfortable silence and then proceeded with filling in the knowledge gaps. The history of teaching

Chicano history in schools or via public media or popular, commercial outlets was one of woeful neglect.

Their reviews of the one-day class were mostly positive with several assigning me high scores. One student wrote a comment that everyone should take the class, while another wrote it was controversial. Many of the articles I wrote for the *Fort Worth Star-Telegram* dealing with Texas history were also considered provocative by many readers. For the most part students listened attentively, some surprised by the history of the struggle of Chicanos in the US. Despite my efforts not to place personal blame, some appeared uncomfortable by the historical, oppressive actions by whites in their quest to fulfill their Manifest Destiny. Unlike the 2015 Texas school book that called slaves "workers," I presented the facts of the white, Texas immigrants' resistance to the Mexican Government's law that had outlawed slavery on Mexican lands. After the creation of the Lone Star State, slavery in Texas boomed.

The topic of this country's demographic changes yielded another silent response from the class. From Texas minority to Texas majority in a few years, Chicanos will face the challenges of assuming political, economic, and educational ascendancy. Non-Chicanos will face the reality of adjusting to cultural and power shifts that will call for them to resist building walls around the borders of their senses.

For older Americans, raised in a culture of Jim Crow laws, blatant discrimination, and segregation, the past is truly gone with the foul wind. For the young, learn from history on how to pursue a Magnificent Destiny.

CONCLUSION

After convincing the Tarrant County Commissioners to approve a paid César Chávez Holiday for county employees in 2000, Chicano activists have staged annual marches and rallies in downtown Fort Worth. In 2015, Sundance Square Management denied the César Chávez's Committee's request to hold the rally in Sundance Square. They explained the rally would disrupt Easter Holiday weekend shopper traffic. They also forbade the march to travel through their privately-owned, one-block portion of Main Street. Indeed, they requested Chávez marchers not use Main Street at all but instead trek several blocks away. On Passion Saturday, Fort Worth Main Street shoppers were the priority.

On Easter eve 2015, festive César Chávez marchers chanted *si se puede*, sang *De Colores* on downtown Main Street, bypassing Sundance Square, and rallied at Tarrant County College–Trinity River Campus. Two costumed Easter Bunnies, handing out plastic, candy-filled eggs and hugging children, hopped in our ranks.

Photo 32. César Chávez March, April 2015

Courtesy of Emerico Pérez, Emerico Photography.
Photo shows the march on Main Street Fort Worth, April 4, 2015

Tarrant County, one of the reddest counties in the State of Texas, was the only Texas major metropolitan area that President Barack Obama didn't win in the 2012 presidential election. Former Texas State Representative Lon Burnam, a Chávez admirer, said he was surprised by our victory to secure a César Chávez paid holiday—I wasn't. After studying Chávez' skills in inspiring others to raise their voices, to assert their rights, to respect themselves, to organize, I was emboldened to propose the Chávez Holiday. *Sí se puede* was more than a slogan; it was my credo.

To sweeten the victory, we persuaded the commissioners to jettison Columbus Day for Chávez Day, resulting in no extra taxpayer cost.

Shedding a holiday for a man responsible for enslavement and slaughter of Indians was not lost on many of the activists.

The 2014 César Chávez March and Rally in Fort Worth, Texas, was one of the biggest yet. With the release of the César Chávez biographical movie, Chicano pride swelled for our activist history. We refused to see ourselves as narcos, sexy maids, dim-witted sidekicks, and womanizers. Instead, we assumed the armor of honorable men and women willing to take moral stands and actions against injustice.

A critic remarked the Tarrant County César Chávez marches weren't as big as the ones held in San Antonio. I agreed, but then pointed out Bexar County employees weren't allowed a paid day off to honor César Chávez as were 4,000 Tarrant County workers.

Raza Rising has shown that Latino presence in the Americas predates all other ethnic groups with the exception of the Indians. Unlike other immigrants from across the seas, Spaniards flew their flags over the Rockies before Kit Carson and Lewis and Clark decided to venture to the other side of the Mississippi River.

Through war, conquest, disease, broken treaties, and superior numbers, Anglos steadily drove Indians and Mexicans to reservations and barrios. In the twenty-first century, the tide has changed. Chicanos follow the work and therefore live everywhere. I venture that when humans colonize Mars and other planets, Mexican *gritos* and guitars will break the silence of space.

Never have I heard among *La Gente* a desire to reconquer lands lost in the Mexican American War or *La Reconquista* as right-wing talk show hosts inflate. Why would we? Through higher education, upper social mobility, political might, and dismantling of discriminatory laws and practices, Mexican Americans will earn their share of the American Pie.

Too many Chicanos and Chicanas have spilled their blood in all the wars for this country. We would dishonor their sacrifices if we weren't loyal to the principles of the United States Constitution. The USA is our home; Texas is our *colonia.* México is our memory.

On cultural and historical stone steps, we have climbed the Chicano pyramid to see a future for the United States where Chicanos can assume political power and educational excellence. An understanding of Chicano history gives us a context for the reality of today's struggle for political might. The history of *La Gente* revealed that Chicanos have been present north of the Río Grande centuries before the first Anglo settler emigrated to *Tejas.* The Mayflower immigration model does not fit the Chicano experience.

La Raza Unida Party movement taught us that Chicanos can take political offices by inflaming political interest and mobilizing voters. *La Causa* demonstrated that organized Chicanos can overcome well-financed, established power interests that value commerce over humanity. Both movements drew on family values, ethnic pride, cultural symbols, sacrifice, and brave leadership.

Chicano culture, heavily influenced by Mexican-Spaniard customs and art, have given us rich, beautiful literature, music, dance and graphic expressions. All children should learn this Mexican American artistic expression to develop healthy self-esteems, and appreciation for Chicano genius. We should encourage more Chicanos to write and talk about their efforts to excel as role models for youths. Chicano TED talks will inspire others to persevere.

Edna Ferber illustrated in her book *Giant* the underlying racism toward Chicanos on the Reata ranch and Texas. By adopting vaquero ranching culture, settlers in the southwest thrived at the cost of oppressing their benefactors. Fort Worth Stock Yards wouldn't exist if not for vaqueros.

Photo 33. Ballet Folklórico Children Dancing in Fort Worth Library, circa 2012

Author's personal collection.

The educational gaps for Chicanos require immediate action. If we're to stay globally competitive and maintain this country's first-world status, many more Chicanos and Chicanas must don mortarboards. I implore Mexican American students to assume their vital academic role for their own, family's and country's future.

At the pyramid top, let us share our vision for a culturally inclusive, educated, economically robust United States of America with Chicano captains at the controls. Let us enlist a long-treasured custom where Chicanos have excelled. Let us work hard and smart . . . for North Texas, America, and *La Raza* to rise along the Trinity.

Photo 34. Nicholas Gonzales standing on one of the Three Sisters Volcanoes Outside of Albuquerque, New Mexico.

NOTES

Section 1: School Blues

1. "Public Education Finances: 2009," *U.S. Census Bureau*, May 2011: 11, http://www2.census.gov/govs/school/09f33pub.pdf.

2. Jacques Soustelle, *Daily Life of the Aztecs on the Eve of the Spanish Conquest,* trans. Patrick O'Brian (London: Weidenfeld and Nicolson, 1961), 173.

3. Miguel León-Portilla, *Aztec Thought and Culture: A Study of the Ancient Nahuatl Mind,* trans. J. Davis (Norman: University of Oklahoma Press, 1963).

4. "More Education Still Means More Pay in 2014," US Department of Labor, Bureau of Labor Statistics, TED: The Economics Daily, September 2, 2015, http://www.bls.gov/opub/ted/2015/more-education-still-means-more-pay-in-2014.htm

5. Texas State Senator Florence Shaprio Press Release, "TAKS Test to Be Replaced With End of Course Exams," news release, March 1, 2007, http://www.shaprio.senate.tx.us/pr07/p030107a.htm.

6. Ibid.

7 Ibid.

8. Marianne Perie, Rebecca Moran, and Anthony D. Lutkus, "NAEP 2004 Trends In Academic Progress: Three Decades of Student Performance in Reading and Mathematics," *US Department of Education, Institute of Education Sciences, National Center of Education Statistics* (Washington, DC: Government Printing Office, 2005), 1-126, http://nces.ed.gov/nationsreportcard/pdf/main2005/2005464.pdf.

9. Ibid., 34-35.

10. Texas Association of Business Press Release, "Most Students Granted Waivers Under New Policy: 86.4 Percent of Students Who Failed Exit Level Tests Still Graduated," press release, November 19, 2015, http://web.txbiz.org/news/newsarticledisplay.aspx?ArticleID=974

11. Erica Frankenberg, Chungmei Lee, and Gary Orfield, "A Multiracial Society with Segregated Schools: Are We Losing the Dream?" The Civil Rights Project, Harvard University (January 2003): 14. http://www.civilrightsproject.ucla.edu/research/reseg03/AreWeLosingtheDream.pdf.

12. Ibid., 11–12.

13. Gary Orfield and John T. Yun, "Resegregation in American Schools," The Civil Rights, Project Harvard University (June 1999): 21–22.

http://www.civilrightsproject.ucla.edu/research/deseg/ResegregationAmerican_Schools

99.pdf.

14. Steve Murdock, "The Population of Texas: Historical Patterns and Future Trends Affecting Texas," *Institute for Demographic and Socioeconomic Research* (University of Texas in San Antonio): www.senate.state.tx.us/75r/senate/commit/c525/handouts06/01242006.c525.Murdock.pdf

15. "Snapshot 2014, District Detail." *Texas Education Agency*, 2014. Check website at:

http://ritter.tea.state.tx.us/cgi/sas/broker?_service=marykay&_program

16. "American Fact Finder," *U.S. Census Bureau*, 2009-2013. http://factfinder.census.gov/faces/tableservices/jsf/pages/productview.xhtml?pid=ACS_13_5YR_DP05&prodType=table.

17. "The 2012 Statistical Abstract, The National Data Book, Educational Attainment by State," *US. Census Bureau*, http://www.census.gov/compendia/statab/cats/education/educational_attainment.html.

18. Cruz Torres, "Texas — A Majority/Minority State: Social and Economic Implications,"

Department of RPTS, Texas A&M University (May 25, 2011):

http://txsdc.utsa.edu/Resources/Presentations/TXSDC/2011/Annual-Workshop/sdc2011_Tx_Majority_Minority_State_Torres.pptx.

19. Bill Gates, "Speech to the 2005 National Education Summit on High School," (February 26, 2005): http://69.36.77.223/Journal/May_05/article01.htm.

20. Ibid.

21. Ibid.

22. Roy Johnson, "More Than 3 Million Students Have Been Lost from Texas High Schools Since 1986," *Intercultural Development Research Association Newsletter* (October 2010): http://www.idra.org/IDRA_Newsletter/October_2010_School_Holding_Power/More_than_3_Million_Students_Have_Been_Lost/.

23. Scott McCown, "Meeting the Needs of Texas: Expanding the Sales Tax Base to Services" (Testimony to the Texas Senate Finance Committee, 78th Legislature, April 27, 2004).

24. Wayne Pierce, Panelist on Texas School Finance Discussion, Fort Worth Independent School District and IBM sponsored breakfast, Fort Worth, Texas, November 2004.

25. John David Thompson, III, Panelist on Texas School Finance Discussion, Fort Worth Independent School District and IBM sponsored breakfast, Fort Worth, Texas, November 2004.

26. Steve Murdock, et al., "Texas Challenge in the Twenty-First Century: Implications of Population Change for the Future of Texas," Department

of Rural Sociology Texas A&M University System (December 2002): http://txsdc.utsa.edu/reports/2002/texaschallange/TxChall2002.pdf.

27. Ibid.

28. Carmen DeNavas-Walt and Bernadette D. Proctor, "Income and Poverty in the United States: 2013," US Census Bureau, (Washington, DC: US Government Printing Office, 2014): 6, https://www.census.gov/content/dam/Census/library/publications/2014/demo/p60-249.pdf?cssp=SERP

29. Murdock, et al. "Texas Challenge."

30. W. Gardner Selby, "Rick Perry Says Texas Education Spending Increased a Phenomenal 70 Percent as Enrollment Escalated 23 Percent," Politifact Texas, January 16, 2013, http://www.politifact.com/texas/statements/2013/jan/16/rick-perry/rick-perry-says-texas-education-increased-phenomen/

31. Ibid.

32. Ryan Murphy and Matt Stiles, "Census 2010 Interactive Map: Race, Hispanic Origin," *Texas Tribune,*February 18, 2011, http://www.texastribune.org/library/data/census-2010/.

33. Jeffrey Passel and D'Vera Cohn, "U.S. Population Projections: 2005-2050." *Pew Hispanic Center*, February 11, 2008, http://www.pewhispanic.org/2008/02/11/us-population-projections-2005-2050/.

34. Clark Mindock, "Donald Trump Tells Jeb Bush to Stop Speaking Spanish," *International Business Times*, September 3, 2014, http://www.ibtimes.com/donald-trump-tells-jeb-bush-stop-speaking-spanish-2081394

35. Ibid.

36. "2015 Texas Higher Education Almanac, A Profile of State and Institutional Performance and Characteristics." *Texas Higher Educa-*

tion Coordinating Board, 2015, http://www.thecb.state.tx.us/index.cfm?objectid=A44B548A-E50C-8417-E09BF83FC11EA1EF.

37. Ibid., 15–16.

38. Ibid., 38–40, 45.

39. "Education: Elementary and Secondary Education: Completions and Dropouts," *2012 Statistical Abstract: U.S. Census Bureau*,

http://www.census.gov/compendia/statab/cats/education/elementary_and_secondary_education_completions_and_dropouts.html.

40. "2005, The Year of Languages," *American Council on the Teaching of Foreign Languages*, http://www.actfl.org/i4a/pages/index.cfm?pageid=3420.

41. Stephen D. Krashen, *Under Attack: The Case Against Bilingual Education.* (Burlingame, CA: Language Education Associates,1996).

42. Wayne Thomas and Virginia Collier, "Bilingual Education—Need For Bilingual

Education, Benefits of Bilingualism and Theoretical Foundations of Bilingual Education," *State University.com*, http://education.stateuniversity.com/pages/1788/Bilingual-Education.html.

43. "Academic Excellence Indicator System, 1996-97 State Performance Report," Texas Education Agency, http://ritter.tea.state.tx.us/perfreport/aeis/97/state-level.html.

44. Roy L. Johnson, "Texas Public School Attrition Study, 2010-2011: High School Attrition Continues Downward Trend—Universal High School Graduation is Still a Quarter Century Away," *Intercultural Development Research Association Report* (November 2011): http://www.idra.org/images/stories/IDRA_Attrition_Study_2011.pdf.

45. Thomas Kuhn, *The Structure of Scientific Revolutions* (Chicago: University of Chicago Press, 1996).

46. "'English Only' ACLU Briefing Paper Number 6," *'Lectric Law Library* (1996): http://www.lectlaw.com/files/con09.htm.

47. James Crawford, "Frequently Asked Questions About Official English," *Institute for Language and Education Policy* (July 2006): 4, http://users.rcn.com/crawj/Crawford_Official_English_testimony.pdf.

48. *Opposition to Arizona Initiative "English Language Education for Children in Public Schools,"* Resolution 15 Passed at LULAC Convention National Convention, July 2, 2000, signed by Rick Dovalina, national LULAC president,

http://www.lulac.net/advocacy/resolutions/resolve00.html.

49. Johnson, "More Than 3 Million Students Have Been Lost."

50. U.S. Census Bureau, "Hispanic Population: 2010," *U.S. Census Bureau* (May 2011): 2, http://www.census.gov/prod/cen2010/briefs/c2010br-04.pdf.

SECTION 2: LA GENTE

1. Alonso Sánchez and Anna Marie Weiss-Armush, "Study of North Texas Immigrant Communities," Prepared for Dallas International, January 28, 2003. www.dfwinternational.org/resource_center/Study_of_North_Texas_Immigrant_ Communities_2003.pdf. 5.

2. Ibid., 6.

3. Luis Zayas, "Toward an Understanding of Suicide Risks in Young Hispanic Females,"

Journal of Adolescent Research 1 (Spring 1987): 1-11.

doi:10.1177/074355488721001.

4. Britt Rios-Ellis, *Critical Disparities in Latino Mental Health: Transforming Research into Action,* National Council of La Raza, Institute

for Hispanic Health (November 3, 2005): 5. Found online at http://www.nclr.org/index.php/publications/

5. Ibid., 16.

6. Ibid., 8.

7. Robert Crosnoe, interview by Michelle Trudeau, National Public Radio "Mexican Kids Have Good Mental Health," December 5, 2005,

http://www.npr.org/templates/story/story.php?storyId=5039214.

8. "Aztec Character," http://www.azteca.net/aztec/nahuatl/charactr.html.

9. "Statement on Ending Fast," Emerson Kent.com: History for the Relaxed Historian, http://www.emersonkent.com/speeches/on_ending_fast.htm.

10. Javier Nájera, interview by author.

11. "The Principles of 'A Noble Man'," National Compadres Network, http://www.nationalcompadresnetwork.com/principles/principles.html.

12. Brent Taylor and Andrew Behuke, "Fathering Across the Border: Latino Fathers in Mexico and the U.S." *Fathering* 3, no. 2 (Spring 2005): 1-25,

http://www.ces.ncsu.edu/depts/fcs/Benke/Taylor%20Behnke.pdf.

13. Francisco Álvarez and Sigifredo Muñoz, interview by author.

14. Robert Jensen, *The Heart of Whiteness: Confronting Race, Racism and White Privilege* (San Francisco: City Lights, 2007), xiii.

15. T.J. Degroat, "A Top-Down Approach: 2006 Top 50 Companies For Diversity," *DiversityInc.Magazine,* (June 2006): 34, http://www.diversityinc-digital.com/diversityincmedia/200606#pg34.

16. "DiversityInc Top 50," DiversityInc.com, http://www.diversityinc.com/the-diversityinc-top-50-companies-for-diversity-2015/

17. Luke Visconti, "Ask the White Guy," *Diversityinc.Magazine*, http://www.diversityinc.com/ask-the-white-guy/ask-the-white-guy-diversity-and-inclusion-apologize.

18. Douglas M. West, Introduction to *The Inclusion Breakthrough: Unleashing the Real Power of Diversity,* by Frederick A. Miller and Judith H. Katz (San Francisco: Berrett-Koehler Publishers, Inc., 2002).

19. Frances Negrón-Muntaner, Chelsea Abbas, Luis Figueroa, and Samuel Robson, "The Latino Media Gap: A Report on the State of Latinos in US Media," Center for the Study of Ethnicity and Race, Columbia University, 2014:1-2, http://www.columbia.edu/cu/cser/downloads/Latino_Media_Gap_Report.pdf

20. Harry Pachon, "Still Missing: Latinos In and Out of Hollywood," The Tomas Rivera Policy Institute (May 2000): 4,

http://www.trpi.org/PDFs/missing_in_action.pdf

21. Ibid., 5.

22. "Latino Films Make Money: Consistently Performing Well at the Box Office," Premiere Weekend Club, http://www.premiereweekend.org/profitsb.html.

23. "Did You Know?" *Premiere Weekend Club*, http://www.premiereweekend.org/didyouknowb.html.

24. Glenn Flores, et al., "The Health of Latino Children, Urgent Priorities, Unanswered Questions, And A Research Agenda," *Journal of the American Medical Association* 288, no. 1 (July 3, 2002): 83. doi:10.1001/jama.288.16.1981.

25. Ibid., 85–86.

26. Ibid., 85.

27. Ibid., 87–88.

28. Ibid., 87.

29. Tammy Gómez, "On Language," performed by Tammy Gómez, poem recital featured in the documentary film *Voices from Texas* produced by SOUND CULTURE, screened at the Rose Marine Theater, Fort Worth Texas, August 30, 2003.

30. Raúl Salinas, lecture featured in the documentary film *Voices from Texas* produced by SOUND CULTURE, screened at the Rose Marine Theater, Fort Worth Texas, August 30, 2003.

31. Pablo Neruda, *Twenty Love Poems and a Song of Despair,* trans. W. S. Merwin (New York: Peguin Classics Deluxe Edition, 2003), 78.

32. Tammy Gómez, lecture at "Siempre Neruda," performance produced by SOUND CULTURE at the Rose Marine Theater, Fort Worth Texas, July 14, 2005.

33. Miguel Humara, "The Relationship Between Athletics, Hispanics and Aggression," *Athletic Insight: The Online Journal of Sports Psychology,* http://www.athleticinsight.com/Vol1Iss1/Hispanic_Aggression.htm.

34. W.M. Leonard, J.M. Reyman, "The Odds of Attaining Professional Athlete Status: Refining the Computations," *Sociology of Sport Journal* 5, (1988): 162-169, http://journals.humankinetics.com/ssjbackissues/ssjvolume5issue2june/researchnotescommentstheoddsofattainingprofessionalathletestatusrefiningthecomputations.

35. Bryan Curtis, "The Juice and I: Jose Canseco and Steroids, A Love Story," *Slate,* February 18, 2005, http://www.slate.com/articles/sports/sports_nut/2005/02/the_juice_and _i.html.

36. "'A Slap in the Face': Astro Owner Accused of Remarks Against Hispanics," *CNN/Sports Illustrated.Com* (June 4, 1999): http://sportsillustrated.cnn.com/baseball/mlb/news/1999/06/04/astros_mclane/index.html.

37. F. Lennox Campello, "Before El Duque There was Duque and Before Robinson There was Estalella," http://campello.tripod.com/firstblackinbaseball.html.

38. Tim Keown, "Is Major League Baseball Too Hispanic?" *ESPN Commentary*, October 4, 2011. http://espn.go.com/espn/commentary/story/_/id/7058357/are-there-too-many-hispanics-major-league-baseball.

SECTION 3: RAZA RISING

1. Frederick Douglass, "Frederick Douglass Quotes," *ThinkExist.com*, http://thinkexist.com/quotation/power-concedes-nothing-without-a-demand-it-never/1273306.html.

2. Thom File, Sarah Crissey, "Voting and Registration in the Election of November 2008: Population Characteristics," *U.S. Census Bureau* (May 2010): 4, http://www.census.gov/prod/2010pubs/p20-562.pdf.

3. Ibid.

4. "The Diversifying Electorate—Voting Rates by Race and Hispanic Origin in 2012 (and Other Recent Elections)," *US Census Bureau*, Current Population Survey Reports, Washington, DC, May 2013, 2. https://www.census.gov/prod/2013pubs/p20-568.pdf

5. "Voting and Registration in the Election of November 2012 - Detailed Tables," US Census Bureau, Table 4b. Reported Voting and Registration by Sex, Race and Hispanic Origin, for States: November 2012, http://www.census.gov/hhes/www/socdemo/voting/publications/p20/2012/tables.html?cssp=SERP 135

6. Since my arrival in Arlington, Texas, in 1969, I have observed few Chicanos take political office. Dan Serna served as the first Chicano elected to the Arlington city council, 1993-1997. Robert Rivera took office in 2005 and currently serves as the only Chicano on the council. On the Arlington school board, Gloria Peña was the first Chicana to be elected in 2005 and had served as a school board president. She held office until 2015 when she was defeated in a re-election bid. Tony Pompa served on the school board for one term, 2011–2014. He stepped down to run for the

Texas Senate District 10 seat but lost this race. The result is that in 2015, Robert Rivera is the only Chicano in an Arlington elected office at a time that Latinos comprise 28 percent of the city population and 43 percent of public school students. Ramón Romero was the first Chicano elected from Tarrant County to the Texas State House of Representative in 2014. He defeated the eighteen-year incumbent Lon Burnam. As a result of Romero's excellent service, his fellow House Democrats chose him in 2015 as the Democrat Freshman of the Year for the 84th Legislative session.

7. Justin Levitt, "The Truth About Voter Fraud," *Brennan Center For Justice at New York University School of Law*, (2007): 4, http://www.truthaboutfraud.org/pdf/TruthAboutVoterFraud.pdf.

8. "Governor Abbott Statement on Texas Voter ID Law," press release, August 5, 2015, http://gov.texas.gov/news/press-release/21284

9. José Ángel Gutiérrez, *The Making of a Chicano Militant: Lessons from Crystal* (Madison: University of Wisconsin Press, 1998), 113.

10. Ignacio García, *United We Win: The Rise and Fall of La Raza Unida Party* (Tuscon: Mexican American Studies and Research Center, University of Arizona Press, 1989), 81.

11. Ibid., 83.

12. Allison Green and Jack Martin, "The Sinking Lifeboat, Uncontrolled Immigration and The U.S. Health Care System," *Federation for American Immigration Reform* (February 2004): 1-25,http://www.fairus.org/site/DocServer/healthcare.pdf?docID=424.

13. Ibid., 5-6.

14. Ibid., 3.

15. Sarita Mohanty, et al., "Health Care Expenditures of Immigrants in the United States: A Nationally Representative Analysis," *American Journal of Public Health* 95, no. 8 (August 2005): 1-8, http://ajph.aphapublications.org/doi/pdf/10.2105/AJPH.2004.044602.

16. Ibid., 7.

17. Jeffrey S. Passel and D'Vera Cohn, "Unauthorized Immigrant Population: National and State Trends, 2010," *Pew Hispanic Center* (February 1, 2011): 1–2. http://www.pewhispanic.org/files/reports/133.pdf.

18. Carel Bailey Germain, *Social Work Practice in Health Care, An Ecological Perspective* (New York: The Free Press, 1984), 13.

19. Karl Eschbach, Jacqueline Hagan, and Nestor Rodríguez, "Causes and Trends inMigrant Deaths Along the US-Mexico Border, 1985-1998," Center for Immigration Research (Houston: University of Houston, 2001),http://web.archive.org/web/20070926034617/http://www.uh.edu/cir/Causes_and_Trends.pdf.

20. Rakesh Kochhar, "Latino Labor Report, 2004: More Jobs for New Immigrants But at Lower Wages," *Pew Research Center: Pew Hispanic Center* (May 2, 2005): 8, http://www.pewhispanic.org/files/reports/45.pdf.

21. "Letter of Arrangement," US Department of Labor, https://www.osha.gov/international/

22. "Revisions to the 2013 Census of Fatal Occupational Injuries (CFOI) Counts," US Department of Labor, Bureau of Labor Statistics, April 15, 2015: 1, http://www.bls.gov/iif/oshwc/cfoi/cfoi_revised13.pdf

23. "Fatal Occupational Injuries Incurred by Hispanic or Latino Workers, 2010–2014," US Department of Labor, Bureau of Labor Statistics: 1-2, http://www.bls.gov/iif/oshwc/cfoi/hispanic.pdf

24. "Number of Fatal Work Injuries Involving Hispanic or Latino Workers, 1992–2007," *US Department of Labor, Bureau of Labor Statistics, Census of Fatal Occupational Injuries, 2009,*

http://www.slideshare.net/delforbes/number-of-fatal-work-injuries-19922007.

25. Ibid.

26. Catherine Singley, "Troubling Indicators of Job Quality," chap. 3, fig. 3.7 in *Fractures in the Foundation: The Latino Worker's Experience in an Era of Declining Job Quality* (National Council of La Raza, September 1, 2009): 18, http://www.nclr.org/index.php/publications/fractures_in_the_foundation_the_latino_workers_experience_in_an_era_of_declining_job_quality/.

27. Hector Flores (ex-national LULAC President), speaking at rally in front of the City Hall of Farmers Branch, August 26, 2006.

28. Overheard by author at rally in front of City Hall of Farmers Branch, August 26, 2006.

29. Rachael Miller, speaking at rally in front of the City Hall of Farmers Branch, August 26, 2006.

30. Bernard Weinstein, presentation at the League of Women Voters immigration forum, February 8, 2007.

31. Ibid.

32. " "Unauthorized Immigration Population Profiles: Tarrant and Dallas Counties, TX," *Migration Policy Institute*, http://www.migrationpolicy.org/programs/us-immigration-policy-program-data-hub/unauthorized-immigrant-population-profiles

33. "States Offering Driver's Licenses to Immigrants," National Conference of State Legislatures, July 8, 2015: 1, http://www.ncsl.org/research/immigration/states-offering-driver-s-licenses-to-immigrants.aspx

34. "Newsroom Diversity: A Look at Diversity on the Front Page," 4thEstate, Infographics Special Reports, October 24, 2012, http://specialreports.4thestate.net/bleached-lack-of-diversity-in-newsroom-front-page-election-coverage/

35. Dr. Don Smith, "The Overrpresentation of Latino Youth in Juvenile Justice, Numbers and Reasons" (lecture, Tarrant County Advocate Program North, Third Annual Latino Youth Issues Conference, Fort Worth, TX, April 5, 2007).

36. "Commitment Profile for New Commitments Fiscal Years 2006-2011," *Texas Juvenile Justice Department*, http://www.tjjd.texas.gov/research/profile.aspx.

37. "Texas Prison Population Increase Expected," *Justice Policy Institute* (April 23, 2003), http://www.prisontalk.com/forums/archive/index.php/t-108650.html.

38. "Texas Population, 2012 (Estimates)," Texas Department of State Health Services, December 16, 2014, http://www.dshs.state.tx.us/Layouts/ContentPage.aspx?PageID=35615&id=8589985884&terms=texas+population%2c+2012

39. "Fiscal Year 2012 Statistical Report," Texas Department of Criminal Justice, 1, https://www.tdcj.state.tx.us/documents/Statistical_Report_FY2012.pdf

40. Ann Del Llano and Ana Yañez-Correa, "Criminal Justice Policy Brief, Proven Pro-Family Criminal Justice Polices That Save Families, Save Tax Payers' Money and Improve the Safety of Our Community," *Texas LULAC State Executive Office* (August, 2004): 13, http://www.realcostofprisons.org/materials/LULAC.pdf.

41. Ibid., 16.

42. "Criminal and Juvenile Justice Cost Report: Fiscal Years 2013 and 2014," Submitted to the 84th Texas Legislature by Legislative Budget Board Staff, February 2015: 1, http://www.lbb.state.tx.us/Documents/Publications/Policy_Report/1440_Criminal_Juvenile_Justice_Uniform_Cost_Report.pdf

43. Del Lano, "Criminal Justice Policy Brief," 4.

44. Ibid., 3.

45. "Senator West's Racial Profiling Bill Passes Full Senate," *From the Office of State Senator Royce West—District 23* (April 11, 2001), http://www.senate.state.tx.us/75r/senate/members/dist23/pr01/p041101a.htm.

46. Alberto Govea, personal interview by author, February 2004.

47. Dwight Steward, *Racial Profiling: Texas Traffic Stops and Searches, A First Look at the Nation's Most Comprehensive Racial Profiling Data Set: Texas Traffic Stops and Searches* (Austin: Steward Research Group 2004),

http://www.employstats.com/pdfs/Steward04.pdf.

48. David Garrett, interview by author, February 2004.

49. Eric Dexheimer and Jeremy Schwartz, "DPS Statistics Showing No Racial Bias in Stops are Wrong, Expert Says," *Austin American-Statesman*, November 22, 2015, http://www.mystatesman.com/news/news/dps-statistics-showing-no-racial-bias-in-stops-are/npSts/

50. Brian Collister and Joe Ellis, "Texas Troopers Ticketing Hispanic Drivers as White," KXAN In-Depth Investigative, November 6, 2015, http://kxan.com/investigative-story/texas-troopers-ticketing-hispanics-motorists-as-white/

51. Brian Collister and Joe Ellis, "Legislative Committee Questions DPS troopers Labeling Hispanics as White; DPS to Change Practice," Latino Centric: Linking Dallas Latinos with News and Information, November 19, 2015, http://latinocentric.com/legislative-committee-questions-dps-troopers-labeling-hispanics-white-dps-change-practice/

52. Franciso A. Villarruel and Nancy E. Walker, *Donde Esta La Justicia? A Call to Action on Behalf of Latino and Latina Youth in the U.S. Justice System* (East Lansing: Michigan State University, Institute for Children, Youth and Families, Building Blocks For Youth, July, 2002), http://www.cclp.org/documents/BBY/Donde.pdf.

53. Ibid., 21.

54. Charles Puzzanchera, "Juvenile Arrests 2010," US Department of Justice, Office of Juvenile Justice and Delinquency Prevention, December 2013, 6, http://www.ojjdp.gov/pubs/242770.pdf

55. Steve Holbert, "The Color of Guilt and Innocence" (lecture, New Orleans, LA, September 7, 2006).

SECTION 4: CHICANO ROOTS

1. Rita Arias Jirasek and Carlos Tortolero, *Mexican Chicago* (Charleston, SC: Arcadia Publishing, 2001).

2. Ibid., 58.

3. Ibid., 8.

4. Texas HCR 38. 77th Regular Session (signed by the Governor June 15, 2001).

5. Andres Tijerina, *Tejanos and Texas Under the Mexican Flag, 1821–1836* (College Station: Texas A & M University Press, 1994), 8.

6. Donald A. Gilbert Y Chávez, *Vaqueros: Origins of the First Cowboys* (New Mexican Hispanic Culture Preservation League) chap. 7: http://www.nmhcpl.org/COWBOY.html.

7. Ed Farmer, "Dedicatory Remarks," Speech, Juan Seguin High School, Arlington, Texas, November 10, 2002.

8. Kirby Warnock, *Border Bandits,* Documentary directed and written by Kirby Warnock, Trans-Pecos Productions.

9. Walter Prescott Webb, *Texas Rangers: A Century of Frontier Defense* (Austin: University of Texas Press, 1965), 14.

10. Americo Paredes, "*With His Pistol in His Hand": A Border Ballad and Its Hero* (Austin: University of Texas Press, 1958), 16.

11. Warnock, *Border Bandits.*

12. Julie Leininger Pycior, *LBJ and Mexican Americans: The Paradox of Power* (Austin: University of Texas Press, 1997), 52–53.

13. Ibid., 53.

14. Robert Caro, *The Years of Lyndon Johnson: Master of the Senate* (New York: Knopf, 2002), 741.

15. Henry A. J. Ramos, *The American GI Forum: In Pursuit of the Dream, 1948-1983* (Houston: Arte Público Press, 1998), 10.

16. Ibid., 11.

17. Caro, *Master of the Senate*, 743.

18. Ibid., 741.

19. Ibid., 742.

20. Pycior, *LBJ and Mexican Americans*, 71.

21. Caro, *Master of the Senate*, 747.

22. Ibid., 753.

23. Ibid., 754.

24. Fernando González, born June 14, 1925, is originally from Rio Grande City, Texas, Starr County. He entered the service at 18, leaving high school with his four older brothers. He joined the U.S. Navy August 17, 1943, until his honorable discharge on April 5, 1946. He said he joined the U.S. Navy to "see the world." All five González brothers returned from World War II alive and well. Seaman González served in the Pacific Theater, participating in several naval battles as a front loader against the Japanese Navy and transporting Marines to Japanese-occupied islands. Three brothers including Fernando went on to join the U.S. Department of Agriculture, hoof and mouth eradication campaign in México in 1949. Mr. González later married, had two children, and joined the U.S. Corps of Engineers, where he retired in 1996. He continues to live in Fort Worth with his daughter. He just celebrated his 90th birthday, and counts his military experience as "One of the proudest moments of my life. I was proud to have the opportunity to fight for the country I was born in. I love the U.S.A."

25. Ken Burns, Lynn Novick, "About the Series: Letters from the Directors: The War," Public Broadcasting System, website: http://www.pbs.org/thewar/about_letter_producers.htm.

26. Rafael Olemda and Ivan Roman, "Open Letter to Ms. Paula Kerger, PBS President and Chief Executive Officer" (February 16, 2007): http://www.nahj.org/nahjnews/articles/2007/february/pbsletter.pdf.

27. Tommy Franks, "Get Motivated Seminar," Lecture, American Airlines Center, Dallas, Texas, March 8, 2005.

28. "Operation Iraqi Freedom (OIF) US Casualty Status: Fatalities as of November 20, 2015," US Department of Defense, http://www.defense.gov/casualty.pdf.

29. Brian Gifford, "Combat Casualties and Race: What Can We Learn from the 2003-2004 Iraq Conflict?" *Armed Forces and Society* 31, no. 2 (Winter 2005): 220.

30. Ibid., 215.

31. "Fact Sheet: Survey of Latino Attitudes on the War in Iraq," *Pew Hispanic Center* (February 7, 2005): http://www.pewhispanic.org/2005/02/07/survey-on-latino-attitudes-on-the-war-in-iraq/

32. "César Chávez Action and Information Center," *UFW: The Official Webpage of the United Farm Worker,*"

_history.html&menu=research.

33. César Chávez, "Letter From César Chávez To Friends Regarding *Peregrinacion*, 1966," http://www.farmworkermovement.org/essays/essays/MillerArchive/016%20Letter%20From%20César%20Chávez%20To%20Friends.pdf.

34. Ibid.

35. Rodolfo Gonzales, *I Am Joaquin*, http://www.latinamericanstudies.org/latinos/joaquin.htm.

36. Ibid.

37. *Rubén Salazar: Border Correspondent, Selected Writings 1955-1970,* ed. Mario T. García (Berkeley: University of California Press, 1955), 235.

38. Ibid., 237.

39. Ibid., 252.

40. Ibid., 253.

41. Peg McMahon, Claudio Pasian, Jim Metzger, and Jeanne Youger-Comaty. "Poinsettia Care in the Home." *Ohio State University Extension Fact Sheet*: http://ohioline.osu.edu/hyg-fact/1000/1248.html.

42. "The History of the Poinsettia, Paul Ecke Ranch."

http://www.ecke.com/ecke/?page_id=1365.

43. Don Adams, Teresa A. Kendrick, "Don Juan de Oñate and the First Thanksgiving," *Historical Text Archive* (2003): http://historicaltextarchive.com/sections.php?action=read&artid=736

BIBLIOGRAPHY

"2005, The Year of Languages." American Council on the Teaching of Foreign Languages. http://www.actfl.org/i4a/pages/index.cfm?pageid=3420.

"2012 Statistical Abstract, The National Data Book, Educational Attainment by State." U.S. Census Bureau. http://www.census.gov/compendia/statab/cats/education/educational_attainment.html.

2012 Statistical Abstract, U.S. Census Bureau. http://www.census.gov/compendia/statab/cats/education/elementary_and_secondary_education_completions_and_dropouts.html.

"2015 Texas Public Higher Education Almanac, A Profile of State and Institutional Performance and Characteristics." Texas Higher Education Coordinating Board. http://www.thecb.state.tx.us/index.cfm?objectid=A44B548A-E50C-8417-E09BF83FC11EA1EF.

"Academic Excellence Indicator System, 1996-97 State Performance Report." Texas Education Agency. http://ritter.tea.state.tx.us/perfreport/aeis/97/state-level.html.

"Academic Excellence Indicator System, 2003-04 State Performance Report." Texas Education Agency. http://ritter.tea.state.tx.us/perfreport/aeis/2004/state.html.

"Academic Excellence Indicator System, 2010-2011 District Performance, Arlington." Texas Education Agency. http://ritter.tea.state.tx.us/cgi/sas/broker.

"Academic Excellence Indicator System, 2010-2011 District Performance, Fort Worth." Texas Education Agency. http://ritter.tea.state.tx.us/cgi/sas/broker.

"Academic Excellence Indicator System, 2010-2011 State Performance Report." Texas Education Agency. http://ritter.tea.state.tx.us/perfreport/aeis/2011/state.html.

Adams, Don, Teresa A. Kendrick. "Don Juan de Oñate and the First Thanksgiving." *Historical Text Archive*, 2003. http://historicaltextarchive.com/sections.php?action=read&artid=736.

"American Fact Finder." U.S. Census Bureau. http://factfinder.census.gov/faces/tableservices/jsf/pages/productview.xhtml?pid=ACS_13_5YR_DP05&prodType=table.

"Aztec Character." http://www.azteca.net/aztec/nahuatl/charactr.html.

Bowman, Tom. "Pentagon Details U.S. Deaths In Iraq." *Baltimore Sun*. January 13, 2005. http://www.globalsecurity.org/org/news/2005/050113-iraq-deaths.htm.

Buck, Rinker. "Researchers Finding Surprises In Figures On Deaths In Iraq." *Hartford Courant*, 2004.

"Bullies at the Voting Booth." *Southwest Voter Registration Education Project*, September 16, 2004.

Burns, Ken, Lynn Novick. "About the Series: Letters from the Directors: The War." Public Broadcasting System, website: http://www.pbs.org/thewar/about_letter_producers.htm.

Campello, F. Lennox. "Before El Duque There was Duque and Before Robinson There Was Estalella. http://campello.tripod.com/firstblackinbaseball.html.

Caro, Robert. *The Years of Lyndon Johnson: Master of the Senate*. New York: Knopf, 2002.

Castellon, David. "Why Don't More Hispanics Vote." *Hispanic Vista*, December 20, 2003.

"César Chávez Action and Information Center." *UFW: The Official Webpage of the United Farm Workers.*" http://www.ufw.org/_page.php?inc=research_history.html&menu=research

"Challenges, 2005 National Education Summit on High Schools." Achieve, Inc., National Governors Association, February 26–27, 2005. http://www.achieve.org/files/Achievebriefingbook2005.pdf.

Chávez, César. "Letter From César Chávez to Friends Regarding *Peregrinacion*, 1966." http://www.farmworkermovement.org/essays/

essays/MillerArchive/016%20Letter%20From%20César%20Chávez%20To%20Friends.pdf

Chávez, César. "Statement on Ending Fast." Emerson Kent.com: History for the Relaxed Historian. http://www.emersonkent.com/speeches/on_ending_fast.htm.

Cockrell, Cathy. "Antonio Villaraigosa: Advocate for Opportunity." *Berkeley Magazine*, Summer 1999. http://berkeley.edu/news/magazine/summer_99/feature_antonio.html.

"Commitment Profile for New Commitments Fiscal Years 2006-2001," *Texas Juvenile Justice Department*. http://www.tjjd.texas.gov/research/profile.aspx.

Crawford, James. "Frequently Asked Questions About Official English." *Institute for Language and Education Policy* (July 2006): 1-14, http://users.rcn.com/crawj/Crawford_Official_English_testimony.pdf.

Crosnoe, Robert. "Mexican Kids Have Good Mental Health." NPR Interview by Michelle Trudeau, December 5, 2005. http://www.npr.org/templates/story/story.php?storyId=5039214

Cuellar, Carlos. *Stories from the Barrio: A History of Mexican Fort Worth*. Fort Worth: Texas Christian University Press, 2004.

Currie, Janet. "Early Childhood Intervention Programs: What Do We Know?" *Northwestern University/University of Chicago Joint Center For Poverty* papers/wpfiles/currie_EARLY_CHILDHOOD.PDF. *Research*, April 2000.http://www.ipr.northwestern.edu/jcpr/working

Curtis, Bryan. "The Juice and I: José Canseco and Steroids, A Love Story." *Slate* February 18, 2005. http://www.slate.com/articles/sports/sports_nut/2005/02/the_juice_and_i.html.

Degroat, T.J. "A Top-Down Approach: 2006 Top 50 Companies for Diversity." *DiversityInc.Magazine* (June 2006): 26-38, http://www.diversityinc-digital.com/diversityincmedia/200606#pg34.

Del Llano, Ann, and Ana Yañez-Correa. "Criminal Justice Policy Brief, Proven Pro-Family Criminal Justice Polices That Save Families, Save Tax Payers' Money and Improve The Safety Of Our Community."

Texas LULAC State Executive Office, August, 2004. http://www.realcostofprisons.org/materials/LULAC.pdf.

"Did You Know?" *Premiere Weekend Club.* http://www.premiereweekend.org/didyouknowb.html.

Douglass, Frederick. "Frederick Douglass Quotes." *ThinkExist.com. http://thinkexist.com/quotation/power-concedes-nothing-without-a-demand-it-never/1273306.html.*

"Early Learning, Later Success: the Abecedarian Study, Early Childhood Educational Intervention for Poor Children, Executive Summary." *The Carolina Abecedarian Project.* http://www.fpg.unc.edu/~abc/summary.cfm.

"Education: Elementary and Secondary Education: Completions and Dropouts." The 2012 Statistical Abstract, U.S. Census Bureau. http://www.census.gov/compendia/statab/cats/education/elementary_and_secondary_education_completions_and_dropouts.html.

"'English Only' ACLU Briefing Paper Number 6." *The 'Lectric Law Library* (1996): http://www.lectlaw.com/files/con09.htm.

Eschbach, Karl, Jacqueline Hagan, and Nestor Rodríguez. *Causes and Trends in Migrant Deaths Along the U.S.-Mexico Border, 1958-1998.* Houston: University of Houston, Center for Immigration Research, 2001. http://web.archive.org/web/20070926034617/http://www.uh.edu/cir/Causes_and_Trends.pdf.

Escuela Tlatelolco. "Rodolfo 'Corky' Gonzales,1928-2005." http://www.escuelatlatelolco.org/website/corky_bio.html.

"Fact Sheet: Survey of Latino Attitudes on the War in Iraq." Pew Hispanic Center, January 4, 2007. http://www.pewhispanic.org/2007/01/04/latinos-and-the-war-in-Iraq.

"Fans Celebrate Neruda Centenary." BBC News, http://newsvote.bbc.co.uk/mpapps/pagetools/print/news.bbc.co.uk/2/hi/entertainment/3860681.stm.

Ferber, Edna. *Giant.* New York: HarperCollins Publishers, 1952.

Figueroa, Ivonne. "America's First Thanksgiving, 400th Anniversary." *Hispano America USA, Inc.* http://www.neta.com/~1stbooks/texas2.htm.

File, Thom, and Sarah Crissey. "Voting And Registration in the Election of November 2008: Population Characteristics." U.S. Census Bureau, May 2010. http://www.census.gov/prod/2010pubs/p20-562.pdf.

Flóres, Glenn, Elena Fuentes-Afflick, Oxiris Barbot, Olivia Carter-Pokras, Luz Claudio, Marielena Lara, Jennie A. McLaurin, et al.,"The Health of Latino Children, Urgent Priorities, Unanswered Questions, and a Research Agenda." *The Journal of the American Medical Association,* 288, no.1 (July 3, 2002). doi:10.1001/jama.288.16.1981.

Frankenberg, Erica, Chungmei Lee and Gary Orfield."A Multiracial Society with Segregated Schools: Are We Losing the Dream?" The Civil Rights Project Harvard University, January 2003. http://www.civilrightsproject.ucla.edu/research/reseg03/AreWeLosingtheDream.pdf.

Franks, Tommy. "Get Motivated Seminar." Lecture, American Airlines Center, Dallas, Texas, March 8, 2005.

Fry, Richard. "High School Drop Out Rates for Latino Youth." *ERIC Clearinghouse on Urban Education.* November, 2003. http://www.ericdigests.org/2004-3/latino.html.

García, Ignacio. *United We Win: The Rise and Fall of La Raza Unida Party.* Tucson: Mexican American Studies and Research Center, University of Arizona Press, 1989.

García y Griego, Manuel, and Roberto R. Calderón. *Más Allá del Río Bravo: Breve Historia Mexicana del Norte de Texas.* Mexico City: Secretaría De Relaciones Exteriores, 2013.

Gates, Bill. "Speech to the 2005 National Education Summit on High School." February 26, 2005.http://69.36.77.223/Journal/May_05/article01.htm.

Georgetown University Center for Child and Human Development, Georgetown University Medical Center. *The Compelling Need for Cultural and Linguistic Competence.* Developed by National Center for Cultural Competence. http://nccc.georgetown.edu/foundations/need.html

Germain, Carel Bailey. *Social Work Practice in Health Care, An Ecological Perspective,* New York: The Free Press, 1984.

Gifford, Brian. "Combat Casualties and Race: What Can We Learn From the 2003-2004 Iraq Conflict?" *Armed Forces and Society* 31, no. 2 (Winter 2005): 201-225.

Gil-Gómez, Ellen M. "Teaching Latino Culture/Creating Paths To Success: Mentoring Latino Students Through the Classroom." Abstract. *Latino Intersections* 1, no.1 (2003). http://journals.dartmouth.edu/cgi-bin/WebObjects/Journals.woa/2/xmlpage/2/article/100.

Gilb, Dagoberto, ed. *Hecho En Tejas: An Anthology of Texas Mexican Literature.* Albuquerque: University of New Mexico Press, 2006.

Gilbert, Donald Chávez Y. *Vaqueros: Origins of the First Cowboys.* New Mexican Hispanic Culture Preservation League. http://www.nmhcpl.org/COWBOY.html.

Gonzales, Rodolfo. *I Am Joaquin.* http://www.latinamericanstudies.org/latinos/joaquin.htm.

González, Ralph, and Gregory González, interview by Richard J. Gonzales of Richard "Pancho" González' brother and nephew.

Goode, Tawara, Suganya Sockalingam, Lisa Lopez Snyder. *Bridging The Cultural Divide in Health Care Settings: The Essential Role of Cultural Broker Programs.* Developed by National Center for Cultural Competence, Spring/Summer 2004. http://gucchd.georgetown.edu/products/CulturalBrokerGuide_English.pdf

Green, Alison, and Jack Martin. "The Sinking Lifeboat, Uncontrolled Immigration and The U.S. Health Care System." *Federation For American Immigration Reform,* February 2004.http://www.fairus.org/site/DocServer/healthcare.pdf?docID=424.

Gutiérrez, Jose Ángel. *Cristal, Ten Years of Struggle, A Photographic Essay.* Crystal City, TX: Crystal City Independent School District, 1979.

———. *A Gringo Manual on How to Handle Mexicans.* Houston: Arte Publico Press, 2001.

———. *The Making of a Chicano Militant: Lessons from Crystal.* Madison: University of Wisconsin Press, 1998.

Gutiérrez, Teresa. "Ramsey Muñiz, La Raza Unida Party and the Chicano Struggle in Texas." *Workers World News Service*, March 13, 1997. http://www.workers.org/ww.laraza.html.

Guzmán, Betsy. "Hispanic Population, Census 2000 Brief." U.S. Census Bureau. http://www.census.gov/prod/2001pubs/c2kbr01-3.pdf.

Hart, Roger. *Children's Participation: The Theory and Practice of Involving Young Citizens in Community Development and Environmental Care.* New York: Earthscan Publications, 1997.

Hirsch, Edward. "Pablo Neruda at 100." *Washington Post.com*, July 11, 2004. www.washingtonpost.com/ac2/wp-dyn/A37885-2004Jul8?longuage=printer.

"Hispanic Population: 2010." U.S. Census Bureau (May 2011): 2, http://www.census.gov/prod/cen2010/briefs/c2010br-04.pdf.

"History of the Poinsettia, Paul Ecke Ranch." http://www.ecke.com/ecke/?page_id=1365.

Holbert, Steve, and Lisa Rose. *The Color of Guilt and Innocence: Racial Profiling and Police Pratices in America.* San Ramon, CA: Page Marque Press, 2004.

Holtorf, Cornelius."The Origins of Historical Consciousness." https://tspace.library.utoronto.ca/citd/holtorf/2.5.html.

Humara, Miguel. "The Relationship Between Athletics, Hispanics and Aggression." *Athletic Insight, The Online Journal of Sports Psychology.* http://www.athleticinsight.com/Vol1Iss1/Hispanic_Aggression.htm.

"Immigration in Tarrant County, Facts and Issues." League of Women Voters of Tarrant County, Unpublished manuscript, February, 2007.

Ito, Robert. "Concentration Camp Or Summer Camp?" *Mother Jones.* September 15, 1998. http://motherjones.com/politics/1998/09/concentration-camp-or-summer-camp.

"It's Back-To-School." *Fathering Times.* Connecticut Department of Social Services, 1, no. 6: (September 2001).

Jensen, Derrick. "Thinking Outside the Classroom: An Interview with Zenobia Barlow." *Sun Magazine*, March 2002. http://www.derrickjensen.org/barlow.html.

Jensen, Robert. *The Heart of Whiteness: Confronting Race, Racism and White Privilege.* San Francisco: City Lights, 2007.

Jirasek, Rita Arias, and Carlos Tortolero. *Mexican Chicago.* Charleston, SC: Arcadia Publishing, 2001.

Johnson, Roy L. "Missing:Texas Youth-Cost of School Dropouts Escalates." *Intercultural Development Research Association Newsletter*, October 2001. http://www.idra.org/IDRA_Newsletter/October_2001_Self_Renewing SchoolsPersistence/Missing%3A_Texas_Youth__Cost_of_School_Dropouts_Escalates/.

———. "More Than 3 Million Students Have Been Lost from Texas High Schools Since 1986." *Intercultural Development Research Association Newsletter*, October 2010. http://www.idra.org/IDRA_Newsletter/October_2010_School_Holding_Power/More_than_3_Million_Students_Have_Been_Lost/.

———. "Schools Continue to Lose Students,Texas Public School Attrition Study, 2002-2003." *Intercultural Development Research Association Newsletter*, October 2003. http://www.idra.org/IDRA_Newsletter/October_2003_Self_Renewing_Schools_Holding_Power/Schools_Continue_to_Lose_Students/

———. "Texas Dropout Alert: Where Are the 147,000 Students Lost from the Freshman Class of 1993-94?" http://www.idra.org/IDRA_Newsletter/October_1997_Leadership_Development/Texas_Dropout_Alert/

———. "Texas Public School Attrition Study, 2010-2011: High School Attrition Continues Downward Trend—Universal High School Graduation Is Still a Quarter Century Away." *Intercultural Development Research Association Report* (November 2011): http://www.idra.org/images/stories/IDRA_Attrition_Study_2011.pdf.

Keown, Tim. "Is Major League Baseball Too Hispanic?" *ESPN Commentary*, October 4, 2011. http://espn.go.com/espn/commentary/story/_/id/7058357/are-there-too-many-hispanics-major-league-baseball.

Kochhar, Rakesh. "Latino Labor Report, 2004: More Jobs for New Immigrants But at Lower Wages." *Pew Research Center: Pew Hispanic Center*, May 2, 2005. http://www.pewhispanic.org/files/reports/45.pdf.

Krashen, Stephen D. *Under Attack: The Case Against Bilingual Education.* Burlingame, CA: Language Education Associates, 1996.

Kreck, Dick. "Latinos Left Out of 'The War.'" *Denver Post.* http://www.denverpost.com/portlet/article/html/fragments/print_article.jsp?articleld=5335238&siteld.

Kuhn, Thomas. *The Structure of Scientific Revolutions.* Chicago: University of Chicago Press, 1996.

"Latino Films Make Money: Consistently Performing Well at the Box Office." Premiere Weekend Club. http://www.premiereweekend.org/profitsb.html.

"Latino Vote 2004 Campaigns." *Southwest Voter Registration Education Project*, September 26, 2004.

Leddy, Chuck. Review of *A Great and Godly Adventure*, by Godfrey Hodgson. *SF Gate*, November 12, 2006. http://www.sfgate.com/cgibin/article.cgi?file=c/a/200611/12/RVGT4M5UML1.DTL&type=prin.

Leonard, W. M., and J. M. Reyman. "The Odds of Attaining Professional Athlete Status: Refining the Computations." *Sociology of Sport Journal*, 5, (1988):162-169. http://journals.humankinetics.com/ssj-back-issues/ssjvolume5issue2june/

researchnotescommentstheoddsofattainingprofessionalathletestatusre-finingthecomputations.

León-Portilla, Miguel. *Aztec Thought and Culture: A Study of the Ancient Nahuatl Mind.* Translated by J. Davis. Norman: University of Oklahoma Press, 1963.

Levitt, Justin. "The Truth About Voter Fraud." *Brennan Center for Justice at New York University School of Law*, 2007. http://www.truthaboutfraud.org/pdf/TruthAboutVoterFraud.pdf.

Mancini, Pierluigi. "Helping Our Youth Succeed in Dangerous Times." *LatinoPapi.com*, June 13, 2004. www.latinopapi.com/html/clmn/clmn_mancinidanger.php

McMahon, Peg. "Poinsettia Care in the Home." *Ohio State University Extension Fact Sheet*: http://ohioline.osu.edu/hyg-fact/1000/1248.html.

Meléndez, Michelle. "Searching for Affordable Medical Treatment Is Often a Painful Task for Undocumented Immigrants in Tarrant County." *Fort Worth Star-Telegram*, Sunday, October 31, 1999.

Meyerson, Harold. "Born to Runoff." *The American Prospect Online Edition*, March 10, 2005. http://prospect.org/article/born-runoff.

Miller, Frederick A., and Judith H. Katz. *The Inclusion Breakthrough: Unleashing the Real Power of Diversity.* San Francisco: Berrett-Koehler Publishers, Inc., 2002.

Mohanty, Sarita A., Steffie Woolhandler, David U. Himmelstein, Susmita Pati, Olveen Carrasquillo, and David H. Bor. "Health Care Expenditures of Immigrants in the United States: A Nationally Representative Analysis." *American Journal of Public Health* 95, no. 8 (August 2005). http://ajph.aphapublications.org/doi/pdf/10.2105/AJPH.2004.044602.

Morin. Raúl. *Among the Valiant: Mexican Americans in WWII and Korea.* Alhambra, CA: Borden Publishing Company, 1963.

Murdock, Steve."The Population of Texas: Historical Patterns and Future Trends Affecting Texas." Institute for Demographic and Socioeconomic Research, University of Texas in San Antonio. www.senate.state.tx.us/75r/senate/commit/c525/handouts06/01242006.c525.Murdock.pdf

Murdock, Steve, Steve White, Md. Nazrul Hoque, Beverly Pecotte, Xiuhong You, and Jennifer Balkan. "Texas Challenge in the Twenty-First Century: Implications of Population Change for the Future of Texas." Department of Rural Sociology Texas A & M University System, December 2002. http://txsdc.utsa.edu/reports/2002/texaschallange/TxChall2002.pdf.

Murphy, Ryan, and Matt Stiles. "Census 2010 Interactive Map: Race, Hispanic Origin." *Texas Tribune*,February 18, 2011. http://www.texastribune.org/library/data/census-2010/.

Murr, Andrew. "The Survivor's Story." *Newsweek*, May 30, 2005: 32-34.

Neruda, Pablo. *Twenty Love Poems and a Song of Despair.* Translated by W. S. Merwin. New York: Peguin Classics Deluxe Edition, 2003.

"Number of Fatal Work Injuries Involving Hispanic or Latino Workers, 1992-2007." US Department of Labor, Bureau of Labor Statistics, Census of Fatal Occupational Injuries, 2007. http://www.slideshare.net/delforbes/number-of-fatal-work-injuries-19922007.

Office of Minority Health and Human Services. *National Standards for Culturally and Linguistically Appropriate Services in Health Care, Executive Summary.* Prepared by IQ Solutions, Inc., March 2001. http://minorityhealth.hhs.gov/assets/pdf/checked/executive.pdf.

Olmeda, Rafael, and Ivan Roman. Open Letter to Ms. Paula Kerger, PBS President and Chief Executive Officer, February 16, 2007. http://www.nahj.org/nahjnews/articles/2007/february/pbsletter.pdf.

Opposition to Arizona Initiative "English Language Education for Children in Public Schools." Resolution 15 Passed at LULAC Convention National Convention, July 2, 2000, signed by Rick Dovalina, national LULAC president. http://www.lulac.net/advocacy/resolutions/resolve00.html.

Orfield, Gary, and John T. Yun. "Resegregation in American Schools." The Civil Rights Project Harvard University, June 1999. http://www.civilrightsproject.ucla.edu/research/deseg/Resegregation_American_Schools99.pdf.

Pachon, Harry. "Still Missing: Latinos In and Out of Hollywood." The Tomás Rivera Policy Institute, May 2000. http://www.trpi.org/PDFs/missing_in_action.pdf.

Pancho González: The Latino Legend of Tennis. Directed by Nick Athas and Danny Haro. Spike TV Documentary, aired September 16, 2006.

Paredes, Americo. *"With His Pistol in His Hand," A Border Ballad and Its Hero.* Austin: University of Texas Press, 1958.

Passel, Jeffrey S., and D'Vera Cohn. "Unauthorized Immigrant Population: National and State Trends, 2010." *Pew Hispanic Center,* February 1, 2011. http://www.pewhispanic.org/files/reports/133.pdf.

Passel, Jeffrey, and D'Vera Cohn. "U.S. Population Projections: 2005-2050." *Pew Hispanic Center*, February 11, 2008. http://www.pewhispanic.org/2008/02/11/us-population-projections-2005-2050/.

Perie, Marianne, Rebecca Moran, and Anthony D. Lutkus. "NAEP 2004 Trends in Academic Progress: Three Decades of Student Performance in Reading and Mathematics." *U.S. Department of Education, Institute of Education Sciences, National Center of Education Statistics.* Washington. DC: Government Printing Office, 2005. http://nces.ed.gov/nationsreportcard/pdf/main2005/2005464.pdf.

Perry, Leonard. "Why Do We Have Poinsettias?" University of Vermont Extension, Department of Plant and Soil Science. http://pss.uvm.edu/ppp/articles/pointhist.html.

"Poinsettia Pages." University of Illinois Extension. http://www.urbanext.uiuc.edu/poinsettia/history.html.

"Principles of *Un Hombre Noble.*" The National Latino Fatherhood and Family Institute. http://www.nationalcompadresnetwork.com/principles/principles.html

Pritchard, Justin. "AP Investigation: Mexican Worker Deaths Rise Sharply Even As Overall U.S. Job Safety Improves." *Associated Press*, http://fmmac2.mm.ap.org/polk_awards_dying_to_work_html/DyingtoWork.html.

"Public Education Finances: 2009." U.S. Census Bureau. May 2011. http://www2.census.gov/govs/school/09f33pub.pdf.

Pycior, Julie Leininger. *LBJ and Mexican Americans: The Paradox of Power.* Austin: University of Texas Press, 1997.

Quintana, Robert. "Going to the Root: Jerry Tello Builds Pride from the Inside Out." *La Prensa San Diego,* May 15, 1998. http://www.laprensa-sandiego.org/archieve/may15/tello.htm.

Ramos, Henry A.J. *The American GI Forum: In Pursuit of the Dream, 1948-1983.* Houston: Arte Público Press, 1998.

"Raza Unida Party" The Handbook of Texas Online. http://www.tshaonline.org/handbook/online/articles/print/RR/war1/html.

Ríos-Ellis, Britt. *Critical Disparities in Latino Mental Health :Transforming Research Into Action.* National Council of La Raza, Institute for Hispanic Health, November 3, 2005. http://www.nclr.org/index.php/publications/critical_disparities_in_latino_mental_health_transforming_research_into_action/.

Rivas-Rodríguez, Maggie. "Ken Burns: Efforts Made to Force Him to Include Latinos in His History of WWII." Email by Maggie Rivas-Rodríguez, Ph.D. Associate Professor, School of Journalism, University of Texas at Austin to *History News Network.* February 16, 2007. http://hnn.us/roundup/entries/35535.html

Rodríguez, Roberto, and Patrisia Gonzales. "Deconstructing Machismo." *Latino Spectrum,* June 20, 1997. http://www.mexica.net/literat/macho.php.

Salazar, Rubén. *Rubén Salazar: Border Correspondent, Selected Writings 1955-1970.* Edited by Mario T. García. Berkeley: University of California Press, 1955.

Sánchez, Alonso, and Anna Marie Weiss-Armush. "Study of North Texas Immigrant Communities." Prepared for Dallas International, January 28, 2003. www.dfwinternational.org/resource_center/Study_of_North_Texas_Immigrant_Communities_2003.pdf.

Schmal, John P. "The Four Latino Mayors of Los Ángeles." *Hispanic Vista,* May 23, 2005.

Seguin, Juan N. *A Revolution Remembered: The Memoirs and Selected Correspondences of Juan N. Seguin.* Edited by Jesús F. De La Teja. Austin:Texas State Historical Association, 2002.

"Senator West's Racial Profiling Bill Passes Full Senate." *From the Office of State Senator Royce West-District 23,* April 11, 2001.

http://www.senate.state.tx.us/75r/senate/members/dist23/pr01/p041101a.htm.

Singley, Catherine. "Fractures in the Foundation: The Latino Worker's Experience in an Era of Declining Job Quality." *National Council of La Raza,* September 1, 2009, 18. See especially chap. 3, fig. 3.7, "Troubling Indicators of Job Quality." http://www.nclr.org/index.

php/publications/fractures_in_the_foundation_the_latino_workers_experience_ in_an_era_of_declining_job_quality/.

Sisson, Pierre et Janine. *Life of the Aztecs in Ancient Mexico.* Translated by David Macrae. Geneve, Spain: Editions Minerva, S.A., 1978.

"'A Slap in the Face': Astro Owner Accused of Remarks Against Hispanics." *CNN/Sports Illustrated.Com* (June 4, 1999). http://sportsillustrated.cnn.com/baseball/mlb/news/1999/06/04/astros_mclane/index. html.

Smith, Don. "The Overrepresentation of Latino Youth in Juvenile Justice, Numbers and Reasons." Lecture presented at Tarrant County Advocate Program North Third Annual Latino Youth Issues Conference, Fort Worth, TX, April 5, 2007.

"Snapshot 2014, District Detail." Texas Education Agency. http://ritter.tea.state.tx.us/cgi/sas/broker?_service=marykay&_program=perfrept.perfmast.sas&prgopt=2014%2Fsnapshot%2Fdistrict.sas&year4=2014&year2=14&topic=snapshot&gifname=g_snapshot2014distsrch&title=Snapshot%A0Report&level=District&search=distback&sublevel=%26SUBLEVEL&ptype=%26PTYPE&distback=057905+

Soustelle, Jacques. *Daily Life of the Aztecs on the Eve of the Spanish Conquest.* Translated by Patrick O'Brian. London: Weidenfeld and Nicolson, 1961.

Steward, Dwight. *Racial Profiling: Texas Traffic Stops and Searches, A First Look At The Nation's Most Comprehensive Racial Profiling Data Set: Texas Traffic Stops and Searches.* Austin: Steward Research Group, 2004. http://www.employstats.com/pdfs/Steward04.pdf.

Suro, Robert, and Jeffrey S. Passel. "The Rise of the Second Generation: Changing Patterns in Historical Population Growth." *Pew Hispanic Center,* October 12, 2003. http://www.pewhispanic.org/2003/10/14/the-rise-of-the-second-generation/.

Sutherland, Jean. "Understanding Hispanic/Latino Culture and History Through the Use of Children's Literature." *Yale-New Haven Teachers Institute.* http://www.yale.edu/ynhti/curriculum/units/1997/2/97.02.06.x.html.

Taylor, Brent, and Andrew Behuke. "Fathering Across the Border: Latino Fathers in Mexico and the U.S." *Fathering* 3, no. 2 (Spring 2005).

http://www.ces.ncsu.edu/depts/fcs/Benke/Taylor%20Behnke.pdf.

Tejada-Flores, Rick, and Ray Telles. *The Fight in the Fields: César Chávez and the Farmworkers' Struggle.* DVD. Documentary produced, directed and written by Rick Tejada Flores and Ray Telles. New York: The Cinema Guild.

Texas HCR 38. 77th Regular Session (signed by the Governor June 15, 2001).

"Texas Prison Population Increase Expected," *Justice Policy Institute,* April 23, 2003. http://www.prisontalk.com/forums/archive/index.php/t-108650.html.

"Texas QuickFacts From the U.S. Census Bureau." http://quickfacts.census.gov/qfd/states/48000.html.

Thomas, Wayne, and Virginia Collier. "Bilingual Education: Need For Bilingual Education, Benefits of Bilingualism and Theoretical Foundations of Bilingual Education." http://education.stateuniversity.com/pages/1788/Bilingual-Education.html.

Tijerina, Andrés. *Tejanos and Texas Under the Mexican Flag, 1821-1836.* College Station: Texas A & M University Press, 1994.

Torres, Cruz. "Texas—A Majority/Minority State: Social and Economic Implications." Department of RPTS,Texas A&M University, May 25, 2011. http://txsdc.utsa.edu/Resources/Presentations/TXSDC/2011/AnnualWorkshop/sdc2011_Tx_Majority_Minority_State_Torres.pptx.

"U.S. Population Projections." U.S. Census Bureau. http://www.census.gov/population/www/projections/natproj.html.

Villarruel, Franciso A., and Nancy E. Walker. *Donde Esta La Justicia? A Call to Action on Behalf of Latino and Latina Youth in the U.S. Justice System.* East Lansing: Michigan State University, Institute for Children, Youth and Families, Building Blocks For Youth, July, 2002. http://www.cclp.org/documents/BBY/Donde.pdf.

Visconti, Luke. "Ask the White Guy." *DiversityInc*. http://diversityinc.com/.

"Voting And Registration in the Election of November 2000." U.S. Census Bureau, February 2002.

Ward, Kathleen. "Poinsettia Inspires Legends, Myths, Sales." *Kstate Research and Extension* (December 9, 2004). http://www.ksre.ksu.edu/news/sty/2004/poinsettia_inspires120904.htm.

Warnock, Kirby. *Border Bandits*. Documentary directed and written by Kirby Warnock, Trans-Pecos Productions.

Webb, Walter Prescott. *Texas Rangers: A Century of Frontier Defense*. Austin: University of Texas Press, 1965.

Why Early Childhood Matters. Hosted by Rob Reiner. Produced by Parents' Action for Children. I Am Your Child Video Series. 2005. DVD.

Zayas, Luis. *Latinas Attempting Suicide, When Cultures, Families, and Daughters Collide*. New York: Oxford University Press, 2011.

———. "Toward an Understanding of Suicide Risks in Young Hispanic Females." *Journal of Adolescent Research* 1 (Spring 1987): 1-11. doi: 10.1177/074355488721001.

Index